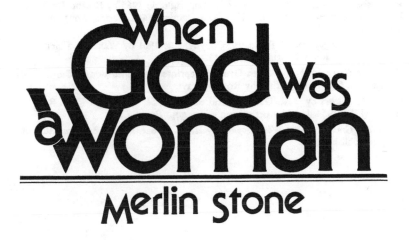

When God Was a Woman

Merlin Stone

Dorset Press
New York

ACKNOWLEDGMENTS

Grateful acknowledgment is made for permission to use the following copyrighted material.

From *They Wrote on Clay* by Edward Chiera: Reprinted by permission of The University of Chicago Press. © 1938, 1966 by The University of Chicago. All rights reserved.

From *Ancient Israel* by Roland De Vaux: Copyright © 1965 by Roland De Vaux. Used with permission of McGraw-Hill Book Company and Darton, Longman & Todd Ltd.

From *Archaic Egypt* by W. B. Emery: Copyright © 1961 by Walter B. Emery. Used by permission of Penguin Books Ltd.

From *The Greek Myths* by Robert Graves: Reprinted by permission of Curtis Brown, Ltd. Copyright © 1955 by Robert Graves.

From *The Hittites* by O. R. Guerney (2nd edition, 1954). Copyright © O. R. Gurney 1952, 1954. Used by permission of Penguin Books Ltd.

From *The Greatness That Was Babylon* by H. W. F. Saggs: Used by permission of Praeger Publishers, Inc.

This edition published by Dorset Press,
a division of Marboro Books Corporation,
by arrangement with Doubleday, a division of Bantam
Doubleday Dell Publishing Group, Inc.
1990 Dorset Press

ISBN 0-88029-533-3

Printed in the United States of America

M 9 8 7 6

To Jenny
and Cynthia
with Love

Contents

Maps

Man enjoys the great advantage of having a god endorse the code he writes; and since man exercises a sovereign authority over women it is especially fortunate that this authority has been vested in him by the Supreme Being. For the Jews, Mohammedans and Christians among others, man is master by divine right; the fear of God will therefore repress any impulse towards revolt in the downtrodden female.

Simone de Beauvoir
The Second Sex 1949

In his statement opposed to the ordination of women, Bishop C. L. Meyers said the Episcopalian priesthood is a "masculine conception."

"A priest is a 'God symbol' whether he likes it or not. In the imagery of both the Old and New Testament God is represented in masculine imagery," he said in a statement that was circulated among some 760 delegates at Grace Cathedral for the 2½ day convention.

"Christ is the source of Priesthood. The Sexuality of Christ is no accident nor is his masculinity incidental. This is the divine choice," the statement said.

San Francisco Chronicle
25 October 1971

In the beginning there was Isis: Oldest of the Old, She was the Goddess from whom all Becoming Arose. She was the Great Lady, Mistress of the two Lands of Egypt, Mistress of Shelter, Mistress of Heaven, Mistress of the House of Life, Mistress of the word of God. She was the Unique. In all Her great and wonderful works She was a wiser magician and more excellent than any other God.

Thebes, Egypt, Fourteenth Century BC

Thou Sun Goddess of Arinna art an honored deity; Thy name is held high among names; Thy divinity is held high among the deities; Nay, among the deities, Thou alone O Sun Goddess art honored; Great art Thou alone O Sun Goddess of Arinna; Nay compared to Thee no other deity is as honored or great . . .

Boghazköy, Turkey, Fifteenth Century BC

Unto Her who renders decision, Goddess of all things, Unto the Lady of Heaven and Earth who receives supplication; Unto Her who hears petition, who entertains prayer; Unto the compassionate Goddess who loves righteousness; Ishtar the Queen, who suppresses all that is confused. To the Queen of Heaven, the Goddess of the Universe, the One who walked in terrible Chaos and brought life by the Law of Love; And out of Chaos brought us harmony, and from Chaos Thou has led us by the hand.

Babylon, Eighteenth to Seventh Centuries BC

Hear O ye regions, the praise of Queen Nana; Magnify the Creatress; exalt the dignified; exalt the Glorious One; draw nigh to the Mighty Lady.

Sumer, Nineteenth Century BC

Preface

How did it actually happen? How did men initially gain the control that now allows them to regulate the world in matters as vastly diverse as deciding which wars will be fought when to what time dinner should be served?

This book is the result of my reactions to these and similar questions which many of us concerned about the status of women in our society have been asking ourselves and each other. As if in answer to our queries, yet another question presented itself. What else might we expect in a society that for centuries has taught young children, both female and male, that a MALE deity created the universe and all that is in it, produced MAN in his own divine image—and then, as an afterthought, created woman, to obediently help man in his endeavors? The image of Eve, created for her husband, from her husband, the woman who was supposed to have brought about the downfall of humankind, has in many ways become the image of all women. How did this idea ever come into being?

Few people who live in societies where Christianity, Judaism or

Islam are followed remain unaware of the tale of Eve heeding the word of the serpent in the Garden of Eden, eating the forbidden fruit and then tempting Adam to do the same. Generally, during the most impressionable years of childhood, we are taught that it was this act of eating the tasty fruit of the tree of knowledge of good and evil that caused the loss of Paradise, the expulsion of Adam and Eve, thus all humankind, from this first home of bliss and contentment. We are also made to understand that, as a result of this act, it was decreed by God that woman must submit to the dominance of man—who was at that time divinely presented with the right to rule over her—from that moment until now.

The expulsion of Adam and Eve from the Garden of Eden is not exactly the latest news, but few contemporary happenings have affected women of today any more directly. In the struggle to achieve equal status for women, in a society still permeated by the values and moralities of Judeo-Christian beliefs (which have penetrated deeply into even the most secular aspects of our contemporary civilization) we soon realize that a thorough examination of this creation legend, alongside its historical origins, provides us with vital information. It allows us to comprehend the role that contemporary religions have played in the initial and continual oppression and subjugation of women— and the reasons for this.

In prehistoric and early historic periods of human development, religions existed in which people revered their supreme creator as female. The Great Goddess—the Divine Ancestress —had been worshiped from the beginnings of the Neolithic periods of 7000 BC until the closing of the last Goddess temples, about AD 500. Some authorities would extend Goddess worship as far into the past as the Upper Paleolithic Age of about 25,000 BC. Yet events of the Bible, which we are generally taught to think of as taking place "in the beginning of time," actually occurred in historic periods. Abraham, first prophet of the Hebrew-Christian god Yahweh, more familiarly known as Jehovah, is believed by most Bible scholars to have lived no earlier than 1800 BC and possibly as late as 1550 BC.

Most significant is the realization that for thousands of years both religions existed simultaneously—among closely neighboring peoples. Archaeological, mythological and historical evidence all reveal that the female religion, far from naturally fading away, was the victim of centuries of continual persecution and suppression by the advocates of the newer religions which held male deities as supreme. And from these new religions came the creation myth of Adam and Eve and the tale of the loss of Paradise.

What had life been like for women who lived in a society that venerated a wise and valiant female Creator? Why had the members of the later male religions fought so aggressively to suppress that earlier worship—even the very memory of it? What did the legend of Adam and Eve really signify, and when and why was it written? The answers I discovered have formed the contents of this book. *When God Was a Woman,* the story of the suppression of women's rites, has been written to explain the historical events and political attitudes that led to the writing of the Judeo-Christian myth of the Fall, the loss of Paradise and, most important, why the blame for that loss was attributed to the woman Eve, and has ever since been placed heavily upon all women.

Introduction

Though to many of us today religion appears to be an archaic relic of the past (especially the writings of the Old Testament, which tell of times many centuries before the birth of Christ), to many of our parents, grandparents or great-grandparents these writings were still regarded as the sacred gospel, the divine word. In turn, their religious beliefs, and subsequent behavior and social patterns, have left their imprint on us in various ways. Indeed, the ancient past is not so far removed as we might imagine or prefer to believe.

In fact, if we are ever to fully understand how and why man gained the image of the one who accomplishes the greatest and most important deeds while woman was relegated to the role of ever-patient helper, and subsequently assured that this was the *natural* state of female-male relationships, it is to these remote periods of human history that we must travel. It is the ancient origins of human civilizations and the initial development of religious patterns we must explore. And this, as you will see, is no easy task.

It is shocking to realize how little has been written about the female deities who were worshiped in the most ancient periods of human existence and exasperating to then confront the fact that even the material there is has been almost totally ignored in popular literature and general education. Most of the information and artifacts concerning the vast female religion, which flourished for thousands of years before the advent of Judaism, Christianity and the Classical Age of Greece, have been dug out of the ground only to be reburied in obscure archaeological texts, carefully shelved away in the exclusively protected stacks of university and museum libraries. Quite a few of these were accessible only with the proof of university affiliation or university degree.

Many years ago I set out upon a quest. It eventually led me halfway round the world—from San Francisco to Beirut. I wanted to know more about the ancient Goddess religion. Along the way were the libraries, museums, universities and excavation sites of the United States, Europe and the Near East. Making my way from place to place, I compiled information from a vast variety of sources, patiently gleaning each little phrase, prayer or fragment of a legend from a myriad of diverse information.

As I gathered this material about the early female deities, I found that many ancient legends had been used as ritual dramas. These were enacted at religious ceremonies of sacred festivals, coinciding with other ritual activities. Statues, murals, inscriptions, clay tablets and papyri that recorded events, legends and prayers revealed the form and attitudes of the religion and the nature of the deity. Comments were often found in the literature of one country about the religion or divinities of another. Most interesting was the realization that the myths of each culture that explained their origins were not always the oldest. Newer versions often superseded and displaced previous ones, while solemnly declaring that "this is as it was in the beginning of time."

Professor Edward Chiera of the University of Chicago wrote of the Babylonian myth of the creation of heaven and earth by the god Marduk that "Marduk, the new god of this rather new city, certainly had no right to appropriate to himself the glory of so great a deed ... But in Hammurabi's time Babylon was the center of the kingdom ... Marduk, backed by Hammurabi's armies, could now claim to be the most important god in the land." Professor Chiera also explained that in Assyria, where the god Ashur eventually became the supreme deity, "The Assyrian priests gave the honor to Ashur simply by taking the old Babylonian tablets and recopying them, substituting the name of their own god for that of Marduk. The work was not very carefully done, and in some places the name of Marduk still creeps in."

In the difficulties I encountered gathering material, I could not help thinking of the ancient writing and statuary that must have been intentionally destroyed. Accounts of the antagonistic attitudes of Judaism, Christianity and Mohammedanism (Islam) toward the sacred artifacts of the religions that preceded them revealed that this was so, especially in the case of the Goddess worshiped in Canaan (Palestine). The bloody massacres, the demolition of statues (i.e., pagan idols) and sanctuaries are recorded in the pages of the Bible following this command by Yahweh: "You must completely destroy all the places where the nations you dispossess have served their gods, on high mountains, on hills, under any spreading tree; you must tear down their altars, smash their pillars, cut down their sacred poles, set fire to the carved images of their gods and wipe out their name from that place" (Deut. 12:2, 3). There can be little doubt that the continuous attacks, as recorded in the Old Testament, destroyed much precious and irretrievable information.

In later periods Christians were known throughout the world for their destruction of sacred icons and literature belonging to the so-called "pagan" or "heathen" religions. Professor George Mylonas wrote that, during the reign of the early Christian Emperor Theodosius, "The Christians, especially in the large cities of Antioch and Alexandria became the persecutors and the pagans the persecuted; temples and idols were destroyed by fire and their devotees mistreated." As the worship of the earlier deities was suppressed and the temples destroyed, closed or converted into

Christian churches, as so often happened, statues and historic records were obliterated by the missionary fathers of Christianity as well.

Though the destruction was major, it was not total. Fortunately many objects had been overlooked, remnants that today tell their own version of the nature of those dread "pagan" rituals and beliefs. The enormous number of Goddess figurines that have been unearthed in excavations of the Neolithic and early historic periods of the Near and Middle East suggest that it may well have been the evident female attributes of nearly all of these statues that irked the advocates of the male deity. Most "pagan idols" had breasts.

The writers of the Judeo-Christian Bible, as we know it, seem to have purposely glossed over the sexual identity of the female deity who was held sacred by the neighbors of the Hebrews in Canaan, Babylon and Egypt. The Old Testament does not even have a word for "Goddess." In the Bible the Goddess is referred to as Elohim, in the masculine gender, to be translated as god. But the Koran of the Mohammedans was quite clear. In it we read, "Allah will not tolerate idolatry . . . the pagans pray to females."

Since a great deal of information was gleaned from university and museum libraries, another problem I encountered was the sexual and religious bias of many of the erudite scholars of the nineteenth and twentieth centuries. Most of the available information in both archaeology and ancient religious history was compiled and discussed by male authors. The overwhelming prevalence of male scholars, and the fact that nearly all archaeologists, historians and theologians of both sexes were raised in societies that embrace the male-oriented religions of Judaism or Christianity, appeared to influence heavily what was included and expanded upon and what was considered to be minor and hardly worth mentioning. Professor R. K. Harrison wrote of the Goddess religion, "One of its most prominent features was the lewd, depraved, orgiastic character of its cultic procedures." Despite the discovery of temples of the Goddess in nearly every Neolithic and historic excavation, Werner Keller writes that the female deity was

how it works

RARELY HAVE we seen a person fail who has thoroughly followed our path. Those who do not recover are people who cannot or will not completely give themselves to this simple program, usually men and women who are constitutionally incapable of being honest with themselves. There are such unfortunates. They are not at fault, they seem to have been born that way. They are naturally incapable of grasping and developing a manner of living which demands rigorous honesty. Their chances are less than average. There are those, too, who suffer from grave emotional and mental disorders, but many of them do recover if they have the capacity to be honest.

Our stories disclose in a general way what we used to be like, what happened, and what we are like now. If you have decided you want what we have and are willing to go to any length to get it—then you are ready to take certain steps.

At some of these we balked. We thought we could find an easier, softer way. But we could not. With all the earnestness at our command, we beg of you to be fearless and thorough from the very start. Some of us have tried to hold on to our old ideas and the result was nil until we let go absolutely.

Remember that we deal with alcohol-cunning, baffling, powerful! Without help it is too much for us. But there is One who has all power—that One is God. May you find Him now!

Half measures availed us nothing. We stood at the turning point. We asked His protection and care with complete abandon.

Here are the steps we took, which are suggested as a program of recovery:

1. We admitted we were powerless over alcohol—that our lives had become unmanageable.
2. Came to believe that a Power greater than ourselves could restore us to sanity.
3. Made a decision to turn our will and our lives over to the care of God as we understood Him.
4. Made a searching and fearless moral inventory of ourselves.
5. Admitted to God, to ourselves, and to another human being the exact nature of our wrongs.
6. Were entirely ready to have God remove all these defects of character.
7. Humbly asked Him to remove our shortcomings.
8. Made a list of all persons we had harmed, and became willing to make amends to them all.

9. Made direct amends to such people wherever possible, except when to do so would injure them or others.

10. Continued to take personal inventory and when we were wrong promptly admitted it.

11. Sought through prayer and meditation to improve our conscious contact with God as we understood Him, praying only for knowledge of His will for us and the power to carry that out.

12. Having had a spiritual awakening as the result of these steps, we tried to carry this message to alcoholics, and to practice these principles in all our affairs.

Many of us exclaimed, "What an order! I can't go through with it." Do not be discouraged. No one among us has been able to maintain anything like perfect adherence to these principles. We are not saints. The point is, that we are willing to grow along spiritual lines. The principles we have set down are guides to progress. We claim spiritual progress rather than spiritual perfection.

Our description of the alcoholic, the chapter to the agnostic, and our personal adventures before and after make clear three pertinent ideas:

(a) That we were alcoholic and could not manage our own lives.

(b) That probably no human power could have relieved our alcoholism.

(c) That God could and would if He were sought.

KEEP COMING BACK!

worshiped primarily on "hills and knolls," simply echoing the words of the Old Testament. Professor W. F. Albright, one of the leading authorities on the archaeology of Palestine, wrote of the female religion as "orgiastic nature worship, sensuous nudity and gross mythology." He continued by saying that "It was replaced by Israel with its pastoral simplicity and purity of life, its lofty monotheism and its severe code of ethics." It is difficult to understand how these words can be academically justified after reading of the massacres perpetrated by the Hebrews on the original inhabitants of Canaan as portrayed in the Book of Joshua, especially chapters nine to eleven. Professor S. H. Hooke, in his collection of essays *Myth, Ritual and Kingship*, openly admits, "I firmly believe that God chose Israel to be the vehicle of revelation."

Albright himself wrote, "It is frequently said that the scientific quality of Palestinian archaeology has been seriously impaired by the religious preconceptions of scholars who have excavated in the Holy Land. It is true that some archaeologists have been drawn to Palestine by their interest in the Bible, and that some of them had received their previous training mainly as biblical scholars." But he then proceeded to reject this possibility of impairment, basing his conclusion primarily upon the fact that the dates assigned to the sites and artifacts of ancient Palestine, by the scholars who took part in the earlier excavations, were subsequently proven to be too recent, rather than too old, as might perhaps be expected. The question of whether or not the attitudes and beliefs inherent in those suggested "religious preconceptions" had perhaps subtly influenced analysis and descriptions of the symbolism, rituals and general nature of the ancient religion was not even raised for discussion.

In most archaeological texts the female religion is referred to as a "fertility cult," perhaps revealing the attitudes toward sexuality held by the various contemporary religions that may have influenced the writers. But archaeological and mythological evidence of the veneration of the female deity as creator and lawmaker of the universe, prophetess, provider of human destinies, inventor, healer, hunter and valiant leader in battle suggests that the title "fertility cult" may be a gross oversimplification of a complex theological structure.

Paying closer attention to semantics, subtle linguistic undertones and shades of meaning, I noticed that the word "cult," which has the implicit connotations of something less fine or civilized than "religion," was nearly always applied to the worship of the female deities, not by ministers of the Church but by presumably objective archaeologists and historians. The rituals associated with the Judeo-Christian Yahweh (Jehovah) were always respectfully described by these same scholars as "religion." It was upon seeing the words "God," and even "He," each time carefully begun with capital letters, while "queen of heaven," "goddess" and "she" were most often written in lower case, that I decided to try it the other way about, observing how these seemingly minor changes subtly affected the meaning as well as the emotional impact.

Within descriptions of long-buried cities and temples, academic authors wrote of the sexually active Goddess as "improper," "unbearably aggressive" or "embarrassingly void of morals," while male deities who raped or seduced legendary women or nymphs were described as "playful," even admirably "virile." The overt sexual nature of the Goddess, juxtaposed to Her sacred divinity, so confused one scholar that he finally settled for the perplexing title, the Virgin-Harlot. The women who followed the ancient sexual customs of the Goddess faith, known in their own language as sacred or holy women, were repeatedly referred to as "ritual prostitutes." This choice of words once again reveals a rather ethnocentric ethic, probably based on biblical attitudes. Yet, using the term "prostitute" as a translation for the title of women who were actually known as *qadesh,* meaning holy, suggests a lack of comprehension of the very theological and social structure the writers were attempting to describe and explain.

Descriptions of the female deity as creator of the universe, inventor or provider of culture were often given only a line or two, if mentioned at all; scholars quickly disposed of these aspects of the female deity as hardly worth discussing. And despite the fact that the title of the Goddess in most historical documents of the Near East was the Queen of Heaven, some writers were willing to know Her only as the eternal "Earth Mother."

The female divinity, revered as warrior or hunter, courageous soldier or agile markswoman, was sometimes described as possessing the most "curiously masculine" attributes, the implication being that Her strength and valor made Her something of a freak or physiological abnormality. J. Maringer, professor of prehistoric archaeology, rejected the idea that reindeer skulls were the hunting trophies of a Paleolithic tribe. The reason? They were found in the grave of a woman. He writes, "Here the skeleton was that of a woman, a circumstance that would seem to rule out the possibility that reindeer skulls and antlers were hunting trophies." Might these authors be judging the inherent physical nature of women by the fragile, willowy ideals of today's western fashions?

Priestesses of the Goddess, who provided the counsel and advice at Her shrines of prophetic wisdom, were described as being fit for this position since as women they were more "intuitive" or "emotional," thus ideal mediums for divine revelation. These same writers generally disregarded the political importance of the advice given or the possibility that these women might in fact have been respected as wise and knowledgeable, capable of holding vital, advisory positions. Strangely enough, emotional qualities or intuitive powers were never mentioned in connection with the male prophets of Yahweh. Gerhard Von Rad commented, ". . . it has always been the women who have shown an inclination for obscure astrological cults."

The word "gods," in preference to the word "deities," when both female and male deities were being discussed, was most often chosen by the contemporary scribes of ancient religion. Conflicting translations, even something as simple as Driver's "He did sweep from the fields the women gathering sticks" to Gray's "To and fro in the fields plied the women cutting wood" raise questions about the accuracy of the use of certain words chosen as translations. It is true that ancient languages are often quite difficult to decipher and to then translate into contemporary words and terms. In some cases a certain amount of educated guessing takes place, and this is temporarily useful, but it is here that preconceived attitudes may be likely to surface.

Unfortunately, instances of possibly inaccurate translation, biased comments, assumptions and speculations innocently blend into explanations of attitudes and beliefs of ancient times. Male bias, together with preconceived religious attitudes, which appears in both major and minor matters, raises some very pressing and pertinent questions concerning the objectivity of the analysis of the archaeological and historical material available at present. It suggests that long-accepted theories and conclusions must be re-examined, re-evaluated and where indicated by the actual evidence, revised.

In 1961 a series of mistakes was described by Professor Walter Emery, who took part in the excavations of some of the earliest Egyptian tombs. He tells us that "The chronological position and status of Meryet-Nit is uncertain, but there is reason to suppose that she might be the successor of Zer and the third sovereign of the First Dynasty." Writing of the excavation of this tomb by Sir Flinders Petrie in 1900 he says, "At that time it was believed that Meryet-Nit was a king, but later research has shown the name to be that of a woman and, to judge by the richness of the burial, a queen." He goes on to say, "In 1896 de Morgan, then Director of the Service of Antiquities discovered at Nagadeh a gigantic tomb which, from the objects found in it, was identified as the burial place of Hor-Aha, first king of the First Dynasty. However later research has shown that it is more probable that it was the sepulchre of Nit-Hotep, Hor-Aha's mother." And again he tells us that "On the mace of Narmer a seated figure in a canopied palanquin was once thought to be that of a man, but a comparison of similar figures on a wooden label from Sakkara shows that this is improbable and that it almost certainly represents a woman." Yet, despite his own accounts of this series of assumptions that the richest burials and royal palanquins of the past were for men, rather than women, in describing the tomb of King Narmer he then states, "This monument is almost insignificant in comparison with

the tomb of Nit-Hotep at Nagadeh and we can *only conclude* that
this was only the king's southern tomb and that his real burial place
still awaits discovery . . ." (my italics). Though some pharaohs did
build two tombs, one might expect a "possibly" or "probably"
rather than such an absolute conclusion and the implied dismissal
of the possibility that, in that period of earliest dynastic Egypt, a
queen's tomb just might have been larger and more richly decorated than a king's.

In *Palestine Before the Hebrews,* E. Anati described a group of
Asiatics arriving in Egypt. In this description he explains that it is
the men who have arrived and with them they bring their goods
and their donkeys, their wives and children, tools, weapons and
musical instruments, in that order. Anati's description of the earliest appearance of the Goddess is no less male-oriented. He writes,
"These Upper Paleolithic *men* also created a feminine figure
apparently representing a goddess or being of fertility . . . the
psychological implications of the mother goddess are therefore of
tremendous importance . . . Here undeniably is the picture of a
thinking *man,* of a *man* with intellectual as well as material
achievements" (my italics). Could it possibly have been the female
ancestors of those women who are listed along with the donkeys
and other goods who were thinking *women, women* with intellectual as well as material achievements?

Dr. Margaret Murray of the University of London, writing on
ancient Egypt in 1949, suggested that the whole series of events
surrounding the "romantic" relationships of Cleopatra, who actually held the legitimate right to the Egyptian throne, was misunderstood as the result of male bias. She points out that, "The classical
historians, imbued as they were with the customs of patrilineal
descent and monogamy, besides looking on women as the chattels
of their menfolk, completely misunderstood the situation and have
misinterpreted it to the world."

These are just a few examples of the sexual and religious biases
that I encountered. As Cyrus Gordon, Professor of Near Eastern
Studies and formerly Chairman of the Department at Brandeis
University in Massachusetts, writes, "We absorb attitudes as well

as subject matter in the learning process. Moreover, the attitudes tend to determine what we see, and what we fail to see, in the subject matter. This is why attitude is just as important as subject matter in the educational process." Many questions come to mind. How influenced by contemporary religions were many of the scholars who wrote the texts available today? How many scholars have simply assumed that males have always played the dominant role in leadership and creative invention and projected this assumption into their analysis of ancient cultures? Why do so many people educated in this century think of classical Greece as the first major culture when written language was in use and great cities built at least twenty-five centuries before that time? And perhaps most important, why is it continually inferred that the age of the "pagan" religions, the time of the worship of female deities (if mentioned at all), was dark and chaotic, mysterious and evil, without the light of order and reason that supposedly accompanied the later male religions, when it has been archaeologically confirmed that the earliest law, government, medicine, agriculture, architecture, metallurgy, wheeled vehicles, ceramics, textiles and written language were initially developed in societies that worshiped the Goddess? We may find ourselves wondering about the reasons for the lack of easily available information on societies who, for thousands of years, worshiped the ancient Creatress of the Universe.

Despite the many obstacles, I sought out and gathered the existing information and began to collate and correlate what I had collected. As I undertook this process, the importance, the longevity and the complexity of this past religion began to take form before me. So often there was just the mention of the Goddess, a part of a legend, an obscure reference, tucked away in some four or five hundred pages of scholarly erudition. A deserted temple site on Crete or a statue in the museum at Istanbul, with little or no accompanying information, began to find its place in the overall picture.

Painstakingly bringing these together, I finally began to comprehend the total reality. It was more than an inscription of an ancient prayer, more than an art relic sitting on a museum shelf behind glass, more than a grassy field strewn with parts of broken columns or the foundation stones which had once supported an ancient temple. Placed side by side, the pieces of this jigsaw puzzle revealed the overall structure of a geographically vast and major religion, one that had affected the lives of multitudes of people over thousands of years. Just like the religions of today, it was totally integrated into the patterns and laws of society, the morals and attitudes associated with those theological beliefs probably reaching deep into even the most agnostic or atheistic of minds.

I am not suggesting a return or revival of the ancient female religion. As Sheila Collins writes, "As women our hope for fulfilment lies in the present and future and not in some mythical golden past . . ." I do hold the hope, however, that a contemporary consciousness of the once-widespread veneration of the female deity as the wise Creatress of the Universe and all life and civilization may be used to cut through the many oppressive and falsely founded patriarchal images, stereotypes, customs and laws that were developed as direct reactions to Goddess worship by the leaders of the later male-worshiping religions. For, as I shall explain, it was the ideological inventions of the advocates of the later male deities, imposed upon that ancient worship with the intention of destroying it and its customs, that are still, through their subsequent absorption into education, law, literature, economics, philosophy, psychology, media and general social attitudes, imposed upon even the most non-religious people of today.

This is not intended as an archaeological or historical text. It is rather an invitation to all women to join in the search to find out who we really are, by beginning to know our own past heritage as more than a broken and buried fragment of a male culture. We must begin to remove the exclusive mystique from the study of archaeology and ancient religion, to explore the past for ourselves rather than remaining dependent upon the interests, interpretations, translations, opinions and pronouncements that have so far been produced. As we compile the information, we shall be better able to understand and explain the erroneous assumptions in the stereotypes that were initially created for women to accept and follow by the proclamations in the male-oriented religions that, according to the divine word, a particular trait was normal or natural and any deviation improper, unfeminine or even sinful. It is only as many of the tenets of the Judeo-Christian theologies are seen in the light of their political origins, and the subsequent absorption of those tenets into secular life understood, that as women we will be able to view ourselves as mature, self-determining human beings. With this understanding we may be able to regard ourselves not as permanent helpers but as doers, not as decorative and convenient assistants to men but as responsible and competent individuals in our own right. The image of Eve is not *our* image of woman.

It is also an invitation to all men—those who have previously questioned the reasons for the roles and images of females and males in contemporary society and those who had never considered the subject before. It is an invitation extended in the hope that becoming aware of the historical and political origins of the Bible, and the role played over the centuries by the Judeo-Christian theologies in formulating the attitudes toward women and men today, may lead to a greater understanding, cooperation and mutual respect between women and men than has heretofore been possible. For men interested in achieving this goal, exploring the past offers a deeper and more realistic understanding of today's sexual stereotypes by placing them in the perspective of their historical evolution.

As with every extensive work or study there are many people who have graciously helped along the way, people to whom I owe much appreciation. First of all I want to thank my mother, my sister and my two daughters for the emotional courage they have given me all through the years of research. I would also like to express my appreciation to Carmen Callil and Ursula Owen of Virago Limited, the feminist division of Quartet Books Limited in London, who both put so much time, effort and personal concern into the original editing and publication of the book in England; and to Joyce Engelson, Debra Manette, Donna Schrader, Anne

Knauerhase and all the others at The Dial Press who have, in turn, each graciously contributed so much to this edition. Next there are the museum directors, museum staff, museum and university librarians, archaeologists and workers at excavation sites, so many that I hesitate to mention their names for fear of leaving someone out, but nearly all extremely helpful. Then there are the archaeologists and historians whose books I have used. (There were many who included the most cursory fragments and even those who somehow managed to ignore the existence of the female deity altogether.) Though some of the comments and conclusions caused me to flinch in astonished dismay at their unquestioned and internalized belief in a natural male dominance, their work in unearthing and deciphering the artifacts of the past has made this book possible. In fact, I cannot help but hope that what I have said, and will say throughout the rest of the book, may have some effect upon their future perception of the Goddess-worshiping people.

The works of the late Stephen Langdon, S. G. F. Brandon, Edward Chiera, Cyrus Gordon, Walther Hinz, E. O. James, James Mellaart, H. W. F. Saggs, J. B. Pritchard and R. E. Witt proved especially useful. But it is primarily to the women scholars, such as the late Margaret Murray, the late Jane Harrison, E. Douglas Van Buren, Sybelle von Cles-Reden, Florence Bennett, Rivkah Harris and Jacquetta Hawkes, to whom I am most indebted for having presented vital information with a unique perception, in turn providing me with the courage to question the objectivity of so much else that had been written, to learn to carefully sift through material to separate opinion from fact and—perhaps most important—to begin to notice what had been left out.

Though archaeology and ancient religion may seem very isolated or esoteric fields, I hope that this book will encourage more people to explore these subjects for themselves, so that some day we may better understand the events of the past, bring what has been carelessly or intentionally hidden out into the open and challenge the many unfounded assumptions that have too long passed for fact.

1

Tales with a Point of View

Though we live amid high-rise steel buildings, formica countertops and electronic television screens, there is something in all of us, women and men alike, that makes us feel deeply connected with the past. Perhaps the sudden dampness of a beach cave or the lines of sunlight piercing through the intricate lace patterns of the leaves in a darkened grove of tall trees will awaken from the hidden recesses of our minds the distant echoes of a remote and ancient time, taking us back to the early stirrings of human life on the planet. For people raised and programmed on the patriarchal religions of today, religions that affect us in even the most secular aspects of our society, perhaps there remains a lingering, almost innate memory of sacred shrines and temples tended by priestesses who served in the religion of the original supreme deity. In the beginning, people prayed to the Creatress of Life, the Mistress of Heaven. At the very dawn of religion, God was a woman. Do you remember?

For years something has magnetically lured me into exploring the legends, the temple sites, the statues and the ancient rituals of

1

the female deities, drawing me back in time to an age when the Goddess was omnipotent, and women acted as Her clergy, controlling the form and rites of religion.

Perhaps it was my training and work as a sculptor that first exposed me to the sculptures of the Goddess found in the ruins of prehistoric sanctuaries and the earliest dwellings of human beings. Perhaps it was a certain romantic mysticism, which once embarrassed me, but to which I now happily confess, that led me over the years into the habit of collecting information about the early female religions and the veneration of female deities. Occasionally I tried to dismiss my fascination with this subject as overly fanciful and certainly disconnected from my work (I was building electronic sculptural environments at the time). Nevertheless, I would find myself continually perusing archaeology journals and poring over texts in museum or university library stacks.

As I read, I recalled that somewhere along the pathway of my life I had been told—and accepted the idea—that the sun, great and powerful, was naturally worshiped as male, while the moon, hazy, delicate symbol of sentiment and love, had always been revered as female. Much to my surprise I discovered accounts of Sun Goddesses in the lands of Canaan, Anatolia, Arabia and Australia, while Sun Goddesses among the Eskimos, the Japanese and the Khasis of India were accompanied by subordinate brothers who were symbolized as the moon.

I had somewhere assimilated the idea that the earth was invariably identified as female, Mother Earth, the one who passively accepts the seed, while heaven was naturally and inherently male, its intangibility symbolic of the supposedly exclusive male ability to think in abstract concepts. This too I had accepted without question—until I learned that nearly all the female deities of the Near and Middle East were titled Queen of Heaven, and in Egypt not only was the ancient Goddess Nut known as the heavens, but her brother-husband Geb was symbolized as the earth.

Most astonishing of all was the discovery of numerous accounts of the female Creators of all existence, divinities who were credited with bringing forth not only the first people but the entire earth and the heavens above. There were records of such Goddesses in Sumer, Babylon, Egypt, Africa, Australia and China.

In India the Goddess Sarasvati was honored as the inventor of the original alphabet, while in Celtic Ireland the Goddess Brigit was esteemed as the patron deity of language. Texts revealed that it was the Goddess Nidaba in Sumer who was paid honor as the one who initially invented clay tablets and the art of writing. She appeared in that position earlier than any of the male deities who later replaced Her. The official scribe of the Sumerian heaven was a woman. But most significant was the archaeological evidence of the earliest examples of written language so far discovered; these were also located in Sumer, at the temple of the Queen of Heaven in Erech, written there over five thousand years ago. Though writing is most often said to have been invented by *man,* however that may be defined, the combination of the above factors presents a most convincing argument that it may have actually been woman who pressed those first meaningful marks into wet clay.

In agreement with the generally accepted theory that women were responsible for the development of agriculture, as an extension of their food-gathering activities, there were female deities everywhere who were credited with this gift to civilization. In Mesopotamia, where some of the earliest evidences of agricultural development have been found, the Goddess Ninlil was revered for having provided Her people with an understanding of planting and harvesting methods. In nearly all areas of the world, female deities were extolled as healers, dispensers of curative herbs, roots, plants and other medical aids, casting the priestesses who attended the shrines into the role of physicians of those who worshiped there.

Some legends described the Goddess as a powerful, courageous warrior, a leader in battle. The worship of the Goddess as valiant warrior seems to have been responsible for the numerous reports of female soldiers, later referred to by the classical Greeks as the Amazons. More thoroughly examining the accounts of the esteem the Amazons paid to the female deity, it became evident that women who worshiped a warrior Goddess hunted and fought in the lands of Libya, Anatolia, Bulgaria, Greece, Armenia and Russia and were far from the mythical fantasy so many writers of today would have us believe.

I could not help noticing how far removed from contemporary images were the prehistoric and most ancient historic attitudes toward the thinking capacities and intellect of woman, for nearly everywhere the Goddess was revered as wise counselor and prophetess. The Celtic Cerridwen was the Goddess of Intelligence and Knowledge in the pre-Christian legends of Ireland, the priestesses of the Goddess Gaia provided the wisdom of divine revelation at pre-Greek sanctuaries, while the Greek Demeter and the Egyptian Isis were both invoked as law-givers and sage dispensers of righteous wisdom, counsel and justice. The Egyptian Goddess Maat represented the very order, rhythm and truth of the Universe. Ishtar of Mesopotamia was referred to as the Directress of People, the Prophetess, the Lady of Vision, while the archaeological records of the city of Nimrud, where Ishtar was worshiped, revealed that women served as judges and magistrates in the courts of law.

The more I read, the more I discovered. The worship of female deities appeared in every area of the world, presenting an image of woman that I had never before encountered. As a result, I began to ponder upon the power of myth and eventually to perceive these legends as more than the innocent childlike fables they first appeared to be. They were tales with a most specific point of view.

Myths present ideas that guide perception, conditioning us to think and even perceive in a particular way, especially when we are young and impressionable. Often they portray the actions of people who are rewarded or punished for their behavior, and we are encouraged to view these as examples to emulate or avoid. So many of the stories told to us from the time we are just old enough to understand deeply affect our attitudes and comprehension of the world about us and ourselves. Our ethics, morals, conduct, values, sense of duty and even sense of humor are often developed from simple childhood parables and fables. From them we learn what is socially acceptable in the society from which they come. They define good and bad, right and wrong, what is natural and what is unnatural among the people who hold the myths as meaningful. It was quite apparent that the myths and legends that grew from, and were propagated by, a religion in which the deity was female, and revered as wise, valiant, powerful and just, provided very different images of womanhood from those which we are offered by the male-oriented religions of today.

"A FORTNIGHT AFTER THE CREATION OF THE UNIVERSE"

As I considered the power of myth, it became increasingly difficult to avoid questioning the influential effects that the myths accompanying the religions that worship male deities had upon my own image of what it meant to be born a female, another Eve, progenitress of my childhood faith. As a child, I was told that Eve had been made from Adam's rib, brought into being to be his companion and helpmate, to keep him from being lonely. As if this assignment of permanent second mate, never to be captain, was not oppressive enough to my future plans as a developing member of society, I next learned that Eve was considered to be foolishly gullible. My elders explained that she had been easily tricked by the promises of the perfidious serpent. She defied God and provoked Adam to do the same, thus ruining a good thing—the previously blissful life in the Garden of Eden. Why Adam himself was never thought to be equally as foolish was apparently never worth discussing. But identifying with Eve, who was presented as the symbol of all women, the blame was in some mysterious way mine—and God, viewing the whole affair as my fault, chose to punish *me* by decreeing: "I will greatly multiply your pain in childbearing; in pain you shall bring forth children, yet your desire shall be for your husband and he shall rule over you" (Gen. 3:16).

So even as a young girl I was taught that, because of Eve, when I grew up I was to bear my children in pain and suffering. As if this was not a sufficient penalty, instead of receiving compassion, sympathy or admiring respect for my courage, I was to experience this pain with guilt, the sin of my wrongdoing laid heavily upon me as punishment for simply being a woman, a daughter of Eve. To make matters worse, I was also supposed to accept the idea that men, as symbolized by Adam, in order to prevent any further foolishness on my part, were presented with the right to control me —to rule over me. According to the omnipotent male deity, whose righteousness and wisdom I was expected to admire and respect with a reverent awe, men were far wiser than women. Thus my penitent, submissive position as a female was firmly established by page three of the nearly one thousand pages of the Judeo-Christian Bible.

But this original decree of male supremacy was only the beginning. The myth describing Eve's folly was not to be forgotten or ignored. We then studied the words of the prophets of the New Testament, who repeatedly utilized the legend of the loss of Paradise to explain and even prove the natural inferiority of women. The lessons learned in the Garden of Eden were impressed upon us over and over again. Man was created first. Woman was made for man. Only man was made in God's image. According to the Bible, and those who accepted it as the divine word, the male god favored men and had indeed designed them as naturally superior. Even now I cannot help wondering how many times those passages from the New Testament were read from the authoritative position of a Sunday pulpit or from the family Bible that had been pulled down from the shelf by father or husband—and a pious woman listened to:

> Let the woman learn in silence with all subjection. But I suffer not a woman to teach or to usurp authority over the man, but to be in silence. For Adam was first formed and then Eve, and Adam was not deceived, but the woman being deceived was in the transgression. . . . (I Timothy 2:11–14)
>
> For the man is not of the woman, but the woman of the man. Let the women keep silence in the churches, for it is not permitted unto

them to speak; but they are commanded to be under obedience, so saith the law. And if they learn anything, let them ask their husbands at home; for it is a shame for women to speak in the church. (I Corinthians 11:3, 7, 9)

Strangely enough, I never did become very religious, despite the continual efforts of Sunday School teachers. In fact, by the time I reached adolescence I had rejected most of what the organized religions had to offer. But there was still something about the myth of Adam and Eve that lingered, seeming to pervade the culture at some deeper level. It appeared and reappeared as the symbolic foundation of poems and novels. It was visually interpreted in oils by the great masters whose paintings glowed from the slide projectors in my art history courses. Products were advertised in high fashion magazines suggesting that, if a woman wore the right perfume, she might be able to pull the whole disaster off all over again. It was even the basis of dull jokes in the Sunday comics. It seemed that everywhere woman was tempting man to do wrong. Our entire society agreed; Adam and Eve defined the images of men and women. Women were inherently conniving, contriving and dangerously sexy, while gullible and somewhat simple-minded at the same time. They were in obvious need of a foreman to keep them in line—and thus divinely appointed, many men seemed quite willing.

As I began to read other myths that explained the creation of life, stories that attributed the event to Nut or Hathor in Egypt, Nammu or Ninhursag in Sumer, Mami, Tiamat or Aruru in other parts of Mesopotamia and Mawu in Africa, I began to view the legend of Adam and Eve as just another fable, an innocent attempt to explain what happened at the very beginning of existence. But it was not long afterward that I began to understand how specifically contrived the details of this particular myth were.

In 1960, mythologist Joseph Campbell commented on the Adam and Eve myth, writing:

This curious mythological idea, and the still more curious fact that for two thousand years it was accepted throughout the Western World as the absolutely dependable account of an event that was supposed to have taken place about a fortnight after the creation of the universe, poses forcefully the highly interesting question of the influence of conspicuously contrived, counterfeit mythologies and the inflections of mythology upon the structure of human belief and the consequent course of civilization.

Professor Chiera points out that "The Bible does not give us one creation story but several of them; the one which happens to be featured in chapter one of Genesis appears to be the one which had the least vogue among the common people . . . It was evidently produced in scholarly circles." He then discusses the differences between the religions of today and the ancient worship, saying:

Just a few years ago we succeeded in piecing together from a large number of tablets the complete story of an ancient Sumerian myth. I used to call it the Darwinian theory of the Sumerians. The myth must have been widely circulated for many copies of it have already come to light. In common with the biblical story, a woman plays the dominant role, just as Eve did. But the resemblance ends there. Poor Eve has been damned by all subsequent generations for her deed, while the Babylonians thought so much of their woman ancestress that they deified her.

Now as I read these other myths, it was apparent that the archetypal woman in ancient religions, as represented by the Goddess, was quite different, in many respects, from the woman Eve. I then observed that many of these origin and creation legends came from the lands of Canaan, Egypt and Babylon, the very same lands in which the Adam and Eve myth had been developed. The other legends of creation were from the mythical religious literature of the people who did not worship the Hebrew Yahweh (Jehovah), but were in fact the closest neighbors of those early Hebrews.

2

Who
Was She?

It was not long before the various pieces of evidence fell into place and the connections began to take form. And then I understood. Ashtoreth, the despised "pagan" deity of the Old Testament was (despite the efforts of biblical scribes to disguise her identity by repeatedly using the masculine gender) actually Astarte—the Great Goddess, as She was known in Canaan, the Near Eastern Queen of Heaven. Those heathen idol worshipers of the Bible had been praying to a woman god—elsewhere known as Innin, Inanna, Nana, Nut, Anat, Anahita, Istar, Isis, Au Set, Ishara, Asherah, Ashtart, Attoret, Attar and Hathor—the many-named Divine Ancestress. Yet each name denoted, in the various languages and dialects of those who revered Her, The Great Goddess. Was it merely coincidence that during all those years of Sunday School I never learned that Ashtoreth was female?

Even more astonishing was the archaeological evidence which proved that Her religion had existed and flourished in the Near and Middle East for thousands of years before the arrival of the patriarchal Abraham, first prophet of the male deity Yahweh. Archaeologists had traced the worship of the Goddess back to the Neolithic communities of about 7000 BC, some to the Upper Paleolithic cultures of about 25,000 BC. From the time of its Neolithic origins, its existence was repeatedly attested to until well into Roman times. Yet Bible scholars agreed that it was as late as somewhere between 1800 and 1550 BC that Abraham had lived in Canaan (Palestine).

Who was this Goddess? Why had a female, rather than a male, been designated as the supreme deity? How influential and significant was Her worship, and when had it actually begun? As I asked myself these questions, I began to probe even deeper into Neolithic and Paleolithic times. Though goddesses have been worshiped in all areas of the world, I focused on the religion as it evolved in the Near and Middle East, since these were the lands where both Judaism, Christianity and Islam were born. I found that the development of the religion of the female deity in this area was intertwined with the earliest beginnings of religion so far discovered anywhere on earth.

DAWN IN THE GRAVETTIAN GARDEN OF EDEN

The Upper Paleolithic period, though most of its sites have been found in Europe, is the conjectural foundation of the religion of the Goddess as it emerged in the later Neolithic Age of the Near East. Since it precedes the time of written records and does not directly lead into an historical period that might have helped to explain it, the information on the Paleolithic existence of Goddess worship must at this time remain speculative. Theories on the origins of the Goddess in this period are founded on the juxtaposition of mother-kinship customs to ancestor worship. They are based upon three separate lines of evidence.

The first relies on anthropological analogy to explain the initial development of matrilineal (mother-kinship) societies. Studies of "primitive" tribes over the last few centuries have led to the realization that some isolated "primitive" peoples, even in our own century, did not yet possess the conscious understanding of the relationship of sex to conception. The analogy is then drawn that Paleolithic people may have been at a similar level of biological awareness.

Jacquetta Hawkes wrote in 1963 that ". . . Australian and a few other primitive peoples did not understand biological paternity or accept a necessary connection between sexual intercourse and conception." In that same year, S. G. F. Brandon, Professor of Comparative Religion at the University of Manchester in England, observed, "How the infant came to be in the womb was undoubtedly a mystery to primitive man . . . in view of the period that separates impregnation from birth, it seems probable that the significance of gestation and birth was appreciated long before it was realized that these phenomena were the result of conception following coition."

"James Frazer, Margaret Mead and other anthropologists," writes Leonard Cottrell, "have established that in the very early stages of man's development, before the secret of human fecundity was understood, before coitus was associated with childbirth, the female was revered as the giver of life. Only women could produce their own kind, and man's part in this process was not as yet recognized."

According to these authors, as well as many authorities who have written on this subject, in the most ancient human societies people probably did not yet possess the conscious understanding of the relationship of sex to reproduction. Thus the concepts of paternity and fatherhood would not yet have been understood. Though probably accompanied by various mythical explanations, babies were simply born from women.

If this was the case, then the mother would have been seen as the singular parent of her family, the lone producer of the next generation. For this reason it would be natural for children to take the name of their mother's tribe or clan. Accounts of descent in the family would be kept through the female line, going from mother to daughter, rather than from father to son, as is the custom practiced in western societies today. Such a social structure is generally referred to as matrilineal, that is, based upon mother-kinship. In such cultures (known among many "primitive" peoples even today, as well as in historically attested societies at the time of classical Greece) not only the names, but titles, possessions and territorial rights are passed along through the female line, so that they may be retained within the family clan.

Hawkes points out that in Australia, in areas where the concept of paternity had not yet been understood, ". . . there is much to show that matrilineal descent and matri-local marriage [the husband moving to the wife's family home or village] were general and the status of women much higher." She writes that these customs still prevail in parts of Africa and among the Dravidians of India, and relics of them in Melanesia, Micronesia and Indonesia.

The second line of evidence concerns the beginnings of religious beliefs and rituals and their connection with matrilineal descent. There have been numerous studies of Paleolithic cultures, explorations of sites occupied by these people and the apparent rites connected with the disposal of their dead. These suggest that, as the earliest concepts of religion developed, they probably took the form of ancestor worship. Again an analogy is drawn between the Paleolithic people and the religious concepts and rituals observed among many of the "primitive" tribes studied by anthropologists over the last two centuries. Ancestor worship occurs among tribal people the world over. Maringer states that even at the time of his writing, 1956, certain tribes in Asia were still making small statues known as *dzuli*. Explaining these he says, "The idols are female and represent the human origins of the whole tribe."

Thus as the religious concepts of the earliest *homo sapiens** were

---

*The term *homo sapiens* (literally "knowing or knowledgeable *man*") illustrates once again the scholarly assumption of the prime importance of the male, in this case to the point of the total negation of the female population of the species so defined. If all *"homo sapiens"* had literally been just that, no sooner than the species had developed would it have died out for lack of the capability to reproduce its own kind.

developing, the quest for the ultimate source of life (perhaps the core of all theological thought) may have begun. In these Upper Paleolithic societies—in which the mother may have been regarded as the sole parent of the family, ancestor worship was apparently the basis of sacred ritual, and accounts of ancestry were probably reckoned only through the matriline—the concept of the creator of all human life may have been formulated by the clan's image of the woman who had been their most ancient, their primal ancestor and that image thereby deified and revered as Divine Ancestress.

The third line of evidence, and the most tangible, derives from the numerous sculptures of women found in the Gravettian-Aurignacian cultures of the Upper Paleolithic Age. Some of these date back as far as 25,000 BC. These small female figurines, made of stone and bone and clay and often referred to as *Venus figures,* have been found in areas where small settled communities once lived. They were often discovered lying close to the remains of the sunken walls of what were probably the earliest human-made dwellings on earth. Maringer claims that niches or depressions had been made in the walls to hold the figures. These statues of women, some seemingly pregnant, have been found throughout the widespread Gravettian-Aurignacian sites in areas as far apart as Spain, France, Germany, Austria, Czechoslovakia and Russia. These sites and figures appear to span a period of at least ten thousand years.

"It appears highly probable then," says Maringer, "that the female figurines were idols of a 'great mother' cult, practised by the non-nomadic Aurignacian mammoth hunters who inhabited the immense Eurasian territories that extended from Southern France to Lake Baikal in Siberia." (Incidentally, it is from this Lake Baikal area in Siberia that the tribes which migrated to North America, supposedly about this same period [there developing into the American Indians], are believed to have originated.)

Russian paleontologist Z. A. Abramova, quoted in Alexander Marshak's recent book *Roots of Civilization,* offers a slightly different interpretation, writing that in the Paleolithic religion, "The image of the Woman-Mother . . . was a complex one, and it included diverse ideas related to the special significance of the women in early clan society. She was neither a god, an idol, nor the mother of a god; she was the Clan Mother . . . The ideology of the hunting tribes in this period of the matriarchal clan was reflected in the female figurines."

THE NEOLITHIC MORNING

The connections between the Paleolithic female figurines and the later emergence of the Goddess-worshiping societies in the Neolithic periods of the Near and Middle East are not definitive, but are suggested by many authorities. At the Gravettian site of Vestonice, Czechoslovakia, where Venus figures were not only formed but hardened in an oven, the carefully arranged grave of a woman was found. She was about forty years old. She had been supplied with tools, covered with mammoth shoulder blade bones and strewn with red ochre. In a proto-Neolithic site at Shanidar, on the northern stretches of the Tigris River, another grave was found, this one dating from about 9000 BC. It was the burial of a slightly younger woman, once again strewn with red ochre.

One of the most significant links between the two periods are the female figurines, understood in Neolithic societies, through their emergence into the historic period of written records, to represent the Goddess. The sculptures of the Paleolithic cultures and those of the Neolithic periods are remarkably similar in materials, size and, most astonishing, in style. Hawkes commented on the relationship between the two periods, noting that the Paleolithic female figures ". . . are extraordinarily like the Mother or Earth Goddesses of the agricultural peoples of Eurasia in the Neolithic Age and must be directly ancestral to them." E. O. James also remarks on the similarity, saying of the Neolithic statues, "Many of them are quite clearly allied to the Gravettian-Paleolithic prototypes." But perhaps most significant is the fact that Aurignacian sites have now been discovered near Antalya, about sixty miles from the Neolithic Goddess-worshiping community of Hacilar in

Anatolia (Turkey), and at Musa Dag in northern Syria (once a part of Canaan).

James Mellaart, formerly the assistant director of the British Institute of Archaeology at Ankara, now teaching at the Institute of Archaeology in London, describes the proto-Neolithic cultures of the Near East, dating them at about 9000 to 7000 BC. He writes that during that time, "Art makes its appearance in the form of animal carvings and statuettes of the supreme deity, the Mother Goddess."

These Neolithic communities emerge with the earliest evidences of agricultural development (which is what defines them as Neolithic). They appear in areas later known as Canaan (Palestine [Israel], Lebanon and Syria); in Anatolia (Turkey); and along the northern reaches of the Tigris and Euphrates rivers (Iraq and Syria). It may be significant that all these cultures possessed obsidian, which was probably acquired from the closest site of availability—Anatolia. One of these sites, near Lake Van, would be directly on the route from the Russian steppes into the Near East.

At the site that is now known as Jericho (in Canaan), by 7000 BC people were living in plastered brick houses, some with clay ovens with chimneys and even sockets for doorposts. Rectangular plaster shrines had already appeared. Sybelle von Cles-Reden writes of Jericho, "Various finds point to an active religious life. Female clay figures with their hands raised to their breast resemble idols of the mother goddess which were later so widely disseminated in the Near East." Mellaart too writes of Jericho: "They carefully made small clay figures of the mother-goddess type."

Another Neolithic community was centered in Jarmo in northern Iraq from about 6800 BC. H. W. F. Saggs, Professor of Semitic Languages, tells us that in Jarmo, "There were figurines in clay of animals as well as of a mother goddess: the mother goddess represented by such figurines seems to have been the central figure in Neolithic religion."

Hacilar, some sixty miles from the Aurignacian site of Antalya, was inhabited at about 6000 BC. Here, too, figures of the Goddess have been found. And at the excavations at Catal Hüyük, close to

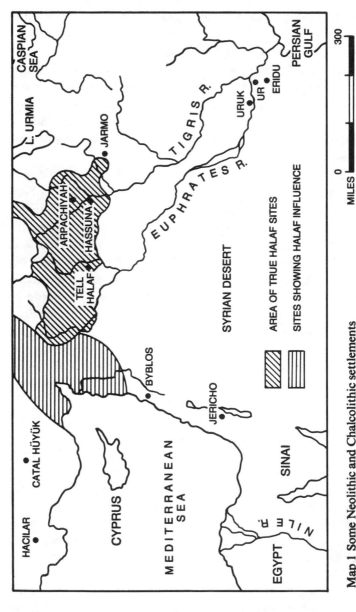

Map 1 Some Neolithic and Chalcolithic settlements
7000–4000 BC

the Cilician plains of Anatolia, near present day Konya, Mellaart discovered no less than forty shrines, dating from 6500 BC onward. The culture of Catal Hüyük existed for nearly one thousand years. Mellaart reveals, "The statues allow us to recognize the main deities worshiped by Neolithic people at Catal Hüyük. The principal deity was a goddess, who is shown in her three aspects, as a young woman, a mother giving birth or as an old woman." Mellaart suggests that there may have been a majority of women at Catal Hüyük, as evidenced by the number of female burials. At Catal Hüyük too red ochre was strewn on the bodies; nearly all of the red ochre burials were of women. He also suggests that the religion was primarily associated with the role of women in the initial development of agriculture, and adds, "It seems extremely likely that the cult of the goddess was administered mainly by women . . ."

By about 5500 BC houses had been built with groups of rooms around a central courtyard, a style used by many architects even today. These were found in sites along the northern reaches of the Tigris River, in communities that represent what is known as the Hassuna period. There, as in other Neolithic communities, archaeologists found agricultural tools such as the hoe and sickle, storage jars for corn and clay ovens. And once again, Professor Saggs reports, "The religious ideas of the Hassuna period are reflected in clay figurines of the mother goddess."

One of the most sophisticated prehistoric cultures of the ancient Near and Middle East was situated along the banks of the northern Tigris and westward as far as the Habur River. It is known as the Halaf culture and appeared in various places by 5000 BC. At these Halaf sites, small towns with cobbled streets have been discovered. Metal was in use, which would place the Halaf cultures into a period labeled by archaeologists as Chalcolithic.

Saggs writes that, judging from a picture on a ceramic vase, "It is probably from the Halaf period that the invention of wheeled vehicles date." Goddess figurines have been found at all Halaf sites, but at the Halafian town of Arpachiyah these figures were associated with serpents, double axes and doves, all symbols connected with Goddess worship as it was known in historical periods. Along with the intricately designed polychromed ceramic ware, at Arpachiyah buildings known as *tholoi* appeared. These were circular shaped rooms up to thirty-three feet in diameter with well-engineered vaulted ceilings. The round structures were connected to long rectangular corridors up to sixty-three feet in length. Since it was close to these *tholoi* that most of the Goddess figurines were discovered, it is likely that they were used as shrines.

By 4000 BC Goddess figures appeared at Ur and Uruk, both situated on the southern end of the Euphrates River, not far from the Persian Gulf. At about this same period the Neolithic Badarian and Amratian cultures of Egypt first appeared. It is at these sites that agriculture first emerged in Egypt. And once again in these Neolithic communities of Egypt, Goddess figurines were discovered.

From this point on, with the invention of writing, history emerged in both Sumer (southern Iraq) and Egypt—about 3000 BC. In every area of the Near and Middle East the Goddess was known in historic times. Though many centuries of transformation had undoubtedly changed the religion in various ways, the worship of the female deity survived into the classical periods of Greece and Rome. It was not totally suppressed until the time of the Christian emperors of Rome and Byzantium, who closed down the last Goddess temples in about 500 AD.

GODDESS—AS PEOPLE TODAY THINK OF GOD

The archaeological artifacts suggest that in all the Neolithic and early Chalcolithic societies the Divine Ancestress, generally referred to by most writers as the Mother Goddess, was revered as the supreme deity. Now She provided not only human life but a controllable food supply as well. C. Dawson, writing in 1928, surmised that "The earliest agriculture must have grown up around the shrines of the Mother Goddess, which thus became social and economic centres, as well as holy places and were the germs of future cities."

W. Schmidt, quoted by Joseph Campbell in *Primitive Mythology,* says of these early cultures, "Here it was the women who showed themselves supreme; they were not only the bearers of children but also the chief producers of food. By realizing that it was possible to cultivate, as well as to gather, they had made the earth valuable and they became, consequently, its possessors. Thus they won both economic and social power and prestige." Hawkes in 1963 added that "There is every reason to suppose that under the conditions of the primary Neolithic way of life mother-right and the clan system were still dominant, and the land would generally have descended through the female line."

Though at first the Goddess appears to have reigned alone, at some yet unknown point in time She acquired a son or brother (depending upon the geographic location), who was also Her lover and consort. He is known through the symbolism of the earliest historic periods and is generally assumed to have been a part of the female religion in much earlier times. Professor E. O. James writes, "Whether or not this reflects a primeval system of matriarchal social organization, as is by no means improbable, the fact remains that the Goddess at first had precedence over the Young-god with whom she was associated as her son or husband or lover."

It was this youth who was symbolized by the male role in the sacred annual sexual union with the Goddess. (This ritual is known from historic times but is generally believed to have been known in the Neolithic period of the religion.) Known in various languages as Damuzi, Tammuz, Attis, Adonis, Osiris or Baal, this consort died in his youth, causing an annual period of grief and lamentation among those who paid homage to the Goddess. The symbolism and rituals connected with him will be more fully explained in the chapter on the male consort, but wherever this dying young consort appears as the male deity, we may recognize the presence of the religion of the Goddess, the legends and lamentation rituals of which are extraordinarily similar in so many cultures. This relationship of the Goddess to Her son, or in certain places to a handsome youth who symbolized the son, was known in Egypt by 3000 BC; it occurred in the earliest literature of Sumer, emerged in later Babylon, Anatolia and Canaan, survived in the classical Greek legend of Aphrodite and Adonis and was even known in pre-Christian Rome as the rituals of Cybele and Attis, possibly there influencing the symbolism and rituals of early Christianity. It is one of the major aspects of the religion which bridges the vast expanses covered both geographically and chronologically.

But just as the people of the early Neolithic cultures may have come down from Europe, as the possible descendants of the Gravettian-Aurignacian cultures, so later waves of even more northern peoples descended into the Near East. There has been some conjecture that these were the descendants of the Mesolithic (about 15,000–8000 BC), Maglemosian and Kunda cultures of northern Europe. As I shall explain more fully later, their arrival was not a gradual assimilation into the area, as the Goddess peoples' seems to have been, but rather a series of aggressive invasions, resulting in the conquest, area by area, of the Goddess people.

These northern invaders, generally known as Indo-Europeans, brought their own religion with them, the worship of a young warrior god and/or a supreme father god. Their arrival is archaeologically and historically attested by 2400 BC, but several invasions may have occurred even earlier. The nature of the northern invaders, their religion and its affect upon the Goddess-worshiping people will be more thoroughly described and discussed in Chapters Four and Five. But the pattern that emerged after the invasions was an amalgamation of the two theologies, the strength of one or the other often noticeably different from city to city. As the invaders gained more territories and continued to grow more powerful over the next two thousand years, this synthesized religion often juxtaposed the female and male deities not as equals but with the male as the dominant husband or even as Her murderer. Yet myths, statues and documentary evidence reveal the continual presence of the Goddess and the survival of the customs and rituals connected to the religion, despite the efforts of the conquerors to destroy or belittle the ancient worship.

Although the earliest examples of written language yet discovered anywhere on earth appeared at the temple of the Queen of Heaven in Erech in Sumer, just before 3000 BC, writing at that time seems to have been used primarily for the business accounts of the temple. The arriving northern groups adopted this manner of writing, known as *cuneiform* (small wedge signs pressed into damp clay) and used it for their own records and literature. Professor Chiera comments, "It is strange to notice that practically all the existing literature was put down in written form a century or two after 2000 BC." Whether this suggests that written language was never considered as a medium for myths and legends before that time or that existing tablets were destroyed and rewritten at that time remains an open question. But unfortunately it means that we must rely on literature that was written after the start of the northern invasions and conquests. Yet the survival and revival of the Goddess as supreme in certain areas, the customs, the rituals, the prayers, the symbolism of the myths as well as the evidence of temple sites and statues, provide us with a great deal of information on the worship of the Goddess even at that time. And to a certain extent, they allow us, by observing the progression of transitions that took place over the next two thousand years, to extrapolate backward to better understand the nature of the religion as it may have existed in earlier historic and Neolithic times.

As I mentioned previously, the worship of the female deity has for the most part been included as a minor addition to the study of the patterns of religious beliefs in ancient cultures, most writers apparently preferring to discuss periods when male deities had already gained prominence. In many books a cursory mention of the Goddess often precedes lengthy dissertations about the male deities who replaced Her. Most misleading are the vague inferences that the veneration of a female deity was a separate, minor, unusual or curious occurrence. Since most books are concerned with one specific geographic area, this is partially the result of the fact that the Goddess was identified by a specific name or names which were native to that location and the overall connections are simply never mentioned.

Upon closer scrutiny, however, it becomes clear that so many of the names used in diverse areas were simply various titles of the Great Goddess, epithets such as Queen of Heaven, Lady of the High Place, Celestial Ruler, Lady of the Universe, Sovereign of the Heavens, Lioness of the Sacred Assembly or simply Her Holiness. Often the name of the town or city was added, which made the name even more specific. We are not, however, confronting a confusing myriad of deities, but a variety of titles resulting from diverse languages and dialects, yet each referring to a most similar female divinity. Once gaining this broader and more overall view, it becomes evident that the female deity in the Near and Middle East was revered as Goddess—much as people today think of God.

In Strong and Garstang's *Syrian Goddess* of 1913, some of the connections are explained. "Among the Babylonians and northern Semites She was Ishtar; She is Ashtoreth of the Bible and the Astarte of Phoenicia. In Syria Her name was Athar and in Cilicia it had the form Ate (Atheh)."

In Robert Graves's translation of *The Golden Ass* by the Roman writer Apuleius of the second century AD, the Goddess Herself appears and explains:

> I am Nature, the universal Mother, mistress of all elements, primordial child of time, sovereign of all things spiritual, queen of the dead, queen also of the immortals, the single manifestation of all gods and goddesses that are. My nod governs the shining heights of Heaven, the wholesome sea breezes, the lamentable silences of the world below. Though I am worshipped in many aspects, known by countless names, and propitiated with all manner of different rites, yet the whole round earth venerates me.
>
> The primeval Phrygians call me Pessinuntica, Mother of the gods; the Athenians sprung from their own soil, call me Cecropian Artemis; for the islanders of Cyprus I am Paphian Aphrodite, for the archers of Crete I am Dictynna; for the tri-lingual Silicians, Stygian Proserpine; and for the Eleusinians their ancient Mother of Corn. Some know me as Juno, some as Bellona of the Battles; others as Hecate, others again as Rhamnubia, but both races of Aethiopians, whose lands the morning

sun first shines upon, and the Egyptians who excel in ancient learning and worship me with ceremonies proper to my godhead, call me by my true name, namely Queen Isis.

Ironically, Isis was the Greek translation for the Egyptian Goddess Au Set.

The similarities of statues, titles, symbols such as the serpent, the cow, the dove and the double axe, the relationship of the son/lover who dies and is mourned annually, eunuch priests, the sacred annual sexual union and the sexual customs of the temple, each reveal the overlapping and underlying connections between the worship of the female deity in areas as far apart in space and time as the earliest records of Sumer to classical Greece and Rome.

The deification and worship of the female divinity in so many parts of the ancient world were variations on a theme, slightly differing versions of the same basic theological beliefs, those that originated in the earliest periods of human civilization. It is difficult to grasp the immensity and significance of the extreme reverence paid to the Goddess over a period of either twenty-five thousand (as the Upper Paleolithic evidence suggests) or even seven thousand years and over miles of land, cutting across national boundaries and vast expanses of sea. Yet it is vital to do just that to fully comprehend the longevity as well as the widespread power and influence this religion once held.

According to poet and mythologist Robert Graves, "The whole of Neolithic Europe, to judge from surviving artifacts and myths, had a remarkably homogenous system of religious ideas based on the many titled Mother Goddess, who was also known in Syria and Libya . . . The Great Goddess was regarded as immortal, changeless, omnipotent; and the concept of fatherhood had not yet been introduced into religious thought."

Much the same religion that Graves discusses existed even earlier in the areas known today as Iraq, Iran, India, Saudi Arabia, Lebanon, Jordan, Israel (Palestine), Egypt, Sinai, Libya, Syria, Turkey, Greece and Italy as well as on the large island cultures of

Crete, Cyprus, Malta, Sicily and Sardinia. There were instances of much the same worship in the Neolithic periods of Europe, which began at about 3000 BC. The Tuatha de Danaan traced their origins back to a Goddess they brought with them to Ireland, long before the arrival of Roman culture. The Celts, who now comprise a major part of the populations of Ireland, Scotland, Wales and Brittany, were known to the Romans as the Gauls. They are known to have sent priests to a sacred festival for the Goddess Cybele in Pessinus, Anatolia, in the second century BC. And evidence of carvings at Carnac and the Gallic shrines of Chartres and Mont St. Michel in France suggests that these places were once sites of the Great Goddess.

"FROM INDIA TO THE MEDITERRANEAN . . . SHE REIGNED SUPREME"

The status and origins of the Great Goddess have been discussed in several studies of ancient worship. The primary interest of most of these scholars was in the son/lover and the transition from the female to the male religions, but each of their statements reveal that the original status of the Goddess was as supreme deity.

In 1962 James Mellaart described the cultures of 9000 to 7000 BC in his *Earliest Civilizations of the Near East.* As I mentioned previously, he pointed out that at that time, "Art makes its appearance in the form of animal carvings and statuettes of the supreme deity, the Mother Goddess." He writes that at Catal Hüyük of the seventh millenium, "The principal deity was a goddess . . ." In describing the site of ancient Hacilar, a Neolithic community by 5800 BC, he directs our attention to the fact that "The statuettes portray the goddess and the male occurs only in a subsidiary role as child or paramour."

One figure of the Goddess from Hacilar is now in the museum in Ankara, which houses most of the pieces found at Hacilar and Catal Hüyük by Mellaart's excavations, their antiquity contrasting strangely with its contemporary architecture and decor. This particular sculpture of the Goddess appears to depict Her in the act of making love, though the male figure is broken and represented only by a small fragment of his waist, thighs and one leg. There is the possibility that this is an older child being held close, but it appears more likely to be an adolescent youth, perhaps intended to portray the son/lover of the female deity some eight thousand years ago.

In *The Lost World of Elam,* published in 1973, Dr. Walther Hinz, Director of the Institute of Iranian Studies at the University of Goettingen in Germany, also discusses the worship of the Goddess in the Near and Middle East. The nation of Elam was just east of Sumer and in early historic periods the two cultures were in close contact. Dr. Hinz writes that "Pride of place in this world was taken by a goddess—and this is typical of Elam . . . She was clearly the 'great mother of the gods' to the Elamites. The very fact that precedence was given to a goddess, who stood above and apart from the other Elamite gods, indicates a matriarchal approach in the devotees of this religion."

Dr. Hinz describes the Goddess as She was known in various centers of the Elamite territories and then tells us, "In the third millenium these 'great mothers of the gods' still held undisputed sway at the head of the Elamite pantheon but a change came during the course of the second. Just as the age old matriarchy of Elam had once yielded in the face of a gradual rise in the position of men, so corresponding arrangement took place among the gods . . . During the third millenium he [Humban, the consort of the Goddess] still occupied the third place, but from the middle of the second millenium he stood at the head of the pantheon."

Explaining the precedence of the female deity among the Semites, which include both the Arab and Hebrew peoples, Robertson Smith, in his prophetic work of 1894, *Religion of the Semites,* asserted that the female divinity in Semitic religion was deified as a direct result of the juxtaposition of ancestor worship and a female kinship system. At that time he wrote:

Recent researches into the history of the family render it in the highest degree improbable that the physical kinship between the god and his worshippers, of which traces are found all over the Semitic area, was originally conceived as fatherhood. It was the mother's, not the father's blood which formed the original bond of kinship among the Semites as among other early people and in this stage of society, if the tribal deity was thought of as the parent of the stock, a goddess, not a god, would necessarily have been the object of worship.

"In Mesopotamia, the goddess is supreme," wrote Professor Henri Frankfort in his 1948 publication of *Kingship and the Gods,* "because the source of all life is seen as female. Hence the god too descends from her and is called her son, though he is also her husband. In the ritual of the sacred marriage, the goddess holds the initiative throughout. Even in the condition of chaos, the female Tiamat is the leader and Apsu merely her male complement."

Within his twelve extensive volumes of research on ancient and "primitive" religion, published in 1907, Sir James Frazer wrote of the Egyptian Goddess Isis (Au Set) and Her brother/husband Osiris (Au Sar). In addition to the volumes of *The Golden Bough,* he published a separate book, *Attis, Adonis and Osiris,* a title also used for several of the sections of *The Golden Bough.* In both works he asserted that, according to Egyptian mythology, Isis was the stronger divinity of the pair. He related this to the system of property and descent practiced in Egypt, which he described as "mother-kinship." He referred to the young lover of the Goddess as "the mythical personification of nature" and explained that it was required that this figure should be sexually coupled with the supreme female divinity. Of the lad's status and position within the religion, he commented, "In each case [Attis, Adonis and Osiris] it appears that originally the goddess was a more powerful and important personage than the god."

In his 1928 *Handbook of Greek Mythology,* H. J. Rose discussed the role of the young male in the sacred sexual union and described him as "her inferior male partner," observing, "So far we have been dealing with legends which represent the goddess, not as married but as forming more or less temporary unions with someone much inferior to herself, a proceeding quite characteristic of Oriental goddesses who are essentially mothers but not wives and besides whom their lovers sink into comparative insignificance."

A description of the relationship between the Goddess and Her son/lover was included by Professor E. O. James in his 1960 publication, *The Ancient Gods.* He explained Her supremacy in this way.

> It was She who was responsible for his recovery and his resuscitation on which the renewal of nature depended. So that in the last analysis Inanna/Ishtar, not Damuzi/Tammuz was the ultimate source of life and regeneration, though the young god as her agent was instrumental in the process . . . With the establishment of husbandry and domestication, however, the function of the male in the process of generation became more apparent and vital and the Mother Goddess was then assigned to a spouse to play his role as the begetter, even though as in Mesopotamia for example he was her youthful son/lover or her servant. From India to the Mediterranean, in fact, she reigned supreme, often appearing as the unmarried goddess.

Arthur Evans, eminent Oxford scholar and noted archaeologist, who located, unearthed and even partially reconstructed the royal complex at Knossos on the island of Crete, commented in 1936, "It is certain that, however much the male element had asserted itself in the domain of government, by the great days of the Minoan civilization, the religion still continued to reflect the older matriarchal stage of social development. Clearly the goddess was supreme . . ."

Discussing Anatolia, which was closely related to Minoan Crete through colonization and trade, Evans wrote, "Throughout a large part of Anatolia, again we recognize the cult of the same great mother with her male-satellite husband, lover or child, as the case may be." Another Oxford scholar of the late nineteenth century, L. R. Farnell, wrote about Crete as early as 1896. In his series of volumes *The Cults of the Greek States* he commented that "We may then safely conclude from the evidence so far available that the earliest religion of civilized Crete was mainly devoted to a great goddess, while the male deity, always inevitable in goddess cult, was subordinate and kept in the background."

Robertson Smith wrote of the position of the Goddess in Arabia, who he had previously suggested was originally deified as the parent of the stock. He described the transition of power that then took place: "In Arabian religion a goddess and a god were paired, the goddess being supreme, the god, her son, a lesser deity. Gradually there was a change whereby the attributes of the goddess were presented to the god, thus lowering the position of the female below the male."

Smith pointed out that the Goddess was still known in later patriarchal religion and claimed that Her worship was attached to "cults" which found their origins in the "ages of mother-kinship." He then discussed the time when:

> . . . the change in the law of kinship deprived the mother of her old pre-eminence in the family and transferred to the father the greater part of her authority and dignity . . . women lost the right to choose their own partners at will, the wife became subject to her husband's lordship . . . at the same time her children became, for all purposes of inheritance and all duties of blood, members of his and not her kin. So far as the religion kept pace with the new laws of social morality due to this development, the independent divine mother necessarily became the subordinate partner of a male deity . . . or if the supremacy of the goddess was too well established to be thus undermined, she might change her sex as in Southern Arabia where Ishtar was transformed into the masculine Athtar.

Summing up, he observed that, upon the acceptance of male kinship, the woman was placed in a subordinate status and the principal position in the religion was no longer held by the Goddess, but by a god. Though Smith presented the change as taking place rather naturally, as I have already mentioned and will describe in greater detail later, the transition was actually accomplished by violent aggression, brutal massacres and territorial conquests throughout the Near and Middle East.

After reading these and numerous other studies on the subject, there was no longer any doubt in my mind of the existence of the ancient female religion, nor that in the earliest of theological systems woman was deified as the principal and supreme divine being. It is this religion, once so widespread throughout the ancient world, its similarities and its local differences, that will be described throughout the rest of the book. It will once more be divided by specific names and locations, since that is how the available material is most comprehensible, but we can hardly avoid perceiving the numerous resemblances and similarities of the religion as it was known and practiced in one culture with its forms and rituals in another. That this religion preceded the male religions by thousands of years was also quite evident. But this information, rather than satisfying my curiosity, simply aroused it further. Most directly meaningful to me were a multitude of questions concerning the position and status of women who had actually lived in the societies in which the Divine Ancestress had been revered.

3
Women— Where Woman Was Deified

The question most pressing—perhaps the one that has most insistently caused this book to come into being—is this: What effect did the worship of the female deity actually have upon the status of women in the cultures in which She was extolled? Hinz, Evans, Langdon and many others have referred to the ancient Goddess-worshiping societies as matriarchal. Exactly what does this imply?

It would be easy to enter into a see-saw type of reasoning here; that is to say, they worshiped a Goddess, therefore women must have held a high status, or because women held a high status, therefore a Goddess was worshiped; though these two factors, if we judge by the attitudes of the societies that worship the male deities of today, may have been closely related. Yet various views on the subject should be considered, even those in which cause and effect appear to be confused or simultaneous events are perceived as linear. What we want to achieve is as comprehensive an understanding as possible of the relationship of the female religion to the position of women.

In *The Dominant Sex,* M. and M. Vaerting, writing in Germany in 1923, asserted that the sex of the deity was determined by the sex of those who were in power:

> The ruling sex, having the power to diffuse its own outlooks, tends to generalize its specific ideology. Should the trends of the subordinate sex run counter, they are likely to be suppressed all the more forcibly in proportion as the dominant sex is more overwhelming. The result is that the hegemony of male deities is usually associated with the dominance of men and the hegemony of female deities with the dominance of women.

Sir James Frazer believed that the high status of women was initially responsible for the veneration and esteem of the female deity. He cited the Pelew clan of Micronesia, where the women were considered to be socially and politically superior to the men. "This preference for goddesses over gods," he wrote, "in the clan of the Pelew Islanders has been explained, no doubt rightly, by the high importance of women in the social system of the people."

Robertson Smith connected the choice of the sex of the supreme deity to the position of dominance of the male or female within the family. He suggested that, as a result of the kinship system, the sexual identity of the head of the family formulated the sexual identity of the supreme deity.

Each of these is an example of the theory that the sex of the deity is determined by a previously existing dominance of one sex over the other—in the case of the Goddess, the higher position of women in the family and in society. Alongside these theories there have been reams of pseudo-poetic material about the deification of the female as the symbol of fertility—by the male—the awe of the magic of her ability to produce a child supposedly making her the object of *his* worship.

As I just mentioned, Frazer suggested that the high status of women led to the worship of the Goddess as supreme being, basing his conclusions on years of study of "primitive" and classical societies. But as a result of this research, he also connected the worship of the female deity to a mother-kinship system and ancestor worship, explaining that, "Wherever the goddess is superior to the god, and ancestresses more reverently worshipped than ancestors, there is nearly always a mother-kin structure." Robertson Smith also related the sexual identity of the supreme deity to the kinship system prevalent in each society.

Whatever the suggested order of cause and effect, one of the major factors which continually appears in the material concerned with the status and role of women in the ancient female religion in historic times is its close connection to female kinship, matrilineality, perhaps the very origins of its development. In examining the position of women, this mother or female kin structure, leading to matrilineal descent of name and property, should be carefully studied.

Matrilineality is generally defined as that societal structure in which inheritance takes place through the female line, sons, husbands or brothers gaining access to title and property only as the result of their relationship to the woman who is the legal owner. Matrilineal descent does not mean matriarchy, which is defined as women in power, or more specifically the mother, as the head of the family, taking this position in community or state government as well. In some matrilineal societies, the brother of the woman who holds the rights to the name and property plays an important role. Yet we cannot ignore the probability that matrilineal and matrilocal customs would affect the status and position of women in various ways. The subtleties of the power and bargaining position that come with the ownership of house, property or title, or as in matrilocal societies, women residing in the village or home of their own parents rather than their in-laws', should be considered.

The economics of the Neolithic and early historic agricultural societies were discussed by sociologist V. Klein in 1946. She suggested that, "In early society women wielded the main sources of wealth; they were the owners of the house, the producers of food, they provided shelter and security. Economically, therefore, man was dependent upon woman."

Societies that followed female or mother kinship customs have been known in the past and still appear in many areas of the world. The theory that most societies were originally matrilineal, matriarchal and even polyandrous (one woman with several husbands) was the subject of several extensive studies in the late nineteenth and early twentieth centuries. Scholars such as Johann Bachofen, Robert Briffault and Edward Hartland accepted the idea of ancient matriarchy and polyandry, substantiating their theories with a great deal of evidence, but they regarded these systems as a specific stage in evolutionary development. They suggested that all societies had to pass through a matriarchal stage before becoming patriarchal and monogamous, which they appear to have regarded as a superior stage of civilization. But as Jacquetta Hawkes observes, "Today it is unfashionable to talk about former more matriarchal orders of society. Nevertheless, there is evidence from many parts of the world that the role of women has weakened since earlier times in several sections of social structure."

Most of the studies of matriarchy were based upon anthropological analogy and the classical literature of Greece and Rome. Since most of these works were researched in the nineteenth and earliest part of the twentieth centuries, these writers did not have access to much of the archaeological evidence that is available today. Despite specific misunderstandings, or biased value judgments, we may yet find that these writers were prophetically ahead of their time.

Today we have the use of a much greater body of material, produced by extensive archaeological excavation of the Near and Middle East throughout this century, as well as the material available to those earlier writers. It is true that the chance fortunes of archaeological finds—what remains undiscovered, what is found too damaged to read, what cannot be deciphered and what has perished as the result of the nature of the original material— present limitations.

Hammurabi's law code of Babylon (about 1790 BC), long regarded as the oldest ever compiled, is now known to have been preceded by several others, more recently discovered. Still, only one of these dates back to about 2300 BC and the others to about 2000 BC or slightly later. So we must still rely on material that appears in written form only after the beginnings of the northern invasions. But carefully sifting through the available evidence and commentary, which differ according to location and era, we may gain some insight into the status of women in Goddess-worshiping societies. The Goddess religion, though slowly declining, still existed.

ETHIOPIA AND LIBYA—"ALL AUTHORITY WAS VESTED IN THE WOMAN . . ."

Forty-nine years before the birth of Christ, a man from Roman Sicily wrote of his travels in northern Africa and some of the Near Eastern countries, recording his observations of people along the way. He was keenly interested in cultural patterns and was certainly one of the forerunners of the fields of anthropology and sociology. This man was known as Diodorus Siculus, Diodorus of Sicily. Many statements reporting the high or even dominant status of women were included in his writings. We may question why he, more than any other classical writer, recorded so much information about women warriors and matriarchy in the nations all about him. He did not belittle the men who lived in such social systems; that did not appear to be his aim. Indeed, he seemed to be rather admiring and respectful of the women who wielded such power.

It was Diodorus who reported that the women of Ethiopia carried arms, practiced communal marriage and raised their children so communally that they often confused even themselves as to who the natural mother had been. In parts of Libya, where the Goddess Neith was highly esteemed, accounts of Amazon women still lingered even in Roman times. Diodorus described a nation in Libya as follows:

All authority was vested in the woman, who discharged every kind of public duty. The men looked after domestic affairs just as the women do among ourselves and did as they were told by their wives. They were not allowed to undertake war service or to exercise any functions of government, or to fill any public office, such as might have given them more spirit to set themselves up against the women. The children were handed over immediately after birth to the men, who reared them on milk and other foods suitable to their age.

Diodorus wrote of warrior women existing in Libya, reporting that these women had formed into armies which had invaded other lands. According to him, they revered the Goddess as their major deity and set up sanctuaries for Her worship. Though he gives no specific name, the accounts probably refer to the Libyan warrior-Goddess known as Neith, who was also revered under that name in Egypt.

EGYPT—"WHILE THE HUSBANDS STAY HOME AND WEAVE"

In prehistoric Egypt, the Goddess held supremacy in Upper Egypt (the south) as Nekhebt, symbolized as a vulture. The people of Lower Egypt, which includes the northern delta region, worshiped their supreme Goddess as a cobra, using the name Ua Zit (Great Serpent). From about 3000 BC onward the Goddess, known as Nut, Net or Nit, probably derived from Nekhebt, was said to have existed when nothing else had yet been created. She then created all that had come into being. According to Egyptian mythology, it was She who first placed Ra, the sun god, in the sky. Other texts of Egypt tell of the Goddess as Hathor in this role of creator of existence, explaining that She took the form of a serpent at that time.

In Egypt the concept of the Goddess always remained vital. The introduction of male deities, just as the dynastic periods begin (about 3000 BC) will be more thoroughly discussed in Chapter Four. This probably lessened Her original supremacy as it was known in Neolithic societies. But Goddess worship continued and in conjunction with this, the women of Egypt appear to have benefited in many ways.

Diodorus wrote at great length of the worship of the Goddess Isis (the Greek translation for Au Set), who had incorporated the aspects of both Ua Zit and Hathor. Isis was also closely associated with the Goddess as Nut, who was mythologically recorded as Her mother; in paintings Isis wore the wings of Nekhebt. Diodorus explained that, according to Egyptian religion, Isis was revered as the inventor of agriculture, as a great healer and physician and as the one who first established the laws of justice in the land.

He then recorded what we today may find a most startling description of the laws of Egypt, explaining that they were the result of the reverence paid to this mighty Goddess. He wrote, "It is for these reasons, in fact, that it was ordained that the queen should have greater power and honour than the king and that among private persons the wife should enjoy authority over the husband, husbands agreeing in the marriage contract that they will be obedient in all things to their wives."

Frazer commented on the relationship between the veneration of Isis and the customs of female kinship and stated that "In Egypt, the archaic system of mother-kin, with its preference for women over men in matters of property and inheritance, lasted down to Roman times . . ."

There is further evidence that Egypt was a land where women had great freedom and control of their own lives, and perhaps of their husbands' as well. Herodotus of Greece, several centuries before Diodorus, wrote that in Egypt, "Women go in the market-place, transact affairs and occupy themselves with business, while the husbands stay home and weave." His contemporary, Sophocles, stated that "Their thoughts and actions all are modelled on Egyptian ways, for there the men sit at the loom indoors while the wives work abroad for their daily bread."

Professor Cyrus Gordon wrote in 1953 of life in ancient Egypt. He tells us that "In family life, women had a peculiarly important position for inheritance passed through the mother rather than through the father . . . This system may well hark back to prehistoric times when only the obvious relationship between mother and child was recognized, but not the less apparent relationship between father and child."

Dr. Murray suggested that "Woman's condition was high, due perhaps to their economic independence." S. W. Baron writes that in Egyptian papyri, "many women appear as parties in civil litigations and independent business transactions even with their own husbands and fathers." One of the earliest archaeologists of the pyramids of Egypt, Sir William Flinders Petrie, wrote in 1925 that "In Egypt all property went in the female line, the woman was the mistress of the house; and in early tales she is represented as having entire control of herself and the place."

Discussing the position of women in ancient Egypt, theologian and archaeologist Roland de Vaux wrote in 1965 that "In Egypt the wife was often the head of the family, with all the rights such a position entailed." Obedience was urged upon husbands in the maxims of Ptah-Hotep. Marriage contracts of all periods attest the extremely independent social and economic position of women. According to E. Meyer, who is quoted in the Vaertings' study, "Among the Egyptians the women were remarkably free . . . as late as the fourth century BC there existed side by side with patriarchal marriage, a form of marriage in which the wife chose the husband and could divorce him on payment of compensation."

Love poems, discovered in Egyptian tombs, strongly hint that it was the Egyptian women who did the courting, oftimes wooing the male by plying him with intoxicants to weaken his protestations. Robert Briffault wrote of an Egyptian woman clerk who later became a governor and eventually the commander-in-chief of an army.

A most enlightening and significant study on the social structure and position of women in Egypt was done in 1949 by Dr. Margaret Murray. Painstakingly tracing the lineage of royal families in Egypt, she eventually proved that, at the level of royalty, the Egyptian culture at most periods was matrilineal. Royalty was studied because records for these people were most available. According to Murray it was the daughters, not the sons, who were the actual inheritors of the royal throne. She suggests that the custom of brother/sister marriage then developed, allowing a son to gain access to the royal privilege in this way. She writes that the matrilineal right to the throne was the reason that Egyptian princesses for so many centuries were married within the family and were not available for international marriage alliances. This may clarify why the Goddess Isis, who Frazer stated was a more important deity than Her brother/husband Osiris, and whom Diodorus cited as the origin of the generally high position of women in Egypt, was known as The Throne.

But even in Egypt women were slowly losing their prestigious position. Sir Flinders Petrie, incidentally a deeply respected colleague of Dr. Murray's at the University of London, discussed the role of priestesses in ancient Egypt. He pointed out how their position had changed between the time of the earliest dynasties (3000 BC onward) to the Eighteenth Dynasty (1570–1300 BC). According to the available records, the Goddess known as Hathor, much the same deity as Isis, was in earliest times served by sixty-one priestesses and eighteen priests, while the Goddess known as Neith was attended solely by priestesses. By the time of the Eighteenth Dynasty women were no longer even part of the religious clergy, but served only as temple musicians. It is in the Eighteenth Dynasty that Egypt was made to feel the greatest influence of the Indo-Europeans, a factor again discussed at greater length in Chapters Four and Five. Incidentally, the use of the word "pharaoh," generally summoning up images even more powerful than the word "king," actually comes from the term par-o, which literally means "great house." It was only from the time of the Eighteenth Dynasty that the word was used to signify the royal male of that household.

SUMER—"THE WOMEN OF FORMER DAYS USED TO TAKE TWO HUSBANDS . . ."

Professor Saggs wrote in 1962 of the societies of Mesopotamia, which included both Sumer and Babylon. Mesopotamia generally refers to the areas of Iraq along and between the Tigris and Euphrates rivers, starting at the Persian Gulf and reaching up to Anatolia. He examined the relationship of the reverence for Goddesses to the status of women in Sumer (about 3000 BC–1800 BC, in southern Iraq), concluding that in the earliest periods women were much better off than in the later periods, and that they gradually lost ground over the years. Professor Saggs reports that

> The status of women was certainly much higher in the early Sumerian city state than it subsequently became . . . There are hints that in the very beginning of Sumerian society, women had a much higher status than in the hey-day of Sumerian culture: this chiefly rests on the fact that in early Sumerian religion a prominent position is occupied by goddesses who afterwards virtually disappeared, save—with the one exception of Ishtar—as consorts to particular gods. The Underworld itself was under the sole rule of a goddess, for a myth explains how she came to take a consort; and goddesses played a part in the divine decision making assembly in the myths. There is even one strong suggestion that polyandry may have at one time been practised, for the reforms of Urukagina refer to women who had taken more than one husband; some scholars shied away from this conclusion suggesting that the reference might be only to the remarriage of a widow but the wording of the Sumerian text does not really support this.

I may add that the Goddess of the Underworld does not merely take a consort but has Her hair pulled, is dragged from the throne and is threatened with death until She agrees to marry Her assailant, the god Nergal, who then kisses away Her tears, becomes Her husband and rules beside Her.

The Urukagina reform is dated at about 2300 BC. It reads, "The women of former days used to take two husbands but the women of today would be stoned with stones if they did this." Polyandry has been reported in the Dravidian Goddess-worshiping areas of India even in this century.

The laws of the Sumerian state of Eshnunna, written about 2000 BC, were found in a small town, thus possibly reflecting older attitudes. In them we read that "If a man rejects his wife after she bears a child, and takes another wife, he shall be driven from the house and from whatever he owns and if any accept him they may follow him." These same laws also state that if a woman is married but has a child with another man while her husband is away at war, she is still legally regarded as the wife of the first man. There is no mention of punishment for adultery. Permission for marriage had to be received from both mother and father.

The position and activities of a group of Sumerian women known as the *naditu* were studied in depth by Rivkah Harris in 1962. Carefully examining Sumerian texts, she found that the *naditu* women were engaged in the business activities of the temple, held real estate in their own names, lent money and generally engaged in various economic activities. She also found accounts at this same period of many women scribes. Yet we read in Professor Sidney Smith's chapter in Hooke's *Myth, Ritual and Kingship* that the word *naditu* "probably means woman thrown down, that is surrendered to the god."

In the Sumerian hymns the female precedes the male. The epic of Gilgamish reveals that the official scribe of the Sumerian heaven was a woman, while the initial invention of writing was credited to a Goddess. As I mentioned previously, it may well have been the priestesses, possibly the *naditu* who kept the temple business accounts, who first developed the art of writing. The earliest examples of writing (from about 3200 BC), discovered in the temple of the Goddess Inanna of Erech, where many of the *naditu* women lived, turned out to be the temple's accounts of payment for land rental.

Stephen Langdon, eminent Oxford scholar, writing in 1930, observed that the legends associated with the Sumerian Queen of Heaven, Inanna, had probably been worked out under a "matriarchal system" of society. This is also suggested by the changes in the image and role of the Goddess Inanna, when we find Her centuries later as the Babylonian Ishtar. In the Sumerian myth, Inanna exhibited Her power and omnipotent wrath at Her son/ lover Damuzi's refusal to show proper respect to Her by turning him over to the demons of the Land of the Dead, while thirteen centuries later, in the Babylonian myth of Ishtar, a newer version of much the same story, the Goddess grieved at the accidental death of the youth.

In general, the records of the Sumerian reforms of Urukagina of about 2300 BC were strongly communally oriented. They referred to the fruit trees and food of the temple lands, which were to be used for those in need rather than by priests, which was apparently fast becoming the custom at that time. The fact that on these tablets it was repeatedly mentioned that these reforms harked back to the way things were done in earlier periods suggests that the earliest societies of Sumer were more communal. Most interesting is the word used to label these reforms, *amargi*, which has received the double translation of "freedom" and "return to the mother."

ELAM—NAKED BEFORE THE HIGH PRIESTESS

In 1973 Dr. Walther Hinz suggested that the original supremacy of the Goddess in Elam (slightly east of Sumer and in close contact by 3000 BC), indicated a "matriarchal approach" in the devotees of Her religion. He explained that, though She was supreme in the third millenium, She later became secondary to Her consort Humban; She was then known as the Great Wife. In Susa, at the northern end of the Elamite territories, the male consort was known as In Shushinak. In earliest times he was known as Father of the Weak, by mid-second millenium he was called King of the Gods and in the eighth century BC he was invoked as Protector of the Gods of Heaven and Earth.

In the early periods of Elam the deities appear to have been served by female and male clergy, the men appearing naked before the high priestess, as was the custom in early Sumer. Hinz explains that in Elam, much like the *naditu* women of Sumer, "One special group among the priestesses was formed by those women or maidens who had dedicated their lives to the Great Goddess." These women were primarily involved in the buying, selling and renting of land.

Legal documents from Elam, primarily from after 2000 BC, reveal that women were often the sole heirs. One married woman refused to make her inheritance joint with her husband and intended to pass the inheritance along to her daughter. Another tablet stated that a son and a daughter were to share equally; the daughter was mentioned first. Several tablets described situations where the husband was leaving everything he owned to his wife and insisted that their children would inherit only if they cared for their mother with the greatest respect.

BABYLON—"TO HOLD AND MANAGE THEIR OWN ESTATES"

In Mesopotamia, the Akkadians, after a rise in position under Sargon in 2300 BC, eventually gained supremacy in about 1900 BC, gradually superseding the Sumerians as the cultural and political leaders of the area. They formed the nation known as Babylonia, installing their capital in the city of Babylon on the central Euphrates. The Akkadian language of the Babylonians became the international language of the Near East, but the religion of the Sumerians was incorporated into the Babylonian culture and the Sumerian language was used much as Latin was employed in the masses of the Roman Catholic Church all over the world. By 1600 BC the Kassites gained control of Babylon. Linguistic evidence suggests that the Kassites were ruled by the northern invaders, the Indo-Europeans, who had gradually infiltrated into Babylon and Assyria.

Despite a loss of status in the position of women in Babylon, compared with their predecessors of Sumer—a loss that was accompanied by the gaining ascendancy of male deities such as Marduk, who mythically murdered the Creator Goddess Tiamat to gain and secure his position—the women of Babylon still continued to hold certain rights of independence. The following quote is based upon the law code of Hammurabi, which preceded total Kassite control, but which may have been somewhat affected by continual Indo-European incursions from the north from at least 2000 BC onward. W. Boscawen, writing in 1894, reported that

> The freedom granted to the women in Babylonia allowed them to hold and manage their own estates and this was especially the case with priestesses of the temple, who traded extensively . . . One of the most interesting and characteristic features of this early civilization of the Babylonians was the high position of women. The mother here is always represented by a sign which means "goddess of the house." Any sin against the mother, any repudiation against the mother was punished by banishment from the community. These are the facts which are evidently indicative of a people who at one time held the law of matriarchal descent.

According to de Vaux, writing in 1965, "In Babylonian law, the father gave the young bride certain possessions, which belonged to her in her own right, the husband having only the use of them. They reverted to the wife if she was widowed or divorced without fault on her part. In Babylon she could acquire property, take legal action, be a party to contracts and she had a certain share in her husband's inheritance."

In Hammurabi's time women were free to request divorce, and one Babylonian law declared that if a wife did not intend to be responsible for her husband's premarital debts she had to obtain a document from him stating that he had agreed. This assumption of the financial responsibility in marriage suggests that most women may have taken part in business and financial affairs (as they did in Egypt) and perhaps at one time had been economically responsible for the family. Seven of Hammurabi's laws were concerned with the priestesses of the temple, their rights to inherit and what they might or might not pass along to offspring, suggesting that the economic position of these women was a matter of concern and probably was quickly changing.

Ishtar was revered as "majestic queen whose decrees are pre-eminent." In one text Ishtar Herself says, "When at a trial of judgement I am present, a woman understanding the matter, I am." At Nimrud, in northern Mesopotamia, records of women judges and magistrates have been unearthed, testifying to the vital and respected position women held there even in the eighth century BC. In several cities there were accounts of Babylonian priestesses who acted as oracular prophetesses, providing military and political advice to kings and leaders, revealing their powerful influence upon the affairs of state. Accounts of women scribes occur in all Babylonian periods, though there were more males in this field than women.

We find in the laws of later Babylonia, which belong to some time at the end of the second millenium, that a married woman might no longer engage in business, unless it was directed by her husband, son or brother-in-law. If anyone engaged in business with her, even if he insisted that he did not know she was married, he was to be prosecuted as a criminal.

ANATOLIA—"FROM OF OLD THEY HAVE BEEN RULED BY THE WOMEN"

Just north of Babylon, and in very close political contact, was the area known as Anatolia, present-day Turkey, sometimes known as Asia Minor. In Neolithic periods in Anatolia, the Great Goddess was extolled. Her worship appeared in the shrines of Catal Hüyük of 6500 BC. Little is yet known of Anatolia directly after the Catal Hüyük period, but sometime before 2000 BC Anatolia was invaded by the Indo-Europeans.

The areas where the northern peoples made the heaviest settlements were in the central and south-central sections of Anatolia. Some of them conquered the land known as Hatti. The invaders as well as the original inhabitants thus came to be known as the Hittites. Most of the Goddesses who appear in the literature and texts of this area, written after the Hittite arrival, were actually the older Hattian deities. One of the most important female deities to survive was the Sun Goddess of Arinna. Upon the Hittite conquests She was assigned a husband who was symbolized as a storm god. Although this storm god gained supremacy in most of the cities where the northern peoples ruled, in Arinna he remained in second place. But curiously enough, Hittite queens appear in several texts in a very close relationship to this Hattian Sun Goddess; they acted as Her high priestess. Though there is no conclusive evidence to substantiate it, the existence of these texts suggests the possibility that the invaders, once martially conquering the land, may then have married Hattian priestesses to gain a more secure legitimate right to the throne in the eyes of the conquered population.

In the western sections of Anatolia, matrilineal descent and Goddess worship continued into classical times. Strabo, shortly before the birth of Christ, wrote of northern Anatolian towns, as far east as Armenia, where children who were born to unmarried women were legitimate and respectable. They simply took the name of their mothers, who, according to Strabo's reports, were some of the most noble and aristocratic of citizens.

It is possible that at the time of the Hittite invasions many of the Goddess-worshiping peoples may have fled to the west. The renowned temple of the Goddess in the city of Ephesus was the target of the apostle Paul's zealous missionary efforts (Acts 19:27). This temple, which legend and classical reports claim was founded by "Amazons," was not completely closed down until AD 380. All along this western section, which included the areas known as Lycia, Lydia and Caria, there were accounts in classical Greek and Roman literature of the widespread veneration of "The Mother of all Deities," along with reports of women warriors, the Amazons. Diodorus wrote of a nation in this area in which "women held the supreme power and royal authority." According to his reports the queen of this land assigned the tasks of spinning wool and other domestic duties to the men, while law was established by the queen.

He claimed that the rights to the throne belonged to the queen's daughter and succeeding women in the family line. It was in the land of Lydia that the legendary Indo-European Greek Hercules was said to have been kept as a servile lover to Queen Omphale. We may at this point question whether the numerous tales of "Amazon" women may not actually have been the later Indo-European Greek accounts of the women who tried to defend the ancient Goddess shrines and repel the patriarchal northern invaders. Yet we read in the *Encyclopaedia Britannica,* "The only plausible explanation of the story of the Amazons is that it is a variety of the familiar tale of a distant land where everything is done the wrong way about; thus women fight, which is man's business."

Throughout the classical Greek period, matrilineal descent and suggestions of matriarchy in western Anatolia were repeatedly reported among the Lycians, where they appear to have lingered the longest or were most noted. Herodotus wrote, "Ask a Lycian who he is and he answers by giving his own name, that of his mother and so on in the female line." Nicholas of Damascus reported, "They name themselves after their mothers and their possessions pass by inheritance to the daughters instead of the sons." Heraclides Ponticus said of the Lycians, "From of old they have been ruled by the women."

CRETE—"DOMINATED BY THE FEMALE PRINCIPLE"

Many classical authors wrote that the Lycians and the Carians had strong affinities with the island of Crete. Some claimed that Lycia had once been a colony of that thriving island culture. Upon Crete, Goddess figures have been found in various Neolithic sites, though none as old as those on the mainland. On the Messara plain of Crete, the buildings known as *tholoi,* extremely similar to those of the Halaf site of Arpachiyah, have also been discovered. From Neolithic periods until the Dorian invasion, Crete was the society that is most repeatedly thought to have been matrilineal and possibly matriarchal.

The former director of the British School of Archaeology in Greece, Sinclair Hood, wrote in *The Minoans, Crete in the Bronze Age*:

It seems likely enough that customs of the kind described as matriarchy (mother rule) persisted in Crete. These arise in primitive societies where people do not comprehend when a baby is born who its father can be. The children are therefore named after the mothers and all inheritance is through the female line. Primeval traditions of this kind survived in western Anatolia into classical times. Thus among the Carians on the west coast of Anatolia succession was still through the mother in the fourth century BC and in Lycia, to the south-east of Caria, children were named after their mothers.

Charles Seltman wrote in 1952 of this highly developed culture of Crete, whose beginnings preceded biblical times by many centuries. He stated that, upon Crete, matriarchy had been the way of life. He discussed the sexual freedom of women, matrilineal descent and the role of the "king," pointing out the high status of women in and around the land in which the Goddess appears to have been the very core of existence.

"Among the Mediterraneans," wrote Seltman, "as a general rule society was built around the woman, even on the highest levels where descent was in the female line. A man became *king* or *chieftain* only by a formal marriage and his daughter, not his son, succeeded so that the next chieftain was the youth who married his daughter . . . Until the northerners arrived, religion and custom were dominated by the female principle."

In *The Aegean Civilization,* Gustave Glotz, writing in 1925, examined the role of woman on Crete and asserted that women initially controlled the form and rites of the religion. He explains that

The priestesses long presided over religious practices. Woman was the natural intermediary with divinities, the greatest of whom was woman deified. Hosts of objects represent the priestesses at their duties . . . the participation of men in the cult was, like the association of a god with a goddess, a late development. Their part in the religious ceremonies was always a subordinate one, even when the king became the high priest of the bull. As if to extenuate their encroachment and to baffle the evil spirits to whose power this act had exposed them, they assumed for divine services the priestly costume of women . . . while private worship was performed in front of small idols, in public worship the part of the goddess was played by a woman. It is the high priestess who takes her place on the seat of the goddess, sits at the foot of the sacred tree or stands on the mountain peak to receive worship and offerings from her acolytes and from the faithful.

Stylianos Alexiou, Director of the Archaeological Museum in Iraklion, writes in the chapter on the religion of Crete in *Minoan Civilization,* "The alabaster throne at Knossos was intended, according to Helga Reusch, for the Priestess-queen, who, flanked by the griffins painted on the wall, personified the goddess. In the Royal Villa the throne which is set apart like a kind of sacred altar, shows that an actual person sat there to receive worship. According to Matz, when the queen descended the palace stairs to the courts within the shrines, she represented an authentic epiphany of the deity to the host of ecstatic worshippers."

In 1958 Jacquetta Hawkes presented some perceptive observations on the status of women on Crete, commenting that, although one may consider the possibility that the Goddess may have been a masculine dream, "Cretan men and women were everywhere accustomed to seeing a splendid goddess queening it over a small and suppliant male god, and this concept must surely have expressed some attitude present in the human society that accepted it." She continued by pointing out that the self-confidence of women and their secure place in society was perhaps made evident by another characteristic. "This is the fearless and natural emphasis on sexual life that ran through all religious expression and was made obvious in the provocative dress of both sexes and their easy mingling—a spirit best understood through its opposite: the total veiling and seclusion of Moslem women under a faith which even denied them a soul."

In viewing the artifacts and murals at Knossos, the Archaeological Museum at Iraklion and other museums on Crete there is little doubt that the female divinity was for several millenia the principal sacred being on Crete, with women acting as Her clergy. It is therefore interesting to follow the manifestations of the Cretan culture as they later appeared in early Greece, about one thousand years before the classical Golden Age (about 500–200 BC), with which we are more familiar.

GREECE—"THE ATTACK UPON THE MATRILINEAL CLANS"

The connections are made by the settlements on Crete and/or the mainland of Greece that are attributed to people known as the Mycenaeans, so named by archaeologists for one of the sites on the mainland—Mycenae. Clues to the origins of the people who inhabited these sites have presented scholars with some intriguing possibilities. Most believe that the Mycenaeans were a group of Indo-Europeans, perhaps the same people as the Acheans, or possibly those from an earlier migration of tribes from the north. Other scholars assert that they were already residents of Crete and that they overthrew the previous government shortly before 1400 BC. Some relate them to the group known as the Sea Peoples, while still others suggest that they were the Philistines or that the Philistines were a branch of the Mycenaeans. There has even been the suggestion that the Mycenaeans were related to the Hyksos, the "shepherd kings" who used horse-drawn war chariots and had previously held Egypt under their rule for several centuries. The Hyksos were driven out of Egypt at much the same time as the Mycenaeans first appeared.

Whatever their initial origins, the reason that the Mycenaeans are important to us here is that their culture, as we best know it, was partially Cretan and partially Greek. Most scholars believe that they carried the Cretan culture from Crete to Greece. The Linear B tablets of the Mycenaeans, which are inventory lists, found at the palace of Knossos and all dated to the same year, about 1400 BC, used a language that scholars believe differed from those previously used on Crete. After many years of debate, most authorities accept that the language used on these tablets (written with many of the symbols and signs that had been used for an earlier language not yet acceptably deciphered, though Gordon has offered a body of evidence suggesting that it was closely related to the Canaanite language used in Ugarit) is an early form of Greek. If the Mycenaeans or their leaders were originally Indo-European, as the tablets suggest, once they settled in Crete they soon adopted much of the subject matter and the style of the crafts techniques, the style of dress, the manner of writing, and the religion of the previous inhabitants of the island.

Cottrell tells us that, "Mycenaean art continued to reflect the "Minoan"* culture of the Mediterranean peoples . . . whose system of writing they had adopted." R. W. Hutchinson of the University of Cambridge writes that, "By the middle of the second millenium, probably, Greeks were already settling in Crete, but only in comparatively small numbers, and these Mycenaean Greeks had already adopted many Cretan cults and religious customs. Even on the mainland we find survivals from Minoan or at least pre-Hellenic religion . . ."

In the Catalog of Prehistoric Collections of the National Archaeological Museum in Athens the curators point out, "In Mycenaean religion, where the adoption of many Cretan features is obvious, we may note above all the appearance of the Cretan nature goddess." In this vast museum is the collection of artifacts discovered in the excavations of the Mycenaean settlements on the mainland of Greece, a collection highlighted by the intricate craftsmanship of gold signet rings and seals that depict scenes of the Goddess and Her priestesses—scenes nearly identical with those produced in "Minoan" Crete.

Discussing the Linear B tablets, in which the names of several deities later known in classical Greece are briefly mentioned, Cot-

*"Minoan" is the name given to the indigenous culture of Crete (pre-Mycenaean) by its excavator, Sir Arthur Evans. The name was based on a classical Greek account of a King Minos of Crete, who, it now appears, may actually have lived during the Mycenaean period.

trell explains, " . . . there is also at Pylos [on the mainland] and at Knossos [on Crete] a frequent reference to *Potnia*—"Mistress" or "Our Lady"; these last inscriptions confirm what archaeologists had long suspected from the evidence on seals discovered on the mainland—that the Mycenaeans also worshipped the Minoan mother goddess."

The Mycenaeans inhabited and ruled Crete at the Palace of Knossos shortly before a major holocaust, possibly caused by an invasion or earthquake. These same people also founded many pre-Greek cities on the mainland—and with them they brought the worship of the Cretan Goddess. The Mycenaean Age is generally placed between about 1450 and 1100 BC. Its beginnings date just before the period generally assigned to Moses. It thrived for centuries before the Greece of Homer and it is likely that it was of events during or just after this period that Homer wrote. The quest for Helen may well have been the quest for the legal rights to the throne of Sparta. Although classical Greece is so often presented as the very foundation of our western culture and civilization, it is interesting to realize that it actually came into being twenty-five centuries after the invention of writing and was itself formulated and deeply influenced by the Near Eastern cultures that had preceded it by thousands of years.

Greece was invaded by northern peoples several times. Robert Graves, in his introduction to *The Greek Myths,* wrote in 1955, "Achaean invasions of the thirteenth century BC seriously weakened the matrilineal tradition . . . when the Dorians arrived, towards the close of the second millenium, patrilineal succession became the rule." With these northern people came the worship of the Indo-European Dyaus Pitar, literally God Father, eventually known in Greece as Zeus and later in Rome as Jupiter. This transitional period of the change from the worship of the Goddess to the male deity, the change most intensively brought about by the Dorian invasions, was the subject of E. Butterworth's *Some Traces of the Pre-Olympian World,* written in 1966.

Butterworth managed to accomplish with Greece what Murray

had done with Egypt. By carefully tracing the lineage of the royal houses, he ultimately showed that many of the greatest pre-Greek cities, which were essentially small nations, were originally matrilineal. He pointed out that Argos, Thebes, Tiryns and Athens, as well as other cities, at one time followed matrilineal customs of descent. He explains that this was the result of the worship of the Goddess and Her Cretan origins, stating that Crete itself was matrilineal and possibly even matriarchal.

His primary interest was in the patrilineal revolution, the time at which the patrilineal clans violently set about superimposing their customs upon all those around them:

> Matrilineality, though not universal in the Greek and Aegean world, was widely spread . . . the effect of the system of succession to the kingship and to the inheritance of property on the life of the times was immense. The majority of the clans were matrilineal by custom, and the greatest revolution in the history of early Greece was that by which the custom was changed from matrilineal to patrilineal succession and the loyalty to the clan destroyed.

From 3000 BC onward, priestesses had been portrayed in sculptures and appeared in murals and other artifacts of Crete, strongly suggesting that it was women who controlled the worship. Crete was later ruled by the Mycenaeans, who then adopted their religion and many aspects of their culture. Since the religious artifacts of the Mycenaeans depict the clergy of the Goddess as female, it is quite probable that the women in the Mycenaean communities of Greece also held this privilege. Butterworth asserted that it was the women, especially the women of the royal houses, who were the protectors of the religion. He further explains that

> The attack upon the matrilineal clans destroyed the power of the clan world itself and with it, its religion . . . the history of the times is penetrated through and through with the clash of patrilineal and matrilineal as the old religious dynasties were broken, swept away and re-established . . . The matrilineal world was brought to an end by a number of murderous assaults upon the heart of that world, the Potnia Mater [The Great Goddess] herself.

I cannot help but recall the Greek legend of the Goddess known as Hera, whose worship appears to have survived from Mycenaean times, and Her thwarted rebellion against Her newly assigned husband Zeus, surely an allegorical reminder of those who struggled for the primacy of the Goddess—and lost. Yet, according to Hawkes, many of the attitudes about the lowly position of the women of classical Greece were greatly exaggerated by "the bias of nineteenth century scholarship." She suggests that, even in the classical period of Greece, women retained some of their Cretan predecessors' freedom:

> Just as in Crete, women shared the power of the Goddess both psychologically and socially; priestesses were of high standing and priestly associations of women were formed round temples and holy places. There was an influential one for example associated with the famous temple of Artemis (Diana) at Ephesus. At this city and indeed in Ionia generally, women and girls enjoyed much freedom. While women certainly won influence and responsibility by serving at the temples and great state festivals of the goddesses, there was also the liberation of the ancient cults. Respectable matrons and girls in large companies would spend whole nights on the bare hills in dances which stimulated ecstasy, and in intoxication, perhaps partly alcoholic, but mainly mystical. Husbands disapproved, but, it is said, did not like to interfere in religious matters.

In the classical age of Sparta, where the veneration of the Goddess as Artemis continued to thrive, women were extremely free and independent. According to both Euripedes and Plutarch, young Spartan women were not to be found at home but in the gymnasia where they tossed off their restricting clothing and wrestled naked with their male contemporaries. Women of Sparta appear to have had total sexual freedom, and though monogamy was said to be the official marriage rule, it was mentioned in several classical accounts that it was not taken very seriously. Plutarch reported that in Sparta the infidelity of women was even somewhat glorified, while Nicholas of Damascus, perhaps as the result of some personal experience, tells us that a Spartan woman was entitled to have herself made pregnant by the handsomest man she could find, whether native or foreigner.

CANAAN—"THE SOCIAL AND LEGAL POSITION OF AN ISRAELITE WIFE . . ."

I have saved the examination of the women in the two Hebrew nations of Judah and Israel for last, since we generally regard them as part of an isolated patriarchal society which worshiped the male deity alone. At this point it will be clarifying to compare the position of Hebrew women not only with their contemporaries in Babylon and Egypt, cultures so intertwined with their own, but also with the other women of Canaan, where they finally settled.

In the city of Ugarit in northern Canaan of the fourteenth century BC, which was not a Hebrew community, there are records of a woman whose title was translated as "Important Lady of the Royal House." She was known as the Adath (meaning "Lady," as the female counterpart of Adon meaning "Lord"). The Goddess in this area was known as Anath, which may be much the same word. The texts of Ugarit (present-day Ras Shamra in Syria), where legends of Anath were also unearthed, revealed that this "Important Lady" took an active part in political affairs.

Claude Schaeffer, co-director of the first excavation at Ugarit, wrote in 1939, "The social status of women, and particularly the mother of the family, thus appears to have been a high one in Ugarit." Ugaritan documents of this same period reveal that upon divorce or widowhood a woman kept her own property. Legal records read much like those of Elam, stating that husbands left their possessions to their wives rather than their children; these children are told not to quarrel but to respect and obey their mother. As I shall explain in the following two chapters, at Ugarit there was a curious combination of the southern and northern cultures, reflected in their religious myths. There are accounts of many Indo-Europeans living in that city by the fourteenth century, yet the status of women does not appear to have been greatly affected by it at that time.

Among the Ammonites of Canaan, a people with whom the Hebrews were in repeated conflict, women acted in official capacities. In 1961 archaeologist G. Landes wrote of "the superior position of women being in agreement with nomadic practice." He stated that queens, such as the Queen of Sheba (about 950 BC), at times led Arab states or tribes and that this was also attested in the eighth and seventh centuries BC.

In contrast to the economic, legal and social position of women all about them, the position of the Israelite women exhibits the effects of the almost total acceptance of the male deity Yahweh, and the patriarchal society that accompanied it. According to the Bible, though no archaeological evidence has yet been found to confirm it, the Israelite laws date from the time of Moses (about 1300–1250 BC). They continue as the law of the Hebrews of Canaan until the fall of the northern kingdom known as Israel in 722 BC and the fall of the southern kingdom known as Judah in 586 BC. These same laws still appear in the Old Testament of the Judeo-Christian Bible to this day.

Through an intensive study of the Bible, archaeologist and priest Roland de Vaux made these observations about Hebrew women in his study of 1965, published as *Ancient Israel*:

> The social and legal position of an Israelite wife was inferior to the position a wife occupied in the great countries round about . . . all the texts show that Israelites wanted mainly sons, to perpetuate the family line and fortune, and to preserve the ancestral inheritance . . . A husband could divorce his wife . . . women on the other hand could not ask for divorce . . . the wife called her husband Ba'al or master; she also called him adon or lord; she addressed him in fact as a slave addressed his master or a subject, his king. The Decalogue includes a man's wife among his possessions . . . all her life she remains a minor. The wife does not inherit from her husband, nor daughters from their father, except when there is no male heir. A vow made by a girl or married woman needs, to be valid, the consent of the father or husband and if this consent is withheld, the vow is null and void. A man had the right to sell his daughter. Women were excluded from the succession.

De Vaux asserted that, unlike all the other cultures of the Near East, there were no priestesses allowed in the Israelite faith. He explained that:

. . . the suggestion that there were women among the clergy of the temple clashes with an important linguistic fact: there were priestesses in Assyria, priestesses and high priestesses in Phoenicia, where they are shown by the feminine of kohen; in the Minaean inscriptions there was a feminine form of lw' [priest] which some scholars would link with the Hebrew lewy, but Hebrew has no corresponding noun to kohen or lewy, no women ever held a place among the Israelite clergy.

I might add that according to Hebrew law a woman had no right to money or property upon divorce and since her vow was invalid, presumably she could not engage in business. Perhaps the most shocking laws of all were those that declared that a woman was to be stoned or burned to death for losing her virginity before marriage, a factor never before mentioned in other law codes of the Near East, and that, upon being the victim of rape, a single woman was forced to marry the rapist; if she was already betrothed or married she was to be stoned to death for having been raped.

Perhaps the clearest explanation of the status of early Hebrew women was revealed by archaeologist D. Ussishkin in 1970. He described an ancient Hebrew tomb recently unearthed in Israel in this way: "Thus it seems that one body, almost certainly that of the husband, was placed higher than the body of the wife, so that the woman's inferior status was also demonstrated after her death."

Despite the lowly position of women decreed by the Hebrew laws and customs, there were two incidents that reveal a possible revival of the ancient Goddess religion, even within the royal house of Israel. Their association with the ancient beliefs suggests that two queens may have gained power through the ancient matrilineal customs, which had perhaps slipped back into Israel along with other "pagan" patterns. Both incidents involved women who were listed as Hebrew queens, one in Israel and the other in Judah.

The first concerns a woman known as Queen Maacah, possibly a descendant of an Aramaean princess of the same name who was in the harem of Hebrew king David. This second Maacah was listed in the Bible as the queen of Rehoboam, king of Israel from about 922 to 915 BC. His own mother was not Hebrew, but an

Ammonite princess. This king is recorded as having erected "pagan" golden calves. Murray suggests that this same Queen Maacah was later the wife of the succeeding king, Abijam, who is listed as the son of Maacah and Rehoboam. Her suggestion is based upon the fact that some versions of the Bible list Maacah as the mother of Abijam's son Asa. Other versions list Maacah as his grandmother, but place her name where the name of the mother would ordinarily be listed and never mention who his mother was, a pattern quite unlike all other descriptions of royal Hebrew sons. Murray wrote, "The only way that Abijam and Asa could have had the same mother, was by marriage of Abijam with his own mother."

It was Asa who brought about many Hebrew reforms, suppressing the then very prevalent "heathen" practices, and who finally had Maacah dethroned. In light of the curious discrepancies in Asa's genealogy, the reason given in the Bible for the dethronement is all the more interesting. In I Kings 15:2–14 we read that Maacah had made an *asherah,* that is, a statue of the Goddess Asherah. Considering the repeated evidence of "paganism" during this period, it seems quite likely that Israel had taken up the religious customs of old, at that time accepting the female religion and the female kinship succession to the throne. If this was so, then Maacah would have been the royal heiress and held this position until Asa, possibly under the influence of Hebrew priests, once again established the religion of Yahweh.

The second incident is dated at about 842 BC, when Athaliah, daughter of Queen Jezebel, claimed the throne of Judah as her own. According to Hebrew law, women were not allowed to reign alone. Yet it required a violent revolution to dethrone her. Jezebel herself was closely identified with the ancient religion. Jezebel's parents, Athaliah's grandparents, were the high priestess and priest of Ashtoreth and Baal in the Canaanite city of Sidon, reigning there as queen and king. The murder of Jezebel, who had reigned alongside Ahab as queen in the northern kingdom of Israel, was actually a political assault upon the religion of the Goddess. This is made clear in the events that followed her murder in the biblical account in Kings I and II. So it is worth noting that it was Jezebel's daughter who ascended to the royal throne of Judah, the only woman ever to rule the Hebrew nation alone. Most significant is the fact that, once Athaliah secured her rights to the throne, she reigned for about six years, re-establishing the ancient "pagan" religion throughout the nation, much to the distress of the Hebrew priests.

SUMMARY

Though cause and effect between matrilineal descent, high female status and the veneration of the Goddess are often confused, we cannot avoid the fact that repeated evidence attests that the religion of the Goddess and a female kinship system were closely intertwined in many parts of the Near East. Though much of the material pertains to royalty, there is enough to suggest that matrilineal customs were practiced in many areas by the general population as well. In examining the transition from the Goddess religion to the worship of the male deity as supreme and the subsequent effects upon the status of women, we find certain patterns emerging.

From the beginning of the second millenium, the Assyrians were in close political and commercial contact with the Indo-European Hittites. Indo-European Hurrian princes appeared in various cities of northern Syria from that same time on. By 1600 BC Babylon was controlled by the Indo-European-led Kassites. By 1500 BC Assyria was completely under the control of the Hurrians who had formed the kingdom of Mitanni.

Accompanying these conquests was the introduction of the myth of Marduk, who, we are told, murdered the Goddess to gain his supreme position in Babylon. In Assyria the same myth was told, the name of Ashur simply substituted for the name of Marduk. Throughout the second millenium, the Indo-Europeans made further inroads into the lands of Canaan and Mesopotamia and, as I shall explain in the next two chapters, may have played an important role in the formation of the Hebrew religion and laws.

It may be helpful at this point to summarize the changes in the laws as they affected various aspects of the lives of women. In Eshnunna (in Sumer) at about 2000 BC, if a man raped a woman he was put to death. In the Old Babylonian period of Hammurabi, before the major incursions of the Indo-Europeans, though many of the northerners were in Babylonia even at that time, the same punishment was given. In the laws of Assyria, which are dated between 1450 and 1250 BC (when Assyria was under Indo-European control), we read that if a man rapes a woman the husband or father of that woman should then rape the rapist's wife or daughter and/or marry his own daughter to the rapist. The last part of the law was also the law of the Hebrews, who added that a raped woman must be put to death if she was already married or betrothed. Assyrian laws appear to be the first to mention abortion, assigning the penalty as death.

The reforms of Urukagina (about 2300 BC) refer to the fact that women used to take two husbands, though at the time of his reign this was no longer allowed. In the laws of Eshnunna a man who took a second wife, after his first had given birth to a child, was to be expelled from the house without any possessions. In Eshnunna, if a woman had a child by another man while her husband was away at war, her husband was expected to take her back as his wife. No punishment for adultery was mentioned. In Hammurabi's laws, if a woman related to another man sexually she was expected to take an oath at the temple and return home to her husband. The Assyrian and Hebrew laws give the husband the right to murder both the wife and lover.

It is somewhat difficult to make comparisons between the various places and periods since the laws seem to have been included to codify very specific incidents and refer to varying situations. The major changes in the laws concerning women affected their right to engage in economic activities, what they might or might not inherit, what they in turn were allowed to pass on to their children, the attitude toward rape, abortion, infidelity on the part of the husband or wife and, among the Hebrews only, the penalty of death —for women—for the loss of virginity before marriage. These laws, since they primarily affected the economic and sexual activities of women, point to the likelihood that they were aimed at the matrilineal descent customs. The very fact that so many of the laws concerned women suggests that both the economic and sexual position of women was continually changing from the time of the first attested northern invasions (about 2300 BC) until the laws of the Hebrews, probably written down between 1250 and 1000 BC— though, as I mentioned, none of the original Hebrew texts have yet been discovered.

In questioning to what extent the female kinship customs and the reverence of the female deity affected the status of women, we may perhaps best judge by our observations of the women of the Hebrew tribes who had accepted the worship of the new male deity alone and the subsequent laws controlling their position and rights in the society in which they lived.

We might also want to consider the possibility that, in an even more personal way, just as the Hebrews prayed for sons and rejoiced when male heirs were born to carry on the family line (not so far removed from the attitudes of many families even today), in matrilineal societies the birth of daughters was likely to have been considered a special blessing. Female children may have been especially cherished for the same reasons. According to the curators of the Archaeological Museum of the University of Cambridge in England, even today, "Among the matrilineal Asanti in Africa, female children are especially valued because of their power to transmit blood *(mogya),* to continue the matriline *(abusua)."* In ancient times the Sun Goddess of Arinna in Anatolia was worshiped along with Her two daughters and a granddaughter. The Khasis of Assam worshiped their Goddess along with Her three daughters and a wayward son. What emotional effects this may have had upon the self-esteem and development of a young girl at that time we can only guess.

A consciousness of the relationship of the veneration of the Goddess to the matrilineal descent of name, property and the rights to the throne is vital in understanding the suppression of the Goddess religion. As I shall explain, it was probably the underlying reason for the resentment of the worship of the Goddess (and all that it represented) by the patriarchal invaders who arrived from the north.

Judging by the continued presence of the Goddess as supreme deity in the Neolithic and Chalcolithic societies of the Near and Middle East, Goddess worship, probably accompanied by the matrilineal customs, appears to have existed without challenge for thousands of years. It is upon the appearance of the invading northerners, who from all accounts had established patrilineal, patriarchal customs and the worship of a supreme male deity sometime before their arrival in the Goddess-worshiping areas, that the greatest changes in religious beliefs and social customs appear to have taken place. Who were these northern people? And how were they able to gradually suppress and eventually destroy the ancient Goddess religion that had existed for so many thousands of years?

4

The
Northern
Invaders

Why and when the more northern tribes came to choose a male deity is a moot question. In their earliest development they left neither tablets nor temples. It is only upon their arrival in the Goddess-worshiping communities of the Near and Middle East, which by that time had developed into thriving urban centers, that they come to our attention.

The lack of evidence for earlier cultural centers in their northern homelands of Russia and the Caucasus region just previous to the invasions suggests that up until their arrival in the Near and Middle East they may still have been nomadic hunting and fishing groups, possibly shepherds just beginning to practice agriculture. These northern peoples are referred to in various contexts as Indo-Europeans, Indo-Iranians, Indo-Aryans or simply Aryans. Their existence, once it surfaced in historical periods, portrays them as aggressive warriors riding two abreast in horse-drawn war chariots; their earlier more speculative appearances in prehistoric times, as big sailors who navigated the rivers and coastlines of Europe and the Near East.

Discussing their origins, Hawkes writes of the Mesolithic and Neolithic groups known as the "battle axe cultures," telling us that:

> On no subject have authorities differed so completely or with greater lack of objectivity than on the origins of these cultures. The reason for this partisanship lies in the one thing the authorities are agreed upon —that the *battle axe* cultures represent the roots of the Indo-European speaking peoples . . . What can be said with some certainty is that the battle axe people had a large ethnic, social and cultural inheritance from the hunter-fishers of the forest cultures such as the Maglemosian and Kunda . . . Though it may not always or everywhere have been so, this character came in time to be dominantly pastoral, patriarchal, warlike and expansive.*

These Maglemosian and Kunda people of Mesolithic times (about 15,000–8000 BC) were generally located in the forest and coastal areas of northern Europe, most especially in Denmark. Their sites were generally further north than those of the earlier Gravettian-Aurignacian groups who left us the heritage of the Venus figures.

The invasion by the northern peoples was not a single major event but rather a series of migrations which took place in waves over a period of at least one thousand and possibly three thousand years. The invasions of the historical period, which began at about 2400 BC, are attested by literature and surviving artifacts and are agreed upon by most historians and archaeologists. Those of pre-historic times are speculative, based upon suggestive evidence and etymological connections. These earlier and less extensive inva-

---

*Some authorities associate the Indo-European speaking people with the people of the Neolithic Kurgan culture of Russia, who lived just north of the Black Sea and the Caucasus. There has been the suggestion that the Kurgan people later dominated the peoples of Neolithic Europe, and one writer has even speculated that it was they who introduced the Indo-European language to European peoples at that time. (Since we do not have evidence of the language of the Kurgan people in Russia or of the European people at that time, the theory must at this time remain speculative.)

sions would take us back to 4000–3000 BC, thus taking place before the time of written records. They are not generally associated with the same invading tribes; yet on the basis of the evidence that does appear, I feel that they should be mentioned along with the more attested periods, so that the reader may draw her or his own conclusions.

What is most significant is that in historic times the northern invaders viewed themselves as a superior people. This attitude seems to have been based primarily upon their ability to conquer the more culturally developed earlier settlers, the people of the Goddess. The Indo-Europeans were in continual conflict not only with the people whose lands they invaded but between themselves as well. The pattern that surfaces in each area in which they make an appearance is that of a group of aggressive warriors, accompanied by a priestly caste of high standing, who initially invaded, conquered and then ruled the indigenous population of each land they entered.

The dates given for their original appearance in the Near East vary. Professor James suggests that the Indo-Europeans were established on the Iranian plateau by the fourth millenium. The curators of the Fitzwilliam Museum in Cambridge, England, date their entry into Anatolia at the late fourth millenium or early part of the third. Professor Albright suggests their appearance in Anatolia at "not later than the early third millenium," while Professor Seton Lloyd writes, "In about 2300 BC a great wave of Indo-European peoples, speaking a dialect known as Luvian, seem to have swept over Anatolia."

Professor Gordon tells us that "Indo-Europeans appear on the Near East scene shortly after 2000 BC. While their chief representatives are the Hittites, the Mitannian kings and gods often bear Indo-European names . . . The Iranian plateau was to become a great stamping ground of the Aryans (as we may call the segment of the Indo-Europeans to which the Iranians belong)." Gordon elaborates further, explaining that "The influx of the Indo-European immigrants into the Near East during the second mil-

Map 2 Location of areas discussed in chapter 4

lenium BC revolutionized the art of war. The newcomers introduced the horse-drawn war chariot, which gave a swift striking
power hitherto unknown in the Near East . . . The elite charioteer
officers, who bear the Indo-European name of *maryannu,* soon
became a new aristocracy throughout the entire area including
Egypt."

From Anatolia and Iran, these tribes continued to push southward into Mesopotamia and Canaan. According to Professor Albright,

There is both archaeological and documentary evidence pointing to a
great migratory movement or movements from the northeast into Syria
in the 18th century BC. As a result of this movement Hurrian and
Indo-Iranian tribes flooded the country. By the 15th century we find
most of eastern and northern Syria occupied predominantly by Hurrians and Indo-Iranians . . . Megiddo, Jerusalem and Ascalon [all in
Canaan] are ruled by princes with Anatolian or Indo-Iranian names.
The cranial type at Megiddo, which was previously Mediterranean in
character, now becomes brachycephalic Alpine.

As the invasions were sporadic, they are difficult to follow and
would probably require a volume on each particular area over a
long period of time to be thoroughly explained. But historical,
mythological and archaeological evidence suggests that it was these
northern people who brought with them the concepts of light as
good and dark as evil (very possibly the symbolism of their racial
attitudes toward the darker people of the southern areas) and of a
supreme male deity. The emergence of the male deity in their
subsequent literature, which repeatedly described and explained
his supremacy, and the extremely high position of their priestly
caste may perhaps allow these invasions to be viewed as religious
crusade wars as much as territorial conquests.

The arrival of the Indo-Aryan tribes, the presentation of their
male deities as superior to the female deities of the indigenous
populations of the lands they invaded and the subsequent intricate
interlacing of the two theological concepts are recorded mythologically in each culture. It is in these myths that we witness the
attitudes that led to the suppression of Goddess worship.

As Sheila Collins writes, "Theology is ultimately political. The
way human communities deify the transcendent and determine the
categories of good and evil have more to do with the power dynam-
ics of the social systems which create the theologies than with the
spontaneous revelation of truth from another quarter."

Judging from the production of religious mythology of the royal
scribes and priests found in the archives of palaces of the Indo-
European-ruled nations of the historic periods, often in the language of the conquered populations, we may surmise that political

aims, rather than religious fervor, may well have been the motivation. The prevalence of myths that explain the creation of the universe by the male deity or the institution of kingship, when none had existed previously, strongly hints at the possibility that many of these myths were written by priests of the invading tribes to justify the supremacy of the new male deities and to justify the installation of a king as the result of the relationship of that king to the male deity.

The Indo-European male deity, unlike the son/lover of the Goddess religion, was most often portrayed as a storm god, high on a mountain, blazing with the light of fire or lightning. This recurrent symbolism suggests that these northern people may once have worshiped volcanoes as manifestations of their god, a factor I will discuss more thoroughly in Chapter Five. In some areas this god was annexed to the Goddess as a husband, such as the storm god Taru and the Sun Goddess of Arinna or Zeus and Hera. In some legends he emerged as a rebellious young man, who heroically destroyed the older female deity, at times upon the previously assured promise of supremacy in the divine hierarchy.

In many of these myths the female deity is symbolized as a serpent or dragon, most often associated with darkness and evil. At times the gender of the dragon seems to be neuter, or even a male (closely associated with his mother or wife who is the Goddess). But the plot and the underlying symbolic theme of the story is so similar in each myth that, judging from the stories that do use the name of the female deity, we may surmise that the allegorical identity of the dragon or serpent is that of the Goddess religion. The Goddess, the original supreme deity of the people conquered and ruled by the invading Indo-Europeans, was not ignored, but was symbolically included in such a manner that these supposedly religious myths allow us to trace Her eventual deposition.

The male deity is invariably the powerful champion of light. With slight variations we find the myth in Hittite Anatolia in the battle between the storm god and the dragon Illuyankas; in India between Indra, Lord of the Mountains, and the Goddess Danu and

Her son Vrtra; in northern Canaan between Baal (who plays a dual role as the storm god of Mount Saphon as well as the brother/consort of the Goddess Anath) and the serpent Lotan or Lawtan (in the Canaanite language Lat means Goddess); in Babylon, probably in the Indo-European period of Kassite control, between Marduk and the Goddess Tiamat; in Indo-European Mitannian-controlled Assyria, Ashur simply assumes the deeds of Marduk; in Indo-European Greece between Zeus and the serpent Typhon (son of the Goddess Gaia), between Apollo and the serpent Python (also recorded as the son of Gaia) and between Hercules and the serpent Ladon who guards the sacred fruit tree of the Goddess Hera (said to be given to her by Gaia at the time of her marriage to Zeus). The myth appears in the ancient Hebrew writings (whose connections to the Indo-Europeans shall also be thoroughly discussed in Chapter Five) as the conquest by the Hebrew god Yahweh (Jehovah) of the serpent Leviathan (another Canaanite name for Lotan). It may even survive in the legends of St. George and the dragon and St. Patrick and the snakes.

The female religion, especially after the earlier invasions, appears to have assimilated the male deities into the older worship and the Goddess survived as the popular religion of the people for thousands of years after the initial invasions. By the time of Marduk and Ashur of the sixteenth century BC, Her position had been greatly lowered in Mesopotamia. But it was upon the last assaults by the Hebrews and eventually by the Christians of the first centuries after Christ that the religion was finally suppressed and nearly forgotten.

It is in these accounts of the Indo-European people that we may find the origins of many of the ideas of the early Hebrews. The concept of the god on the mountain top, blazing with light, the duality between light and dark symbolized as good and evil, the myth of the male deity's defeat of the serpent as well as the leadership of a supreme ruling class, each so prevalent in Indo-European religion and society, are to be found in Hebrew religious and political concepts as well. This influence or possible connection with the

Indo-European peoples may provide the explanation for the extreme patriarchal attitudes of the Hebrews which will be thoroughly discussed in Chapter Five. By first becoming aware of the Indo-European political patterns and religious imagery, Hebrew attitudes and ideas, that were later adopted into Christianity, may be better understood.

INDIA—"ORIGIN OF THE CASTES . . ."

In India there is some of the clearest evidence of the Indo-Aryan invasions and the conquest of the original Goddess-worshiping people. The language of the Indo-Aryans of India was what we today refer to as Sanskrit. Upon their arrival, the northern peoples did not yet possess a method of writing. They adopted two alphabets, possibly from the Akkadians. With these scripts they wrote their hymns and other literature. Thus the most comprehensive records of the Indo-Aryans in India were in the books known as the Vedas, written sometime between 1500 and 1200 BC in the Indo-European Sanskrit language, using the borrowed scripts.

In 1963 Professor E. O. James wrote:

> It appears that the sky gods in the ancient Vedic pantheon were already established among the Aryan tribes when they began their migrations in the second millenium BC . . . On their arrival in India they found, contrary to belief prior to the archaeological excavations in and around the Indus Valley since 1922, not a primitive aboriginal population but a highly developed urban civilization superior to their own relatively simple way of life as depicted in the Rg Veda.

Writing in 1965, Guiseppi Sormani also tells us that "The Aryans came into contact with highly civilized and already ancient forms of settled society, in comparison with which they were mere barbarians." He also explains that "They had long since abandoned matriarchy and had a patriarchal family system as well as a patriarchal form of government."

According to the hymns in the Indo-Aryan Rg Veda, in the very beginning of time there was only *asura*—living power. The *asura* then broke down into two cosmic groups. One was the enemies of the Aryans, known as the Danavas or Dityas, whose mother was the Goddess Danu or Diti; the other group, clearly the heroes of the Aryans, were known to them as the A-Dityas. This title betrays the fact that this mythical structure was created in reaction to the presence of the worshipers of Diti, since A-Ditya literally means "not Dityas," not people of Diti. This strongly suggests that these mythical hymns were not only written down after the Aryans came into contact with the Goddess people, but were conceived and composed after that time as well.

One of the major Indo-Aryan gods was known as Indra, Lord of the Mountains, "he who overthrows cities." Upon obtaining the promise of supremacy if he succeeded in killing Danu and Her son Vrtra, he does accomplish the act, thus achieving kingship among the A-Dityas. In a hymn to Indra in the Rg Veda which describes the event, Danu and Her son are first described as serpent demons; later, as they lie dead, they are symbolized as cow and calf. Both images of cow and serpent are associated with the worship of the Goddess as it was known in the Near and Middle East. After the murders, "the cosmic waters flowed and were pregnant." They in turn gave birth to the sun. This concept of the sun god emerging from the primeval waters appears in other Indo-European myths and also occurs in connection with two of the prehistoric invasions.

The Indo-Aryan attitude toward women is made clear in two sentences attributed to Indra in the Rg Veda. "The mind of woman brooks not discipline. Her intellect has little weight." We may find this statement rather ironic in light of the level of the culture of the patriarchal male-worshiping Indo-Aryans compared with that of the more female-oriented Goddess-worshiping people they forcibly subdued.

The Rg Veda also refers to an ancestral father god known both as Prajapati and Dyaus Pitar. He appears as an almost abstract idea in the Rg Veda. Yet Dyaus Pitar is known in later Brahmanic writings as "supreme father of all." Evidence of ancestor worship of the father occurs in several hymns of the Rg Veda. The Indo-Aryans daily recited the Pitriyajna, the worship of the ancestral fathers. In this ritual the father of the family acted as high priest, later passing these rites on to his eldest son. In Sanskrit, *pitar* means father, but *pati* has various meanings. The connections assure us of the position of men in these northern tribes. *Pati* has the alternative translations of lord, ruler, master, owner and *husband*.

The spread of the Indo-Aryan culture brought with it the origins of the Hindu religion and the concept of light-colored skin being perceived as better than darker skins. The Brahmins, the priests of the lighter Indo-Aryans, were considered to be the epitome of the racial hierarchy. Sormani reports that:

> Much study has been given to the real origin of the castes and the most dependable theories trace these back to the invasions of ancient times. The white skinned Aryans did not wish to mingle with the dark skinned Dravidians who were the original inhabitants (the Sanskrit word for caste, *varna,* means colour). The first measures towards dividing the populations into castes were laws that forbade mixed marriages between Aryans and Dravidians.

In the later Bhagavad Gita, the Aryan hero Arjuna speaks of his fear of undermining the "very structure of society." His concern is that he might produce "lawlessness," which is then described as meaning "the corruption of women," which in turn would lead to "caste mixture."

A figure who appears in the Indo-Aryan mythology of 400 BC, though he may have been known in legend before that time, is Rama, who symbolizes the Brahmanic tradition. Norman Brown, Professor of Sanskrit at the University of Pennsylvania, describes him in this way:

> Rama is the mythic agent for spreading Aryan (that is Brahmanic or Sanskrit) culture to the then un-Aryanized south of India, where even now culture is primarily a possession of the Brahmins overlying a substratum which is chiefly Dravidian . . . Rama's conquest is by force

of arms . . . he is thus represented as having brought culture and light to the aborigines, who when intransigent are called demons and when willing converts, monkeys and bears.

Thus it may have been that the patriarchal invaders, who saw women as inferior, are responsible for the origins of racist attitudes as well.

Light to the Aryans may have been the blinding light of volcanic eruptions, later symbolized by the light of their ever-present fire sacrifices, the light of the astral bodies, especially the sun, the lightning bolts of their storm god, perhaps the lightness of their own skin color as compared with the Mediterranean people and the "realm of eternal light" where the spirits of the Aryan dead were supposed to reside. The "gracious fathers dwell in glowing light, light primeval." Brahma, whose name eventually came to be that of the supreme god, is described as "he whose form is light." *Dev*, the Sanskrit word for god, literally means shining or bright. Mithra, still another god who appears in the Rg Veda, later to emerge in a more important role in the Iranian Avesta, is continually associated with light, while Varuna, which seems to be another name of Dyaus Pitar, has the task of performing daily sacrifices to bring the "shining sun" out of the "deep dark space under the earth."

Archaeological evidence, especially the work of Sir John Marshall, reveals that before the Aryan invasions the indigenous population of India revered the Goddess. The earliest cultures of the Indus Valley seem to have been in contact with Sumer and Elam at about 3000 BC. Religious attitudes and beliefs are often firmly entrenched in family and social custom. If the major part of the population once held the Goddess as sacred, it does not seem too surprising to find that these beliefs were revived at times when it was safe to do so openly, though we may find the time span rather astonishing.

In later periods of Indian history, as in many other areas where the worship of the male deity was superimposed upon the female

religion, many people, perhaps those who remained in more isolated areas, still retained the worship of the Goddess. As late as AD
600 the worship of the female divinity once again surfaced in India.
She appeared in the Puranas and Tantras under many names, but
the name *Devi*, simply meaning Goddess, combined them all. Yet
the name Devi was from the Sanskrit Dev; Her name as Danu or
Diti had been forgotten.

Professor Brown explains that:

> The reason why we do not hear of her sooner doubtless is that the Great
> Mother is not Aryan in origin and was late in getting Brahmanic
> recognition. She is quite different from any of the female deities in the
> Rg Veda . . . The Great Mother Goddess is widely worshipped in India
> today in non-Aryan circles; in south India every village has its collec-
> tion of Ammas, or Mothers, and their worship is the chief religious
> exercise of the village . . . the priests of these deities [they have pries-
> tesses as well] are not Brahmins . . . but are members of lower castes,
> thus indicating the pre-Aryan or at least non-Aryan worship of these
> goddesses.

Brown tells us that the Goddess was eventually incorporated into
Brahmanic literature but points out that "The Great Mother conception still has a dubious position in Brahmanic circles."

IRAN—". . . THE SEED OF THE ARYAN LANDS"

Indo-Aryan beliefs are also found in the writings of Iran, though
at a much later period. The oldest written material from Iran
unfortunately dates back only as far as 600 BC to the Zend Avesta
of Zarathustra. But this mythological material is enlightening, for
as James explains, "Indians and Iranians alike were, as we have
seen, Aryans derived from the same Indo-European ethnological
stock established on the Iranian plateau since the fourth millenium
BC and apparently spoke a Vedic Sanskrit dialect."

Professor M. J. Dresden also tells us that "A substantial body
of linguistic, religious and social evidence warrants the assumption
that, at one time, the bearers of the two cultures, which find their

expression in the Indian Rg Veda on the one hand and in parts of the Iranian Avesta on the other, formed a unity."

Though there certainly must have been considerable change from the time of the Rg Veda until the writing of the Avesta, we again find the concept of a great father who represents light, now known as Ahura Mazda. He is generally referred to as the Lord of Light and his abode is on a mountain top, glowing in golden light. This dwelling is said to be on Mount Hara, supposedly the first mountain ever created. In the language of the Indo-Iranians, *hara* actually meant mountain.

The duality of light and dark as good and evil is everywhere evident in Iranian religious thought. Ahura Mazda is on high in goodness, while a devil-like figure called Ahriman is "deep down in darkness." In one account Ahriman dared to come up to the border between them, there to be blinded by the light of Ahura. Seeing valor and supremacy "superior to his own," he fled back to the darkness. In the Iranian texts of AD 200 known as Manichean, once again we find good and evil equated with light and dark. In these statements we are told that the "problems of humanity are caused by the mixture of the two." Mithra, who appears in the Rg Veda, emerges more significantly in Iranian thought: now it is Mithra who defeats the "demons of darkness."

Most interesting is the Iranian figure known as Gayo Mareta, the first man created. Gayo Mareta may have once been much the same figure in Iran as Indra was in India. *Gauee* or *gavee* in Sanskrit means cow. *Mrityu* in Sanskrit means death or murder, surviving in the Indo-European German language as *mord,* meaning murder, and in the Indo-European English language as the word *murder* itself. Thus Gayo Mareta appears to be named "Cow Murderer." Just as Danu was symbolized as the cow Goddess, whose worship is best known from Egypt, and Indra Her murderer, so Gayo Mareta may once have held this position in Iran. In the Pahlavi books of about 400 BC it was written, "From Gayo Mareta, Ahura fashioned the family of the Aryan lands, the seed of the Aryan lands."

A later addition to Iranian mythology as we know it again appears to be a revival of the Goddess religion. According to Iranian texts of the fourth century AD, the Goddess Anahita was in charge of the universe. Curiously enough they tell us that "Ahura Mazda has *given* her the task of watching over all creation."

THE HURRIANS—". . . A RULING CASTE OF INDO-ARYANS"

An earlier group of people who further explain the identity and cultural patterns of the invading northerners were known as the Hurrians. The greater percentage of Hurrian people were not Indo-European; at least they did not use an Indo-European language. But they were from an area either north of Anatolia or northern Iran and were a brachycephalic (Alpine) group, as were the Indo-Europeans. It was perhaps in that area that they too were first conquered and then ruled by Indo-Europeans.

"These people," says Professor Saggs, "long known in the Old Testament as the Horites or Horims spoke a language having no recognized affinities except in the later Urartian. They must have reached the mountains north of Assyria, presumably from the Caucasus region, in the second half of the third millenium BC."

By 2400 BC there was an isolated Hurrian settlement at Urkish, in the Habur Valley, west of Assyria. At this same time, at Nuzi and Tell Brak, later to become important centers of the Hurrian kingdom, Hurrian names began to appear. Some were found as far south as Babylon, while by 2300 BC Hurrian names appeared in the Sumerian city of Nippur, some forty miles from Erech.

Archaeologist O. R. Gurney wrote *The Hittites* in 1952. In this book he suggested that the original homeland of the Hurrians was in northern Iran. He records that "The Hurrian people are known to have spread gradually southward and westward from their home in the mountainous region south of the Caspian Sea from about 2300 BC onwards, and to have become organized during the second millennium into several powerful kingdoms . . . situated near the upper waters of the Euphrates and the Habur."

Although most of the Hurrian people were not Indo-European, our interest in the Hurrians or Horites is based on the evidence that their kings and leaders were. Saggs explains that ". . . the kings of Mitanni bore not Hurrian but Indo-European names, whilst the old Indian gods, Mitra, Varuna and Indra were worshipped . . . All this points to the presence of an Aryan warrior caste ruling over a largely non-Aryan population." Gurney agrees, stating that Mitanni ". . . was ruled by a dynasty of kings whose names have an Aryan etymology, and Indian deities such as Indra and Varuna, figure prominently in its pantheon. It is thus clear in Mitanni a population of Hurrians was dominated by a ruling caste of Indo-Aryans."

The legend of Indra may have been known, since he is mentioned in the Hurrian tablets, but as yet no actual Hurrian accounts of the legend have been found. One Hurrian myth known through Hittite copies, though not a typical dragon story, revolves around the efforts to destroy Teshub, consort of the important Anatolian Goddess Hepat, whom Hittite queen Pudu-Hepa considered to be much the same deity as the Sun Goddess of Arinna. The major protagonist is the god known as Kumarbi, whose religious center is listed as the early Hurrian settlement of Urkish. In this myth he is called "father of all gods." His Aryan connections are visible in his name; Rajkumar in Sanskrit means prince. Kumarbi gives birth to a child made of stone named Ullikummi, which is the name of a mountain in the Kizzuwatna territory of Cilcia in south-central Anatolia, possibly the double-peaked volcanic mountain known today as Hasan Dag. It is Ullikummi's job to destroy Teshub. The text is quite long and involved and broken at many vital sections, but the major point is that Ullikummi is told to "suppress the city of Kummiya," to "hit Teshub," "pound him like chaff" and "crush him with your foot like an ant." It is not certain but the city of Kummiya in the legend may refer to the city of Kummani, which was a major religious center of the Goddess Hepat.

The origins of the meaning of the name Hurrian, Horite or

Horim may be associated with the meaning of the Iranian word *hara,* mountain. This word may survive in the German word for hill, *höhe,* and the word for higher, *höher* (possibly in the English word *higher* itself). This suggests that the Hurrians may simply be designated by the word "mountains" or "hills," a description of their original homeland.

It is also possible that the term was originally related to the Sanskrit word *hari,* which means golden yellow. This word is generally associated with Indra, Lord of the Mountains, used to describe his bow, his horse, his sandals and other symbolic possessions. It may even refer to the possession of gold which in Sanskrit is *hiran,* later becoming *oro* in Latin.

But to go even further, both of these groups of words may derive from an earlier idea of a golden mountain, the realm of eternal light, where the ancestors of the Aryans supposedly reside upon death. This image is most clearly presented in the later image of Ahura in his glowing home on the top of Mount Hara.

THE UBAID PERIOD—ERIDU, URARTU, ARARAT AND ARATTA

Along with these historically attested appearances of the Indo-Europeans from the middle of the third millenium onward, there is the speculative suggestion that the Indo-Europeans, or closely related groups such as the predecessors of the Hurrians, may have entered southern Iraq as early as the fourth millenium BC. A group generally known as the people of the Ubaid culture (so called by archaeologists for the modern name of the site at which they were first noticed, al'Ubaid) entered the Tigris-Euphrates area at this time. It is most often suggested that the Ubaid people came from the highlands of Iran, though some authorities are now beginning to believe that they moved down from the north of Iraq.

Though it is uncertain, since there was no form of writing at that time, some writers suggest that the Ubaid people brought the Sumerian language with them. This language, neither Semitic nor

Indo-European, has long puzzled many language experts. Professor S. N. Kramer, who has done extensive work deciphering Sumerian tablets, suggests that Sumerian is "reminiscent to some extent of the Ural Altaic languages." Some of the areas in which these languages have been noted are just north and west of the Caspian Sea. It has been suggested that Aratta, a place name often mentioned in Sumerian texts, may be in that same area or just slightly south, in the northwestern stretches of Iran along the Caspian Sea.

From whichever direction their entrance was made, the Ubaid people seemed to have established their major settlement in the town later known as Eridu, quite close to the junction where the Tigris and Euphrates join with the Persian Gulf. These same people are known to have spread across the Tigris and Euphrates area. Mellaart tells us that, as a result, the Halaf culture "broke up" and "at Arpachiyah there was destruction and massacre." The Ubaid people extended as far north as Lake Urmia and Lake Van, close to the Iranian-Russian border, perhaps the area from which they originated as a more nomadic group. This section was later known as Ararat or Urartu, a name which may have been derived from Aratta. It is possible that the name Eridu was once meant to remind its people of the name Aratta or Urartu (Urartu was known in later periods to have been inhabited by the Hurrian people and at times is suggested as their original homeland).

In about 4000 BC the Ubaid people built a temple at Eridu. Though shrines to the Goddess had been built in many Neolithic and Chalcolithic towns along the Tigris and Euphrates from 7000 BC onward, this temple at Eridu appears to be the first built on a high platform. Could this have been an attempt to simulate a mountain where there was none? Curiously enough, the Sumerian word for mountain is *hur* or *kur*. Unlike the other communities present in Iraq at that time, at the Ubaidian temple of Eridu not a single Goddess figurine was found.

The Maglemosian and Kunda people, who as mentioned previously seem to have been the cultural ancestors of the Indo-European peoples, used "dug-out" canoes, even in Mesolithic

Map 3 Some major waterways from Estonia
to the Persian Gulf

times. These boats were basically logs with holes burned out for the
occupants. In earlier periods these people were located in northern
Europe and Denmark. Two canoes, one in the Netherlands and one
on the coast of Scotland, have both been attributed to the Maglemosian people. Maglemosian steering paddles, fish nets and
fishing traps reveal that these boats were used for fishing activities,
apparently a major aspect of Maglemosian life.*

---

*The Maglemosians, who appear to have been exceptionally interested in mobility
and means of transportation, also developed skis and sleds.

With rivers and streams that flow across Europe and the Near East more numerous at a time closer to the melting of the Ice Age glaciers and pluvial rains that were still occurring in 10,000 BC, it may have been some of these ancient sailors, possibly over many generations, who eventually made their way to the warmer climate of Eridu. Evidence of the Maglemosians has also been found in Estonia, suggesting that they may have traveled down the Volga, which pours into the Caspian Sea. Many of them may have wandered into the numerous river inlets along the western edge of the Caspian into the Caucasus region. One of the major rivers, even today, that joins with the Caspian Sea is the Araks. Following the mainstream of the Araks would have led some of them into the Lake Urmia and Lake Van areas, that is, the land of Urartu. Branches of the Tigris in Urartu join up with the mainstream of that river, leading directly to the Persian Gulf, where the Tigris and Euphrates meet.

Hawkes tells us that "On the Euphrates the men of the al'Ubaid culture were probably the first regular navigators of the river . . . A model found in a late al'Ubaid grave at Eridu represents the oldest sailing boat known in the world."

The deity worshiped at Eridu in historic times was known as the god Enki. In prehistoric periods the god of this shrine appears to have been a fish or water god; offerings of fish were burned on his altar. In historic times Enki was thought of as a god of the waters, often described as riding about in his boat or simply called "he who rides." This concept of the fish or water god is quite like one found in a fragment of an Indo-European Hittite tablet which tells of a sun god who rose from the water with fish on his head. It is also reminiscent of the sun god who was born from the cosmic waters supposedly released by Indra, upon the deaths of Danu and Vrtra. Though Enki is not generally designated as a sun god, in the myth of Marduk he is named as Marduk's father, whereupon Marduk is called "the son of the sun."

The Ubaid people are credited with first developing irrigation canals in Eridu. Though these later salted up from the Persian

Gulf, we may see the concept of irrigation canals as a natural idea for people who had lived their lives on rivers and streams, later settling in dryer areas.

Another possible clue to the identity of the people of the Ubaid period of Eridu is the institution of kingship and the mention of the name Alalu as the very first king of Sumer in the king lists of the earliest part of the second millenium. His residence was listed as Eridu. According to these tablets, which appear to refer back to prehistoric periods, it was in the city of Eridu that "kingship was first lowered from heaven." The name Alalu also occurs in the Hurrian myth of Kumarbi, which was previously mentioned. The Hurrian myth begins, "In former years when Alalu was king in heaven, when Alalu was sitting on the throne . . ." Though it is most often suggested that the Hurrian use of the name Alalu was based on the writings of Sumer, which are older, it is possible that this name remained in the memory of those Ubaidians who later sailed back to the area of Lake Urmia; their presence there is attested by sites later than that of earliest Eridu. It is perhaps in this way that the name survived in the Hurrian myths of the people who lived in that area.

SUMER AND BABYLON—NEW PEOPLE, NEW GODS AND A REVEALING ACCOUNT OF THE MURDER OF THE GODDESS

Somewhere between 3400 and 3200 BC another group of people appear to have entered Sumer. Professor Saggs writes of the manner of construction of a temple in what is known as the Uruk Level Five period as "indicating the arrival of a mountain race familiar with the techniques of stone working." At this same time the areas of Nippur and Kish began to develop as populated centers.* At Nippur of historical periods, a god known as Enlil appears to have

---

*The Sumerian king lists mention a great flood, stating that after the flood kingship was lowered from heaven a second time, this time in Kish.

taken the limelight from Enki. In myths and inscriptions we read of Enlil as the "bright eyed great mountain," his temple described as the House of the Mountain, despite the fact that Nippur, in fact most of Sumer, is no higher than about 600 feet above sea level. His introduction into the city of Nippur is associated mythologically with the rape of the daughter of the Goddess in Nippur, Nunbarshegunu. The daughter's name is then given as Ninlil and later she is described as Enlil's wife. Enlil was also known as Lord Air, a title also associated with a deity in Egypt, where the sign for the word air is a sail. In Hurrian myths, Kumarbi is associated with the town of Nippur; they claim that it is Kumarbi's town.

In Sumerian tablets we find the Goddess under many names. In earlier times, each of these may have been revered as the Divine Ancestress of a particular community or town. Ninsikil was the patron deity of Dilmun, the Paradise of the Sumerians, but is also listed as an actual place in many records. Nammu was known as "She who gives birth to heaven and earth," as well as "the mother of all deities." Nina was worshiped as the "Prophetess of Deities." Nanshe of Lagash was "She who knows the orphan, knows the widow, seeks justice for the poor and shelter for the weak." On New Year's Day, She judged all of humankind. Nidaba of Erech was known as the learned one of the holy chambers, She who teaches the decrees, the great scribe of heaven. Shala, a title of Ininni, described Herself as "Mighty queen Goddess who designs heaven and earth am I."

Ningal or Nikkal ("Great Lady"), who in historical times was known as the wife of a moon god named Nannar (Sin in Akkadian), may at one time have been worshiped as the sun. In Anatolia, several high priestess-queens of the Sun Goddess of Arinna had the name Nikkal as part of their names. In historical periods She was said to be the mother of Utu, the sun, which may have been a later innovation. A shrine in Ur, which in the earliest periods may have been just that of Ningal, was in most periods shared with Her husband. In the Kassite period of Ur She was totally removed from the main shrine and placed in a smaller annex. There is a long poem to Her as the "mother and queen of Ur," with Nannar mentioned as Her *ishib* priest.

The Goddess Ninhursag, also known as Ninmah, seems to be closely identified with the worship of Enki, as his wife and sister, though in earliest legends She plays a rather dominating role and Her name often precedes those of Enki and Enlil. One legend explained that, with the help of Nammu, She created the first people. The Goddess, known as Ereshkigal, whom we later hear of as the Mistress of the Underworld, in one early Sumerian legend is carried off to the Underworld as a prize—at the time that Enlil took possession of the earth. But as we just read, even in the Underworld She was given no peace, eventually being forced to accept a consort to rule beside Her, to whom She was made to present the Tablets of Destiny.

The name of the Goddess as Inanna appears to have been derived from Innin, Innini or Nina. She may have become the daughter of Ningal at the same time that Utu became the sun. By the time we meet Her in the period of written legend (shortly after 2000 BC), though She still receives great reverence, She has clearly lost what was previously Hers. Though Nammu had created heaven and earth and Ninhursag, Nintu or Ninmah the first people, one myth tells us that Enki established world order. In this myth we read that he created the irrigation canals, "making the Tigris and Euphrates eat together." We next learn that he had appointed various deities to certain positions and that Enki himself or the personage appointed in charge of the canals "has carried off like fat the princely knee from the palace." Though this line is rather obscure, it may refer to the murder of a young prince at that time. Shortly afterward we twice read that Inanna has given up Her royal scepter, upon which She twice asks Enki, "Where are my royal powers?" As if to console Her, he tells Her that She is still in charge of "the words spoken by the young lad," words which She had established, and that the crook, the staff and the "wand of shepherdship," were still Hers. As if in further explanation of

Her loss of powers as a result of the canal building, he ends with, "Inanna, you who do not know the distant wells, the fastening ropes, the inundation has come, the land is restored, the inundation of Enlil has come."

In this legend we may be reading an explanation of the diminished powers and status of the Goddess upon the arrival of the Ubaidians of Eridu or by the advocates of Enlil at Nippur, to whom, according to Sumerian legend, Enki presented many gifts. Since the myth was not written until after 2000 BC, it would be difficult to say whether these changes occurred during the arrival of the Enki people or at the time of the settling of Nippur. Though the position of women and the supremacy of the Goddess certainly lost ground all through the historical period of Sumer, these changes may have been happening for centuries, even millenia. Yet throughout the historical period the Goddess, as Inanna, was still deeply revered, especially in Erech; She appears to have been regarded continually as the one who bestowed the rights of shepherdship or kingship, suggesting that the matrilineal rights to the royal throne continued to exist, a factor that will be more thoroughly discussed in Chapter Six.

There may even have been a revival of the religion of the Goddess between the two periods, since one myth is concerned with the transfer of the cultural center from Eridu to Erech, Enki claiming that Inanna had stolen all the gifts of civilization from him. Alongside the archaeological evidence that many of these "gifts of civilization" had been developed in the Goddess-worshiping communities of Neolithic times, it is also interesting to note that the words the Sumerians used for farmer, plow, furrow, smith, weaver, leatherworker, basketmaker, potter and mason were not Sumerian words but apparently borrowed from another, perhaps earlier, language.

A third male deity was introduced to Sumer probably shortly before the beginning of the second millenium, a period when Hurrians are known to have been entering the area. He is known as An or Anu, generally defined as the Sumerian word for sky. Yet the word *an* or *ahn* appears in several Indo-European languages as "ancestor," while in German, *ür-ahn* is defined as primeval ancestor. This title occurs in the Indo-European Greek name Uranus, a sky god. Professor Hooke tells us that "In the early Sumerian period the name Anu is relatively obscure, and his name does not appear on any of the eighteen lists belonging to this period . . ."

Anu appears as the successor to Alalu in the Hurrian and Hittite Kumarbi myth previously discussed. But most interesting is his appearance in the later myth of Marduk, "the son of the sun." Here we learn that Enki was first asked to subdue the Creatress-Goddess, whom they call Tiamat, and was not able, though he did manage to kill Her husband Apsu, thus becoming Lord of the Abzu (primeval waters) himself. Then Anu was asked, but according to the legend when he confronted Her, he cringed in fear and refused to complete his mission. Finally Marduk, son of Enki, was willing, though only upon the promise of the supreme position among all other deities if he succeeded. This previously secured promise brings to mind the one Indra requested before murdering Danu and Her son Vrtra; both of these myths were probably written about the same period (1600–1400 BC).

This legend, known as the *Enuma Elish,* which explains the supremacy of Marduk, has long been designated as Babylonian and therefore Akkadian and Semitic. But latest research suggests that, though Marduk was known in the Hammurabi period, the myth claiming his supremacy did not actually appear until after the Kassites had conquered Babylon. Professor Saggs points out that "none of the extant texts belonging to it is earlier than the first millenium" and that "it has been suggested that in fact this work arose only in the Kassite period, a time now known to have been one of intense literary activity." As I mentioned before, the Kassites were also ruled by the Indo-Europeans. Gurney tells us that "The names of Indian deities are found to form an element in the names of the Kassite rulers of Babylonia," though once again the greater part of the Kassite people were not Indo-European.

In about 2100 BC a Sumerian king named Ur Nammu declared

that he would establish justice in the land, somewhat like the reforms of Urukagina, who preceded him. It was said that he did away with the heavy duties and taxes that were burdening the people at that time and "rid the land of the *big sailors* who seized oxen, sheep and donkeys" (my italics).

In many of the legends and inscriptions of Sumer, the people of Sumer are often referred to as "the black-headed people." This designation, which was probably a description of the hair coloring of most of the inhabitants of Sumer at that time, is interesting when one begins to question why the phrase first came into use. Usually people are identified by whatever is different about them. We would not refer to a group as "the two-eyed people" unless there was also a group of people with only one eye, or with more than two eyes. This description, so often applied to the people of Sumer in the writings of Sumer itself, may well be another indication that those who first coined the term and used it, were themselves, or were at least familiar with others who were, not "black-headed people," but people with hair of a lighter color.

Each of these connections, when viewed side by side, may suggest that Enki, Enlil, Anu and Marduk were each introduced by Indo-European or closely related northern groups entering the Goddess cultures of Mesopotamia. Enlil, Enki and Anu appear to have become gradually assimilated into the vaster numbers of Goddess-worshiping people. But the later figure of Marduk, and especially Ashur, who succeeded to his position in Hurrian-controlled Assyria, were worshiped in societies where the position of women had certainly lost ground.

EGYPT—A BOAT IN THE HEAVENS?

The other possible, though also speculative, appearance of these same northern invaders may have occurred shortly before the earliest dynastic period of Egypt. Just before 3000 BC, there is evidence of an invasion in Egypt, shortly after which, just as in Eridu, kingship was first instituted. Upper and Lower Egypt were then joined together for the first time—under that one king. Until the time of the invasion, the Neolithic cultures of Egypt appear to have held the Cobra Goddess of the north (Ua Zit) and the Vulture Goddess of the south (Nekhebt) as the two supreme deities, though there were many other local deities worshiped in each community. After the invasion the two Goddesses were demoted, though they continued to symbolize the royal crowns of Upper and Lower Egypt, both of which were now worn on the king's head—one inside the other.

M. E. L. Mallowan writes that "The inference that there was some contact between Egypt and Sumer at the time is confirmed by the presence of Jemdet Nasr type seals." The Jemdet Nasr period of Sumer was the time of the settling of Nippur and apparently the introduction of Enlil. Mallowan, judging from methods of construction and style, also suggested that the First Dynasty tombs may have been inspired by the temples of Mesopotamia.

Discussing the Jemdet Nasr period, Saggs reports that "Abundant evidence of Mesopotamian cultural influence is found at this time in Egypt. Significant is the fact that cylinder seals (a specifically Mesopotamian invention) occur there, together with methods of building in brick foreign to Egypt but typical of the *Jemdet Nasr* culture. In Egypt also at this time Mesopotamian motifs and objects are represented in art, a striking example being a boat of Mesopotamian type found carved on a knife handle . . . whilst the principle of writing (though not the technique) was certainly taken over by the Egyptians from Mesopotamia."

It may be that the same people who were known as the Ubaid in Sumer, perhaps leaving during the Jemdet Nasr period when the newer groups were entering Sumer, made their way into Egypt at that time. Paintings in early dynastic tombs portray a conical basket type of fish trap, nearly identical to those of the Ertebølle people of northern Europe who were descended directly from the Maglemosians. In Egypt, the god who was assigned the role of father to the ancient Goddess Nut was known as Shu, Lord Air. As I mentioned before, in Egypt the sign for air is a sail, while the sign for the word gods is a series of banners or pendants, which are otherwise seen at the prow of boats. The male deity of Egypt, who arrived with the invaders, was portrayed as a sun god riding in his boat, much as Enki was known as "he who rides."

Professor Walter Emery spent some forty-five years excavating the ancient tombs and pyramids of Egypt. Discussing the arrival of these people, he writes:

> Whether this incursion took the form of gradual infiltration or horde invasion is uncertain but the balance of evidence, principally supplied by the carving on an ivory knife handle from Gebel-el-Arak and by paintings on the walls of a late predynastic tomb at Hieraconopolis, strongly suggests the latter. On the knife handle we see a style of art which some think may be Mesopotamian, or even Syrian in origin, and a scene which may represent a battle at sea against invaders, a theme which is also crudely depicted in the Hieraconopolis tomb. In both representations we have typical native ships of Egypt and strange vessels with high prow and stem of unmistakable Mesopotamian origin.
>
> At any rate, towards the close of the fourth millenium BC we find the people known traditionally as the "Followers of Horus" apparently forming an aristocracy or master race ruling over the whole of Egypt. The theory of the existence of this master race is supported by the discovery that graves of the late predynastic period in the northern part of Upper Egypt were found to contain the anatomical remains of a people whose skulls are of greater size and whose bodies were larger than those of the natives, the difference being so marked that any suggestion that these people derived from the earlier stock is impossible.

He also describes a scene on a mace head of one of the earliest kings which portrays him building a canal, apparently amid great ceremonial activity, and adds that "There is strong evidence to show that the conqueror of the North attempted to legitimize his position by taking the Northern princess as his consort."

The invaders of this period were known to the Egyptians as the Shemsu Hor—people of Hor. The Hor tribes eventually made Memphis their capital. Upon their arrival the new male deity was introduced. He was called Hor-Wer—Great Hor. Writing of the origins of the Hor figure in Egyptian mythology. Rudolf Anthes, professor of Egyptology, explains, "The time was the beginning and middle of the third millenium BC, starting with the earliest documentation of history, and the circumstances were prompted by the establishment of the kingship in Egypt."

By 2900 BC pictures of the sun god Hor-Wer show him riding about in his boat of heaven. We may find this conceptual imagery of the sun god riding in his boat in the heavens not unlike the later Indo-European imagery of India and Greece, where the sun god then rode across the heavens in a horse-drawn chariot.

According to Professor Emery, the name of the first king of the First Dynasty, known as Narmer or Menes in Manetho's history of 270 BC, was actually Hor-Aha. But the name of Hor appears to then have been incorporated into the more ancient religion of the Goddess as "the son who dies." This has led to much confusion between the two Hors, one the elder god of light of the invaders, the other the son of the Goddess Isis.

Hor (later known as Horus to the Greeks) was described in various texts as fighting a ritual combat with another male deity known as Set. Set is generally identified as the uncle or brother of Hor. The fight symbolized the conquest of Hor over Set, Hor symbolizing light and good, Set standing for darkness and evil. Dr. E. Wallis Budge wrote that "The fight which Horus the sun god waged against night and darkness was also at a very early period identified with the combat between Horus, the son of Isis, and his brother Set . . . Originally Set or Sut represented the natural night and was the opposite of Horus."

In Sanskrit the word *sat* means to destroy by hewing into pieces. In the myth of Osiris, who is Horus after his death (though also known as the father of Horus at the same time), it was Set who killed Osiris and cut his body into fourteen pieces. But it may be significant that the word *set* is also defined as "queen" or "princess" in Egyptian. Au Set, known as Isis by the Greeks, is defined as "exceeding queen." In the myth of the combat Set tries to mate sexually with Horus; this is usually interpreted as being an insult. But the most primitive identity of the figure Set, who is also closely related to the serpent of darkness known as Zet, and often referred to by classical Greek writers as Typhon, the serpent of the Goddess Gaia, may once have been female, or in some way symbolic of the Goddess religion, perhaps related to Ua Zit, Great Serpent, the Cobra Goddess of Neolithic times.

The followers of Hor who invaded Neolithic Egypt established the institution of kingship. Hor was often symbolized as a hawk or falcon, the Horus name of the king always being designated by a hawk. In Indo-European Iran, the word *xvarnah* meant the legitimate royal authority. In one Iranian myth this *xvarnah* left its owner and flew away from him—in the form of a hawk.

The Shemsu Hor occur in the remote periods of predynastic Egypt. Information on them is sparse. But may the Shemsu Hor at one time have been related to the people we later know as the Hurrians or Horites, first having made their home in northern Iran, later in Sumer, eventually to become the Shemsu Hor of Egypt?

Around the time of the Second Dynasty the town of Heliopolis (known to the Egyptians as Annu), some ten miles north of Memphis, became the home of a school of scribal priests who also worshiped a sun god who rode in a boat. In this town they used the name Ra. In Sanskrit, Ra means royal or exalted on high. This prefix is found in the Sanskrit word for king, *ra*ja and queen, *ra*ni. It survives in the German word *ragen,* to reach up, in French as *roi,* meaning king, as well as in the English words *royal, reign* and *regal.*

In the Pyramid Texts of the Fifth Dynasty (about 2400 BC) Horus was equated with Ra. Both Horus and Ra were closely connected, at times competitively, with the right to kingship. As Ra-Harakhty, Ra is identical with Horus of the Horizon, both meaning the sun at rising. Ra too is portrayed as the sun who rides across the heavens sitting in his sacred boat. Why a boat in the heavens? Was it because the men who brought the idea of a god of light actually did arrive in their boats? Ra's boat was said to emerge out of the primeval waters, much as Enki was said to ride his boat in the deep waters of the Abzu of Eridu, or as the Indo-Aryan sun god was said to have emerged from the cosmic waters. As in the Indo-European Hittite myth of the sun god in the water who rises from the sea with fish on his head, so too Ra rose from the waters each morning.

As sun god, Ra was known as the "shining one," the "forefather of light," "the lord of light." And once again we find the dragon myth, so suggestive of the Aryan religion. Daily, Ra fought the serpent of darkness known as Zet, later called Apophis. Why it should have been seen as such a difficult task for the sun to rise, especially in the climate of Egypt, is puzzling. One might better understand this type of thought originating in northern Europe. But the darkness of night was seen as a power that had to be fought daily, just as the Indo-Aryan Varuna had to perform daily sacrifices to bring the sun out of the deep dark space under the earth.

As the name of Horus was assimilated into the Goddess religion, as the son of Isis, the priests of Memphis proposed another concept of the great father god. This time his name was Ptah, curiously like the Sanskrit Pitar. The texts concerning him describe the creation of all existence, suggesting that Ptah was there first. This time we are told that it was through an act of masturbation that Ptah caused all the other gods to come into being, thus totally eliminating the need for a divine ancestress.

Yet, despite the inroads of male deities who replaced the Cobra and Vulture Goddesses as the supreme deities of Egypt, we find the concept of the Goddess far from forgotten. The ancient Egyptians, so adept at incorporating new deities into their religion (at times to the point where the myriad names and interweaving of myths is overwhelming), seem to have assimilated the male deities of the invaders, synthesizing the religion into various new forms. Judging from the retention of matrilineal descent patterns well into historical periods, they probably assimilated the invaders as well, though many may have remained in the royal house.

The nature of the Cobra Goddess, Ua Zit, was retained in several other later female deities. One is the Goddess known as Hat-Hor, literally defined as House of Hor. She is generally symbolized as a cow who wears the cobra upon her forehead. But She is described in one text as the primeval serpent who first created the world. Au Set too, portrayed in human form, wore the cobra upon Her forehead. The name Au Set appears to have been taken from the name Ua Zit.

Most interesting is the Egyptian Goddess known as Maat. Maat symbolized the order of the universe, all that was righteous and good. Depending upon the location of the text, She came to be known as the Eye of Horus, the Eye of Ra or the Eye of Ptah. Eye in Egyptian is *uzait*, again a word most similar to Ua Zit. But in Indo-European Greek the word for eye is *mati*. Maat was the embodiment of the ancient uraeus cobra. She seems to have been allowed to retain Her qualities and nature as long as She was assigned to one of the male deities as his possession. Professor Anthes writes, "As long as the king lived, the Uraeus was, as the Pyramid texts express it, magically guarded by the king. When the king died, however, the venomous viper would escape unless it was taken into custody."

This suggests that law and order, as perceived by the followers of Hor, Ra or Ptah, was possible only as long as the Cobra Goddess was controlled by the king. The strange combination of qualities assigned to the uraeus cobra, then known as Maat—ultimate wisdom and dangerous, perhaps rebellious, chaos—suggests that the cobra symbolized to the kings of Egypt the Goddess-worshiping society She originally represented.

One reference in the Pyramid Texts of the Fifth Dynasty has long puzzled students of ancient Egyptian culture. This was the account that in earlier times, men were sacrificed at the grave of Osiris—men with red hair. If the Shemsu Hor were related to the people we later recognize as the Indo-Europeans or Horites, this reference becomes more understandable.

The question of whether the people of the Ubaid period of Eridu, those of the Jemdet Nasr period of Nippur or the Shemsu Hor of Egypt were actually groups of early Indo-Europeans or closely related peoples from the Caucasus and Urartu areas, must at this time remain as hypothetical speculation, at least until further research is undertaken. What is certain is that these groups brought the worship of the male deity with them as they entered the lands of the people who held the Goddess as sacred, and both the Ubaidians and Shemsu Hor appear to have first initiated the concept of kingship, while the Jemdet Nasr people at Nippur and Kish revived it.

THE HITTITES ". . . THE CREATION OF AN EXCLUSIVE CASTE"

Returning to the more historically attested periods of the Indo-European invasions, the Hittites are believed to have entered Anatolia from the Caucasus region at about 2200 BC, though there are instances of earlier arrivals of small numbers of these same people.

According to Professor Gurney, "Examination of the skulls which have been found on several sites in Anatolia shows that in the third millenium BC the population were preponderantly long-headed or doliocephalic [Mediterranean] with only a small admixture of brachycephalic [Alpine] types. In the second millenium the proportion of brachycephalic skulls increases to about 50%."

It was these brachycephalic or Alpine people who eventually came to be known as the ruling class of the Hittite Empire. Before their arrival, the inhabitants of the land were known as the people of Hatti. It was actually the name of Hatti that led to the name of these people as Hittites, so called by early scholars who were still unaware that the Hittite kingdom was composed of two quite distinct groups of people. This was further complicated by the fact that several Hittite kings took the name Hattusili and the invaders named the capital Hattusas, perhaps thus identifying themselves as belonging to the people. Now better understood, it is clear that the original inhabitants of the land became the subservient or conquered class, while the invading Indo-Europeans assumed the roles of royalty and leadership, much as the Shemsu Hor did in Egypt and the historically attested Aryans did in India, Hurrian Mitanni, among the Kassites and later in Greece and Rome.

"The Hittite state," says Gurney, "was the creation of an exclusive caste superimposed upon the indigenous population of the country . . . a group of Indo-European immigrants became dominant over an aboriginal race of Hattians." Professor Saggs tells us that "After the period of confusion resulting from the incursion of Indo-European invaders into the region of the Halys, one of their princes, a certain Labarnas, carved out a kingdom for himself, which according to Hittite tradition, he rapidly enlarged by military successes until he made the sea his frontiers." Saggs agrees with Gurney, stating that "government in the Hittite kingdom was at this time essentially restricted to a noble and closed caste ruling over the indigenous population and alone concerned in military activities and the central administration of the state."

The Indo-Europeans, with their horse-drawn war chariots and iron weapons, as well as their greater physical size (even further emphasized by conical hats that appear to be about eighteen to twenty-four inches high) possessed a military supremacy never before encountered. The wheeled vehicle occurs in the Goddess-worshiping cultures of the Halaf period, but up until the arrival of the Hittites and Hurrians, wagons and chariots were apparently hitched only to donkeys, primarily as a means of transportation of people and products. It was only upon the advent of the Indo-European *maryannu* warriors that the horse was used and horse-drawn war chariots were introduced into the Near East. According to Rg Veda descriptions, these chariots were pulled by horses, two abreast, and driven by two riders. It is generally stated that sometime during the second millenium BC the Hittites discovered the process of mining and smelting iron, though one iron dagger was found in a grave dated about 2500 BC. Compared with the copper, gold and bronze of the Goddess cultures, iron obviously provided more "efficient" weaponry. The word iron may be related to the word Aryan, for it was closely associated with these people, who managed to keep the process a secret for many centuries after its discovery. The Neolithic Egyptians had used meteoric iron, which they referred to as "metal from heaven." It was perhaps this association of iron, though scientifically attested terrestrial iron, with the Aryans that led to the legends that suggested their heavenly origins and the idea that kingship had been lowered from heaven. Between the monopoly on iron weapons and the speed and force (as well probably as the intimidating effects upon peaceful urban people) of the horse-drawn war chariots, the Indo-European invaders held a military power unknown in the Near East until their arrival.

The conquered Hattians must have been kept tightly in line through fear of this well-armed warrior caste that ruled their country. One Hittite law stated, "If anyone opposes the judgement of the king, his household shall become a ruin; if anyone opposes the judgement of a dignitary, his head shall be cut off."

Before the invasions, the Hittites had not yet developed a written language, at least not one that was used for recording myths and literature. (Hittite hieroglyphs do appear, which I shall discuss more fully later.) Upon their arrival and contact with the Akkadian people, they began to use the Akkadian cuneiform alphabet, which was based on the writing of the Sumerians. Though in the writing of many of their myths the Hittites actually used the Akkadian language, their own language was also transferred into the Akkadian manner of writing. It is this Hittite language that appears as one of the earliest forms of Indo-European speech. In early historic times this language is most closely associated with Sanskrit, Latin and Greek. At the present time we find it related to German, French, English, Danish and nearly all other European languages.

Gurney reports that "The discovery that Hittite had affinities with the Indo-European languages was made by Czech scholar B. Hrozny and published in 1915. The suggestion that an Indo-European language was spoken by the population of Asia Minor in the second millenium before Christ was so startling that it was first received with great scepticism." He goes on to say that it has now been proven without a doubt.

The original Hattians, who may have been related to the much earlier Goddess-worshiping people of Catal Hüyük, which is about 125 miles south of the Hittite capital of Hattusas, seem also to have held the Goddess as their supreme deity. Goddesses such as HannaHanna, Hepat, Kupapa and the Great Sun Goddess of Arinna all appear to have survived from the earlier Hattian religion. In several texts the Goddess was simply called The Throne, the title associated with Isis in Egypt.

Though there is evidence in their texts that the Hittites worshiped Indra, Mitra and Varuna, Hittite myths and accounts of these deities have not yet been unearthed. Mountain storm gods were introduced by the Hittites and in the writings of Hittite Anatolia we are treated to some of the attitudes toward these new male deities. In the inscriptions of King Annita, one of the earliest Hittite kings, the storm god Taru is mentioned as the supreme deity. Yet centuries later in the city of Arinna, said to be a day's journey from Hattusas but not yet located, there is a different story. Gurney observes from the texts of Boghazkoy that "At Arinna the principal deity was apparently the Sun Goddess, Wurusemu; her consort, the Weather-god Taru, takes second place, and there are daughters named Mezulla and Hulla and even a granddaughter Zintuhi."

Some texts describe the rituals observed by a series of Hittite queens for the Sun Goddess of Arinna, revealing that the queen also held the role of high priestess to the Goddess. As I mentioned before, this close relationship of the Hittite queens to the Sun Goddess suggests that at one time the invading Indo-Europeans may have gained popular acceptance and legitimacy upon the throne by marrying Hattian priestesses who may have held the rights to the throne through matrilineal descent. Gurney explained that the Aryan kings retained the old Hattian shrines ". . . while at the same time assuming in their own person the office of supreme high priest of the realm."

Once more we find the myth of the defeat of the dragon. The Hittite king Mursilis II wrote of having to celebrate the festivals of the storm god in several cities. In this same letter he referred to the major festival of this nature being celebrated at the capital at Hattusas, at the mausoleum of the Goddess known as Lilwanis. At these festivals a ritual combat was either recited or enacted, perhaps much like the one between Hor and Set in Egypt. This combat was between the storm god and the dragon Illuyankas. It seems that Mursilis, as king, may even have played a role in the drama, possibly as the storm god. But the other figure involved in the story, that of a young man named Hupisayas, who upon sleeping with the Goddess known as Inara gained enough strength to help the storm god defeat the dragon, seems a more likely role. The story of Hupisayas gaining strength by making love with the Goddess may have been enacted by an annual sacred sexual union, much like those described in the texts of Sumer and Babylon, which will be more thoroughly explained in Chapter Six. In those countries the king played the role of the son/lover to the high priestess of the Goddess, who then endowed him with the rights of kingship. If this is so, it again suggests that the early Indo-European kings may have played this role with Hattian priestesses to legitimatize their position. The name of the dragon Illuyankas may be related to the Goddess Lilwanis. In the end the dragon was killed, just as the Goddess Tiamat, symbolized as a dragon, was killed by Marduk. Is it merely coincidence that the festival took place not in the temple of Lilwanis but in Her mausoleum?

The name of the Hittite god Taru is at times related to the Hittite word *tarh,* to conquer. In Sanskrit the word *tura* means mighty, while in India Tura Shah was another name for Indra. This word may survive in the words *taurus* and *toros* meaning bull. But it may also be connected with mountains, as is the word *Hor, Hur* or *Hara.* Alongside the fact that one of the major mountain ranges in Anatolia is called the Toros Mountains and one of its highest peaks known as Mount Toros, we find that in the Indo-European Celtic language *tor* means rocky hill top, in German *türm* means tower and in English we have the word *tower* itself. This name appears as that of the Etruscan storm god Tarchon and may even in some way be associated with the well-known Viking storm god Thor.

The Hittites were often in conflict with Egyptian armies, both trying to gain control of Canaan (the area today known as parts of Syria, Lebanon and Israel [Palestine]). Possibly as a result of these conflicts, in an effort to make peace or perhaps to infiltrate, Hittite, Hurrian and Kassite princesses were sent as wives to Egyptian kings of the Eighteenth Dynasty (1570–1300 BC) for several generations in succession. Both queens Tiy and Nefertete, respectively mother and wife of the religious revolutionary king Ikhnaton, are thought by some authorities to have been of Hittite or Hurrian descent. If this is true, it may account for the religious revolution of about 1350 BC, which made Ikhnaton move his capital to El Amarna, rejecting all other deities than Ra as the disc of the sun, which he called Aten. If these marriages were an attempt to infiltrate, the plan worked, for Ikhnaton, supposedly so interested in his religious activities, ignored his colonies and allies in Canaan, which in turn allowed the Hittite and Hurrian armies to gain control.

Still another curious event was the receipt of a letter by a Hittite king shortly after the deaths of Ikhnaton and his son-in-law Tutenkhamon. There is some argument as to whether it was sent by Nefertete or her daughter Anches-en-Amun. In the letter the writer, identifying herself as the Queen of Egypt, asked the Hittite king to send her one of his sons, so that she might make him her husband.

The Hittites, as well as other Indo-European ruled nations, were continually involved in international wars and politics. Under King Mursilis, the Hittites raided Babylon in about 1610 BC, though when Mursilis was assassinated, the Kassites took over the reins of government. The Hurrian state of Mitanni from about this same time controlled Assyria for several centuries, while the Kassites conquered the ancient Sumerian cities of Ur and Erech.

From the twentieth to the sixteenth centuries BC, the archaeology of Canaan shows continual nomadic disruption. This is generally attributed to local nomadic warfare. But as Professor Albright, who describes the entrance of the Indo-Europeans into Canaan as a "migratory movement," tells us, "by the fifteenth century Indo-Aryan and Horite princes and nobles were established almost everywhere." It is seldom suggested that the "nomadic disruption" may have been the result of the original invasions of these Indo-Aryan and Horite tribes entering the country and battling until they were finally accepted as rulers. Describing letters found in the archives of Ikhnaton at El Amarna, Werner Keller writes, "Though it may sound extraordinary, a third of these princely correspondents from Canaan have Indo-Aryan ancestry."

The name Baal, eventually used as the name of the male consort of the Goddess in Ugarit, Canaan, in the fourteenth century BC and the consort of Ashtoreth in the biblical period of southern Canaan after Moses (about 1250–586 BC), may also find its origins in the Indo-European language. By the fourteenth century a large percentage of the population of Ugarit was Hurrian. Hittite and Hurrian texts used the same sign for Baal as the Akkadians did. In Sanskrit *bala* means much the same as *tura,* that is, bull and mighty or powerful. It is used especially in conjunction with army troops. This may help to explain the dual role of Baal. As the possibly Indo-European storm god in Ugarit, he is lord of Mount Saphon, asking the Goddess Anath to have a proper temple built for him. Mount Saphon is also mentioned in the Hurrian myth of Kumarbi. In classical times it was known as Mount Casius and described as the location of the battle between Zeus and the serpent Typhon, who, according to Greek legend, was born in a mountain cave in Cilicia, Anatolia, where Zeus first attacked him. It may be significant that the volcanic mountain north of Lake Van is still known as Mount Suphan, though the Mount Saphon of Baal is generally described as the Saphon near Ugarit (today known as Jebel-el-Akra). Just as Hor became the name used for the son of the Goddess Isis in Egypt, the name Baal appears to have been used to replace the name of Tammuz as the consort of the Goddess, though the name Tammuz was still used as late as 620 BC in Jerusalem.

Another male deity of Ugarit, known as El, is considered to be the consort of the Goddess known as Asherah and thought to have been a part of the Goddess religion from the most ancient times. Yet we may once again suspect the nature of El in Ugarit, for the texts there continually refer to him as Thor-El, suggesting his ties with the Indo-European storm god as well.

LUVIANS, LUVISCHEN OR LOUVITES

Close by Hittite territory in Anatolia existed yet another group of Indo-Europeans, known as the Luvians or Luwians, depending upon the translation. Some of the Luvians lived directly south of the Hittites in the area known as Cilicia, close to the Toros Mountains. This is much the same area as the one in which the Goddess-worshiping culture of Catal Hüyük once flourished. The Luvians have long been regarded as part of the Hittite nation and it is only in the past few decades that their existence as a separate group has been clarified.

Very little is known of these people except that they were the authors of what have long been referred to as the Hittite hieroglyphs, picture words appearing most often on royal monuments and in a few texts. These hieroglyphs have been extremely difficult to decipher and even today many remain a mystery.

Varying dates for the Luvian entry into Anatolia are given. Albright writes that "The Luwians occupied most of southern Asia Minor not later than the early third millenium BC." R. A. Crossland, in the *Cambridge Ancient History,* suggests a later date, stating, "the deduction that Luwians were current in western Anatolia from 2300 BC onwards is not improbable in itself." Professor Lloyd agrees with Crossland, saying, "In about 2300 BC a great wave of Indo-European peoples, speaking a dialect known as Luvian, seems to have swept over Anatolia . . . Their progress was marked with widespread destruction . . ."

Some authorities claim that Luvian is archaic compared to Hittite. The name Luvian comes to us through the Hittite texts which referred to the land in which these people lived as Luviya and their language as Luvili. Much as the people of Hatti were called Hittites and the Hurrians at times known as Horites, they may as likely have been called Luwites or Luvites. French archaeologists refer to them as Louvites. The Germans call them Luvischen. Their actual name may be a significant factor, as I shall explain in the following chapter.

Experts in linguistics describe Luvili as an Indo-European language, closely related to Hittite. It is only as the hieroglyphs of these people are gradually translated that we have come to learn a little about them. Hans Güterbock, professor of Hittitology, wrote in 1961, "We have to assume that the Luwians too, superseded a population that spoke another language, but this substrate still remains unknown and un-named. The language written with the so called Hittite hieroglyphs is nothing else but a Luwian dialect."

Because of the problems in deciphering the hieroglyphs, the poor state of what has so far been discovered and the limitations of the material itself, little is yet known of the Luvian religion. We do know that the major deity was the storm god, whose name was much like the Hittite god Taru. In Luvian he was known as Tarhund, Tarhunta or Tarhuis. Güterbock tells us that no mythological material has yet been found in the hieroglyphs and that they are for the most part of votive character. These are what he refers to as the "magic type," "spells and incantations inserted into ritual texts." This prevalence of totally religious material in their own archaic hieroglyphs, while other means of writing were readily available, suggests that the Luvians, perhaps much like the Brahmins of India or the priestly scribes of Ra at Annu in Egypt, may also have been a priestly caste. Other indications that seem to affirm this possibility include the fact that scribal schools producing myths in Hurrian, Hittite and Akkadian appear to have been located in the Luvian territory of Kizzuwatna.

Güterbock observes that "Kizzuwatna, the region in south eastern Anatolia, including the Cilician plain, was the one Hittite province in which Hurrian scribal schools must have flourished most prominently." He suggests this on the basis of the fact that there are many Luvian loanwords in texts written in the Hittite language but which deal with Hurrian myths. But it is equally as possible that it was the Luvians themselves who were making these translations.

Little else can be stated about the Luvians until further interpretations of the hieroglyphs are made or more material is discovered. But their role in religious history may have been extraordinary, as I will explain in the following chapter, which continues our examination of the patriarchal cultures that eventually destroyed the religion of the Goddess.

5

One of Their Own Race

Unlikely as it may seem, the next group of people whose connections to the Indo-Europeans will be considered are the Hebrews. As George Mendenhall writes, "Ancient Israel can no longer be treated as an isolated independent object of study; its history is inseparably bound up with ancient oriental history, whether we are concerned with religion, political history or culture."

Mendenhall also comments that "Hypotheses are basic to sound research and eminently practical; they are constructed not as a substitute for facts but to suggest possibilities and guide future investigation." It is in the spirit of this attitude that I hope what I am about to say will be understood.

Abraham, father of the Hebrew tribes, first prophet of the Hebrew god Yahweh, may have either been related to, or deeply influenced by, the conclave of Indo-Europeans who lived in the town of his kinsmen, Harran. It is possible that the name of the Judeo-Christian God, known in the Old Testament as Yahweh, though perhaps more familiar to us as Jehovah, was originally derived from the Sanskrit word *yahveh*, meaning everflowing. The name Abraham itself may be related to the name of the Aryan priestly caste of India, the Brahmins, and the patriarchal attitudes of the Hebrews may have been formed, not in a cultural vacuum, as is generally assumed, but by their connections to the male-oriented northern invaders.

Certainly the Hebrew people have never been thought of as Indo-European, and by the time they were settled in Canaan, after their stay in Egypt, the majority of them may have been Semitic. Yet there is one group that stands apart from the Hebrews and yet is counted as one of their tribes. These are the priestly Levites. This is surely the most controversial hypothesis yet suggested, but at the risk of overwhelming religious, emotional and academic reactions, I suggest that the Levites may have in some way been related to the Indo-Europeans, most especially the Luwians, Luvians, Luwites or Luvites as the various translations will have it. Despite the almost universally accepted belief that the Hebrews were always a totally Semitic people, there are many curious pieces of evidence that suggest that their connections with the Indo-Europeans should at least be considered in this context.

Before going any further it is important to realize that the oldest extant texts of the Old Testament in Hebrew are the ones recently found at Qumran, which date back to two or three centuries before Christ. The oldest version before these discoveries was a Greek translation from about this same period. The earliest Hebrew text available before the Qumran discoveries was from about the tenth century AD. Judging from the vocabulary, language structure, and the names of places and people, it is generally believed that part of the Old Testament, known as the Yahwist account, was written about 1000 BC, while the other sections, known as the Priestly, were written about 600 BC.

We should also take into account that the Bible as we know it is the result of many changes throughout the centuries, this factor made most evident in its contradictory passages. Professor Edward Chiera remarks that

In the case of the Bible, besides this process of expansion that belongs to all literary products of antiquity, there was another and contrary trend, namely, the jealous censorship on the part of the priest, who did not want the book to contain episodes or explanations which might not agree with his own conception either of the god or what was fit to be incorporated into the history of the founders of the race, and who piously but nonetheless ruthlessly eliminated what he did not approve.

George Widengren, professor of Oriental languages at the University of Uppsala in Sweden, also writes that "We must not lose sight of the fact that the Old Testament, as it is handed down to us in the Jewish Canon, is only one part—we do not even know if the greater part—of Israel's national literature. And, moreover, this preserved part has in many passages quite obviously been exposed to censorship and correspondingly purged."

INDO-EUROPEANS IN THE BOOK OF GENESIS

Biblical scholars generally date Abraham at about 1800–1700 BC. But many of these same scholars assign Moses to about 1300 or 1250 BC. If we carefully trace the generations as listed in the Bible, however, we find that there are only seven generations between and including these two patriarchal figures. Five or even four hundred years seems a long time for seven generations. Since the dates on Moses are based on more historical evidence and lead more directly into the more historical accounts of Saul, David and Solomon, I would place Abraham at about 1550 BC. Placing Moses at 1300 BC, this would still allow more than forty years between each generation, which is more likely than the sixty to seventy years the other dates would suggest. Using these same biblical lists of generations, unless we assume that names were omitted, and allowing thirty-five to forty years for each generation, we find that even the primeval figure of Noah, who is only ten generations before Abraham, would be dated at about 2000–1900 BC, well within the time of the arrival of the Indo-Europeans into the Near East.

The Old Testament tells us that Abraham had been living in Ur of the Chaldees. This is generally considered to be the city of Ur in Sumer, some five miles from Eridu. Yet after the first mention of Ur, Harran is continually referred to as Abraham's country, the land of his kinsmen and his father's house. After leaving Ur, the Bible states that, "When they reached Harran, they settled there" (Gen. 11:32). But once in Harran, "The Lord said to Abram, Leave your own country, your kinsmen and your father's house . . ." (Gen. 12:1). Some Bible scholars have suggested that since there were towns at that time with names such as Urkish, Uruk, Ura, Urfa and others ("ur" meaning old or great), one of these others actually may have been the Ur of the Bible. Though Harran does seem to be his actual homeland and the city of his kinsmen, this connection being further evident in the stories of Isaac and Jacob, we may even conjecture that Abraham or his family moved from Harran to Ur at some earlier time. We know that there were Hurrians in Nippur by 2300 BC. In any case the Bible relates that Abraham moved from Ur to Harran with his wife and family.

The information on the Indo-European invasions has made it clear that even by 1800 BC many Hurrian people had moved into the area eventually known as Mitanni. Harran was located in the very center of that kingdom. The name of the city itself probably results from its position in the Hurrian territories; it is not far from the early Hurrian settlement of Urkish, which is dated at about 2400 BC. Abraham's relationship to this town may also be indicated in the names of his relatives. His grandfather and one brother were both named Na Hor. His other brother was named Haran.

Throughout the Bible, but most especially in Genesis, there are references to the Hittite and Horite people, some very closely associated with the family of Abraham. We read in Gen. 23:6 that later, when Abraham was in Canaan, he needed a place to bury his wife Sarah. Now when people bury their dead, they generally try to find consecrated or at least familiar ground. Therefore it is perhaps curious that the man Abraham approached to request the use of his land for Sarah's burial was Ephron the Hittite. Even more surprising was Ephron's answer when Abraham offered to pay for the land. "You are a mighty prince among us," the Hittite said to Abraham. "Bury your dead in the best grave we have." This same plot of land on Hittite territory was used once again when Abraham died. Even his grandson Jacob, before he died in Egypt, requested that his sons carry his body all the way back to Canaan, to bury it in the land that Abraham bought from Ephron the Hittite.

Abraham's son was Isaac. Isaac had two sons, Jacob and Esau. When it was time to choose a wife for Isaac, Abraham sent his servant back to Harran to find the daughter of Abraham's brother Na Hor. And once again, when Jacob married, it was the granddaughter of Na Hor who was chosen, also from Harran. Esau married two wives. One was the daughter of Elon the Hittite, the other the daughter of Zibeon the Horite. Esau then moved with his family to an area in Canaan known in the Bible as "the hill country of Seir, the land of the Horites." In the generation lists (genealogies), which abound in biblical writings, we are given a list of Esau's descendants, but oddly enough we are also treated to a list of the descendants of Seir the Horite, grandfather of Esau's wife.

Most of these connections to the Hittites and the Horites occur in Genesis, the first book of the Bible. Later, in the Book of Ezekiel, we twice read a rebuke to the people of Israel as Ezekiel says, "Your father was an Amorite, your mother was a Hittite." This might suggest that it was then Sarah who was Indo-European, or even Abraham's mother, who is notable by her absence throughout the Book of Genesis. Certainly there is no conclusive proof of the exact connections, but the repeated association of Abraham's family with people and places we know to be connected with Indo-European kingdoms, at the exact time of their existence, should certainly be taken into account.

SOME OF THE LINKS

Another curious similarity is the Hebrew custom of levirate marriage, that is, the law by which the widow of a man is assigned to her dead husband's brother or, if there is none, to her father-in-law. Professor Gordon writes, "Since it is well attested in ancient India, and crops up in the Near East only in the wake of the Indo-European invasions, it was apparently introduced, or at least popularized, by the Indo-Europeans." Professor Gurney also discusses this custom of levirate marriage among the Hittites and comments. "The law is remarkably similar to the Hebrew law of levirate marriage." Something as close to home as the concept of levirate marriage was not likely to be a lightly adopted custom but probably had deep origins within the societies in which it was practiced.

Professor Gordon has long pointed out the close relationship between the Indo-Europeans and the Hebrew peoples in terms of literature, linguistics and custom. Though he does not present as close a relationship as the one I am suggesting he does say, "We can now surmise why it was the Hebrews and Greeks who first emerged as the historians of the west. Both of them started their historiographic careers on Hittite substratum." Robert Graves also suggests a close relationship between Hebrew and Indo-European Greek concepts and literature, even defending his stand by commenting that he is not a "British Israelite."

As I mentioned before, the Hebrews also retained the memory of a myth of a battle between Yahweh and the serpent Leviathan, though the major portion may later have been removed, possibly at the time of the addition of the legend of Adam and Eve. In Job 26:13 and in Psalm 104 we may still read that Yahweh destroyed the primeval serpent. In Psalm 74 we also find, "By Thy power Thou didst cleave the sea monster in two [just as Marduk did] and break the sea serpent's head above the waters. Thou didst crush Leviathan's many heads." Now this serpent Leviathan was also known in the texts of Ugarit in northern Canaan as the foe of the storm god Baal. Though we do not yet know of them as Indo-European, the rulers of Ugarit, just a few miles south of Hittite and Luvian territory, were on extremely friendly terms with the kings of the Hittites. We do know that a great number of Hurrians were in Ugarit at the time the texts were written, about the fourteenth century BC. Baal's father in Ugarit was Dagon. *Dag* is still the word used in Turkey to mean mountain. Texts of Ugarit describe Baal's conquest of the dragon Lotan, Lawtan or Leviathan. As I mentioned before, Lat or Elat in Canaanite meant goddess. The name emerged again in the Indo-European Greek myth of Hercules who kills the serpent Ladon, who was said to be guarding the sacred fruit tree of the Goddess.

The biblical descriptions of Yahweh's conquest of the primeval serpent may well have been simply another version of the by now familiar tale of the Indo-European male deity defeating the serpent of darkness, the Goddess. After the time of Moses until the fall of the two Hebrew states, the Hebrews despised the name of Baal, as the storm god's name appears to have been assimilated into the religion of the Goddess in the role of Tammuz, the son/lover. In Akkadian, Baal simply came to mean Lord, as Baalat came to mean Lady. By about 1000 BC the name Baal was closely associated with Ashtoreth, as Her consort. But in the times of the earliest introduction of the name Baal into Ugarit (possibly originating in the Sanskrit *bala,* meaning mighty), the time before he had a temple of his own, he and Yahweh may have been much the same deity. In Ugaritan texts we read, "Behold, thine enemies, O Baal; Behold thine enemies shalt thou crush." In biblical Psalm 92 we find, "For behold thine enemies, O Lord; for behold Thine enemies shall perish." In Ugarit, Baal was referred to as Rider of the Clouds. In Psalm 104:3 Yahweh is described as using the clouds for his chariot.

Still another enigmatic passage in the Bible may reveal itself as a reference to early Indo-European connections. Once one is aware that the Aryans viewed themselves as a race superior to the people whom they had conquered and ruled, the passage may perhaps be understood as a reflection of this attitude. In the first part of the Bible (Gen. 6:2–4) it was written, "When mankind began to increase and spread all over the earth and daughters were born to them, the sons of the gods saw that the daughters of men were beautiful; so they took for themselves such women as they chose . . . In those days when the sons of god had intercourse with the daughters of men and got children by them, the Nephilim [giants] were on earth. They were heroes of old, men of renown."

This passage, which has figured so largely in the current spate of books suggesting that spacemen have been responsible for the development of human culture, may actually refer to the Aryan image of themselves as physically larger and at that time the lone worshipers of the god of light on the mountain top, as compared to the smaller Mediterranean people who worshiped the Goddess. This interbreeding, which we know was so despised by the Aryan priests, seems to be the underlying reason for the great flood in which only Noah and his arkful of relatives survived.

Iranian literature occurs four centuries after the period generally assigned to Yahwist portions of the Old Testament, though simultaneous with the Priestly sections. Similarities between Hebrew and Iranian myths may be the result of connections at that period (about 600 BC), though it would be difficult to decide which culture was the originator. But there is the possibility that both were derived from the same Indo-European religious thought. In the Pahlavi texts of 400 BC, based on the Avesta of 600 BC, the creation of the universe is described as having taken place in seven acts. These correlate extraordinarily closely with the Hebrew account. First the sky; second, water; third, earth; fourth, plants; fifth, cattle; sixth, man; and on the seventh day was Ohrmazd (Ahura Mazda) himself. The account is certainly similar and yet in the ways that it differs one may have reason to assume that neither was a direct loan but more likely the result of two lines of development, originally stemming from the same earlier source.

Another text in the Pahlavi books deals with the Indo-Iranian view of the first woman. She was known as Jeh, "queen of all whore demons." The story takes on the characteristics of the legend of Adam and Eve in that it relates that Jeh arrived at the Creation in the company of the devil (Ahriman). In this account she does not converse with him, but relates to him sexually instead. It is then stated that she was joined with the devil so that she might afterward defile all women, who in turn would defile all men. We are then told, "Since women are subservient to the devil, they are the cause of defilement in men." Surely not the same story, but certainly much the same underlying thought and attitude. Moreover, we may question why the Hebrews' stories should have been so closely aligned to the Indo-European Iranians at all.

Yet another story with a biblical counterpart is the Iranian tale of a man named Yima. Ahura warned him that destruction would come to the world in the form of floods, because people had sinned. He instructed Yima to build a *vara,* generally translated as fortress. Into this *vara* he was told to bring fire, food and animals and humans—in pairs. The ancient legend of a great flood not only occurs in Iranian and Hebrew literature but in early Sumerian legend as well. It is most often assumed that the Hebrews borrowed the legend from the Sumerians. But the account of the flood may have been known among the "mountain race" that arrived shortly before the Jemdet Nasr period in Sumer, perhaps once told as the mythical memory of their ancestors' arrival in the mountain lands of Aratta. It may later have been associated with their own arrival in Sumer, perhaps describing extensive rainfall throughout that area at the time, leading to the line, "the Inundation of Enlil has come, the land is restored." Along with its appearance in Sumerian myth, it may also have remained in the memories of those who stayed behind in Aratta (Ararat?), eventually being connected with Abraham's ancestor Noah and the Iranian Yima as well.

This appears all the more likely when we realize that Sumer has no high elevations, no mountain for the ark to land on (which the Sumerians also claim that it did). The Hebrew account describes the landing of the ark in Ararat or on Mount Ararat itself. Mount Ararat is known by that name even today. It towers over all the other mountains nearby, reaching a height of nearly 17,000 feet. It is located at the easternmost tip of Turkey, close to the Iranian and Russian borders, in the land once known as Urartu, which is much the same name as Ararat. It is, in fact, just alongside the Araks River, which joins with the Caspian Sea. We may also find it significant that the Hebrews state that Noah, primeval ancestor of the Hebrews, started out after the flood from the very same area from which the historically attested Indo-Europeans are known to have entered Anatolia.

Another similarity between the legends of the Bible and those of Sumer concerns the irrigation canals. The Bible records that after Yahweh created the world, there was still no vegetation because there was no water. In Gen. 2:6 we read, "A flood was used to rise out of the earth and water all the surface of the ground." In the legend of the Sumerian Paradise, Dilmun, water was also lacking, so that no vegetation grew. Enki, god of the Eridu temple, then ordered water to be brought up from the earth to water the ground. In the myth of Enki establishing world order, we also read of Enki's canal-building activities. Each of these stories is describing a land where there is little or no rainfall. Water must come from the ground. This was certainly the situation in Ubaidian Eridu, where irrigation canals were first developed—accounts of this period were still being told two thousand years later, at the beginning of the second millenium in Sumer. Again we may surmise that they found their way back to Aratta, considering the continual contact between the two places.

The connections of Moses, Joseph and even Abraham with Egyptian royalty should also be considered as a factor in the relationship between the Hebrews and the Indo-Europeans. As I mentioned before, throughout the Eighteenth Dynasty (about 1570–1300 BC) there were records of Hittite and Hurrian princesses being sent to Egyptian kings as wives, certainly a break in the matrilineal descent patterns. It was during this period that we find no priestesses in the Egyptian temples and the word Par-O (pharaoh) applied only to the king rather than to the royal house. It is also during this period that the religious revolution of Ikhnaton took place, allowing Hittite and Hurrian armies to gain greater control in Canaan; a third of the correspondence found in Ikhnaton's palace archives was received from princes with known Indo-Aryan names.

Thus we may find it significant that, according to the Bible, Moses was the "adopted son" of the pharaoh's daughter, said to have been found as an infant. We read in Exod. 2:5–10 that he was first found by the pharaoh's daughter who gave him to a woman, supposedly his real mother, to be tended as an infant. But then we read that, "when the child was old enough she brought him to pharaoh's daughter, who adopted him and called him Moses." Many pharaohs of the Seventeenth, Eighteenth and Nineteenth Dynasties had names such as Kamosis, Amosis, Tutmosis and Rameses. It is perhaps somewhat curious that the pharaoh's daughter gave this "foundling" child such a royal name.

But even before Moses, Joseph, another son of Jacob, was also closely connected with Egyptian royalty. He was said to have gained his position through his ability to interpret dreams. We read in Gen. 41:41, "Pharaoh said to Joseph, 'I hereby give you authority over the whole land of Egypt.'"

Even Abraham, before them, seems to have had close contact with Egyptian royalty. In Gen. 12:10–20 Abraham and Sarah also find themselves in Egypt, supposedly as the result of a famine in Canaan. This time we learn that Abraham has asked Sarah to pretend that she is his sister. Supposedly as a result of her great beauty, she is then taken into the household of the pharaoh—as his wife.

Again, we have no conclusive evidence, since the Bible does not mention the pharaohs by specific names. But both Abraham's and Joseph's periods may have occurred during the time of the Eighteenth Dynasty, while the period of Moses would have taken place shortly afterward. Once again we may ask if there was some possible connection, this time between the Indo-European princesses and those who probably accompanied them and the biblical ac-

counts of Abraham, Joseph and Moses, each so closely related to
the pharaohs of Egypt at that particular period.

GODS AND GLOWING MOUNTAINS

Another puzzling, and perhaps the most significant and revealing
connection between the Indo-Europeans and the Hebrews is the
symbolism of the mountain, most especially the great and shining
light upon the mountain. The Aryans of India worshiped their
ancestral fathers "who soared up to the realms of eternal light."
Indra was the Lord of the Mountains, his possessions described as
golden. The abode of the Indo-Iranian Ahura was said to be lumi-
nous and shining, set upon the top of Mount Hara. As I mentioned
before, in Indo-European Iranian, *hara* actually meant mountain.

In the Hebrew texts the story of Moses is most often associated
with Mount Sinai, located in the southern end of the Sinai Peninsula. But in many biblical references to the mountain on which
Moses spoke with Yahweh, this mountain is referred to as Mount
*Hor*eb. Long before Moses led the Hebrews out of Egypt he had
found this mountain. We read in Exod. 3:1 that when Moses was
alone in the desert, before the time of the Exodus, he "came to
Horeb, mountain of God." After the Exodus and the more familiar
ascent of Moses on Mount Sinai we again read, "You must never
forget that day when you stood before the Lord your God on Horeb
(Deut. 4:10). And in Deut. 4:15, "On the day when the Lord spoke
to you out of the fire on Horeb . . ."

The association of Yahweh with, or as, a mountain is evident
throughout the Book of Psalms, certainly some of the oldest parts
of the Bible. In Ps. 31, 62, 71, 89 and 94 Yahweh is referred to as
a "rock of refuge." In Ps. 62 he is the "rock of deliverance." In Ps.
18 he is "my rock where I find safety." In Ps. 19 he is "my rock
and my redeemer." In Ps. 28 we read "O my rock" and in Ps. 42,
"God is my rock." In Ps. 78 it was written, "He brought them to
His holy mountain." In Ps. 48 we learn that Yahweh is "upon His
holy hill" and in Ps. 99 the writer tells the reader to "bow down
to His holy hill." In Ps. 92 it was simply written, "The Lord is my

rock." If there were not so many other allusions to the mountain we might see these as simply symbolic of stability, but we also read of the close connections and importance of the mountain itself.

In Exod. 24:17 the appearance of Yahweh is not only described as being on a mountain top but on a crest glowing with fire. "The glory of the Lord looked to the Israelites like a devouring fire on the mountain top." And in Deut. 5:4, "The Lord spoke with you face to face on the mountain out of the fire." In Ps. 144 Yahweh is asked to "shoot forth Thy lightning flashes." In Ps. 104 Yahweh is simply described as "wrapped in a robe of light."

The Indo-European Zeus, with his fiery lightning and thunderbolts, was to be found on the top of Mount Olympus. Baal, with this same lightning symbol, resided upon Mount Saphon. The storm gods of the Hittites and Hurrians are often portrayed with lightning bolts in one hand, standing upon one or even two mountains. Indra, glowing in gold, also holding his lightning bolt known as *vajra,* was known as Lord of the Mountains. Ahura dwelled in his glowing home on top of Mount Hara. Is the Hebrew Yahweh who spoke out of the fire on Mount Horeb to be considered as an image and concept much different from these Indo-European gods? Or may he also be regarded as the Indo-Aryan "father who dwells in glowing light" as portrayed in the Rg Veda? Strangely enough, the Hebrew word for hill is *har.*

LOUVITES AND LEVITES

Though we have observed the connections the Hebrews had with the Indo-European groups generally, it may well have been the Luvians who were most closely connected to the emergence of the Hebrew religion. There is further evidence that suggests that the Luvians (or Luvites) may well have been the origins of the priestly Levites of the Hebrews.

Luvian texts are still being deciphered. As I mentioned previously, the Luvians were very closely related to both the Hurrian and Hittite peoples and had long been considered by archaeologists to be Hittites. Judging from the prevalence of votive, ritual and incantation texts so far attributed to them, the Luvians may have been a separate priestly caste of the Indo-Europeans, much like the Brahmins of India. We may question why they continued to use the less flexible hieroglyphs when other scripts were so readily available and used by the other Indo-Europeans, and why the hieroglyphs were used exclusively for votive rituals and inscriptions on royal monuments. Many of the scribal schools appear to have been located in their territory, suggesting that it may have been the Luvians who used the Hurrian, Hittite and Akkadian languages to disseminate their ideas while retaining the ancient hieroglyphs as their own perhaps more sacred manner of writing (as the Jewish people of later times have done with Hebrew).

Among the Indo-Aryans, the priestly caste known as the Brahmins made fire sacrifices one of the most important aspects of the religion. Professor Norman Brown writes of the Brahmins in the fourth century BC, describing ". . . the overriding power of the elaborate Vedic sacrifice performed by Brahmins according to an ancient ritual of the greatest complexity and carrying unrivalled authority." He tells us that "The Brahmins arrogated to themselves, as custodians and sole competent officiants of this all-important ritual, a position of moral and social superiority to both the old temporal military and governing aristocracy . . ."

Guiseppi Sormani writes that in the early Sanskrit Yajurveda, a collection of Brahmin sacrificial and ritual prayer formulas dated shortly after the Rg Veda, "The priests commanded society; they were the lords even over the gods, whom they bent to their own will by means of ritual. The priestly power of the Brahmins was already evident in this Veda."

These descriptions could as well be applied to the Hebrew Levites as to the Brahmins. If the Luvians were a similar priestly caste, and a group of them was later known as the Levite priestly caste of the Hebrews, this connection would perhaps explain the extraordinary position that the Levites held among the other Hebrew tribes.

According to the Books of the Bible known as Exodus, Leviticus, Numbers and Deuteronomy, that is, the last four of the first five books of the Old Testament, the Levites were to remain a very exclusive group. Moses is described as the son of a Levite mother and father, as is his brother Aaron. In Num. 8:14 we read Yahweh's words, "You shall thus separate the Levites from the rest of the Israelites and they shall be mine." In Num. 18:2 Yahweh says to Aaron, "You and your sons alone shall be fully answerable for your priestly office."

Only Levites were acceptable as members of the priesthood of Yahweh. Moses, Aaron and the sons of Aaron were the highest priests. A Levite high priest was forbidden to marry not only a foreign woman but even a woman of any other Hebrew tribe. Even within his own tribe he was not to marry a widow, a divorced woman or in fact any woman who had ever had sexual relations with another man.

No one but a Levite was allowed to enter into the Tent of the Presence, where Yahweh was worshiped. It was implied that to do so was at the risk of life. When the Israelites marched across the deserts of Sinai the Levites led them, keeping a "day's journey ahead of them," to decide upon the next encampment. Though at first Moses is said to have acted as the sole judge in all disputes he eventually appointed officers in charge of distinct units. These were arranged in numbers of ten, fifty, one hundred and one thousand, much like an army, each with a watchful officer. The Levites were the judges of the law of the community. "Their voice shall be decisive in all cases of dispute" (Deut. 21:6).

The Levites alone had the possession and use of two silver trumpets which were to be used for summoning the community and breaking camp. The blast of one trumpet was a summons to the chiefs of the other tribes to appear before the Tent of the Presence, clearly exhibiting their authority over even the chiefs of the other tribes. The blast of two trumpets was to summon the entire Israelite community. Only Aaronite priests were allowed to use the two trumpets, which were also to be sounded during battle to urge the Israelites on, possibly to command all military strategy as the Qumran scrolls suggest.

While in the desert, probably in preparation for the battle as they entered Canaan, a counting or numbering of the tribes was ordered. At first this was only for the eleven other tribes. Every man aged twenty-one and over who was fit for military service was to be included. Later, when the Levites were counted, all males over one month were listed, and no military eligibility was required. In Num. 13:1–15 a spy party was formed to check out the situation on the approach into Canaan: though every other tribe was represented by one man, no Levite was listed.

At times there was mention of rebellion among the other tribes who complained about lack of food and the loss of comforts they had known in Egypt, despite the fact that they were supposed to have been badly used as slaves. But the penalties for breaking the rules of the Levites were severe. Lev. 24:16 tells of one man being stoned to death for speaking blasphemously of Yahweh. Num. 15:32 gives the account of a man who was found gathering sticks on the Levite-appointed Sabbath: "So they took him outside the camp and all stoned him to death as the Lord had commanded Moses." When Joshua took over the command from Moses the men are said to have promised, "As we obeyed Moses, so we will obey you. Whoever rebels against your authority, and fails to carry out all your orders, shall be put to death" (Josh. 1:18).

Fire sacrifices were an extremely important and major aspect of the rituals of the Levites, much like those of the Brahmins of India. The first ten sections of Leviticus are totally concerned with fire sacrifices. In these sections, as well as throughout Numbers and Deuteronomy, which also describe the laws and rituals of the Levites, we learn that fire sacrifices are to be made twice daily, as well as on the sabbath, at seasonal changes, for uncleanliness, for guilt and for sin.

The Levites were assigned the sole rights to eat the food offerings that were brought to the Tent of the Presence for the sacrifices listed above. In this way they were supplied by the other Israelites with cattle, sheep, rams, pigeons, corn, flour, bread, oil and wine. This right of the Levites and their families (though most often just the male members) was mentioned so repeatedly that I hesitate to include these laws here. Perhaps one passage concerning these rules will be sufficient to explain the situation.

For all the various fire sacrifices, referred to as "burnt offerings" the above listed foods were to be brought to the priests at the Tent. The law then stated that

> The Levitical priests, the whole tribe of Levi, shall have no holdings or patrimony in Israel; they shall eat the food offerings of the Lord. This shall be the customary due of the priests from those of the people who offer sacrifice whether a bull or a sheep: the shoulders, the cheeks and the stomach shall be given to the priest. You shall give him also the first fruits of your corn and new wine and oil, and the first fleeces at the shearing of your flocks. For it was he whom the Lord your God chose from all your tribes to attend on the Lord. [Deut. 18:2–8]

Gifts to the Levites of silver, gold and property were also repeatedly commanded by Yahweh. Each man over twenty had to give half a shekel as ransom for his life. In yet another ransom-for-life system, 1,365 shekels of silver were reported to be given to the Levites. "You shall give the money with which they are ransomed to Aaron and his sons" (Num. 3:48).

Levites who sold their houses always had the right of redemption, and if they did not pay to redeem it, it would be returned automatically at the seven-year jubilee. If a man of another tribe chose to sell his house to a Levite, the Levite had the sole right to decide upon the price. If the man wanted to buy it back he was expected to pay another twenty percent of the value.

Another command offering included six covered wagons and twelve oxen: "Assign them to the Levites" (Num. 7:5). In still another section we read that silver vessels worth 2,400 shekels, gold worth 120 shekels, 36 bulls, 72 full-grown rams, 72 he-goats and 72 yearling rams were the dedication offerings for the Tent (Num. 7: 84–88). And in Num. 18:8 it was written, "The Lord said to Aaron: I the Lord commit to your control the contributions made to me, that is all the holy gifts of the Israelites. I give them to you and your sons for your allotted portion due to you."

Num. 18:20 states, "To the Levites I give every tithe in Israel."

As we read above, the Levites were not to have any patrimony, which was often given as the reason they should receive so much else. But in Num. 35:2–6 we read, "Tell the Israelites to set aside towns in their patrimony as homes for the Levites and give them also the common lands surrounding the towns." Forty-eight towns were given in all.

Very specific instructions for the clothing of the Levites, made of violet and scarlet fabrics and fine linen, gold and precious gems, were described in Exod. 28. Along with their robes, Aaron's sons were also to be provided with headdresses which would give them "dignity and grandeur," perhaps reminiscent of the tall hats of the Hittites. Even perfume was to be provided for Aaron and his sons. If anyone else dared to wear it, he would be "cut off from his father's kin."

The other Israelite tribes were reminded, "You must not neglect the Levites who live in your settlements" (Deut. 14:27) and "Be careful not to neglect the Levites in your land as long as you live" (Deut. 12:19).

In Deut. 31:24 we read, "When Moses had finished writing these laws in a book, from beginning to end, he gave this command to the Levites . . . Take this book of the law and put it beside the Ark of the Covenant of the Lord your God to be witness against you." So it was that these laws, first written by the Levites, were then placed in the sole possession of the Levites, who were thus the only ones who had access to them, to interpret, censor or change in any way they saw fit.

The general picture rendered is not one of monastic priests or ascetic gurus, but rather a well clothed, well fed, well housed, well transported, perfumed aristocracy, who ruled with supreme authority over the other Hebrew people.

Reading through the laws concerning the Levites, we may find their position compared with the other Israelites somewhat extraordinary. The Levites, according to the Bible as we know it, are said to be the descendants of Levi, one of Jacob's twelve sons.

Again, tracing the genealogies, Moses would have been Levi's great-grandson. This doesn't quite tally with the number of males that were counted shortly after leaving Egypt. Though the figures may have been somewhat exaggerated, the Levites claimed that there were 22,000 males among them, quite a family in three generations.

Their position as the ruling class of the Hebrew people, certainly an Indo-European pattern, suggests that they may have been assigned this heritage to justify their relationship to the other tribes. However, the stories of Abraham, Isaac, Jacob and Esau are the ones that most closely relate to the Hittites and Horites, even more strongly suggesting that Jacob and Abraham may actually have been the ancestors of Moses and his brother Aaron, who were leaders of the Levites, while even other Levites, as well as members of the other eleven tribes, understood that this ancestry was symbolic rather than biological. Judging from their numbers, the other tribes may have been gathered together under this same symbolism, which in turn may explain why Jacob, supposedly the father of the twelve sons who spawned the twelve tribes of the Hebrews, was actually called Israel, rather than Abraham, who is generally considered as the first father of the Hebrew people.

The suggestion that the original Hebrews were not all of one race is further made in the Psalms. In Ps. 107 we find, "So let them say who were redeemed by the Lord, redeemed by him from the power of the enemy, and gathered out of every land, from east and west and north and south . . ." We also read in Ps. 87 that Zion, which is another name for the nation of Israelites, "shall be called a mother in whom men of every race are born." This suggests that at the time of the writing of these psalms Israel saw itself as a group of races, each gathered together under the emblem of Israel, perhaps including Semitic desert people, Egyptians, Canaanites and others, all possibly joined together under the direction of the Levites.

Still another curious passage in our consideration of the Levites as an Indo-European group occurs in Deut. 18:14–22. Here we find an account of Yahweh speaking to Moses on the top of the mountain. Moses descends and explains to the other Israelites that Yahweh has told him, "I will raise up for them a prophet like you, one of their own race."

Lewi and Levi, the Hebrew name for their priests, are much the same word, as is made evident in the English, German and French translations. I suggest that both this name and that of the Luvians may derive from the material of volcanic eruptions, the glowing molten mass pouring from the peak of a mountain.

In Latin, *lavo* means to wash in a stream which flows, while *lavit* means to pour. In Hittite, *lahhu* also means to pour. We find the word surviving in the French *laver,* to wash. Now this would suggest that the word was primarily associated with liquids. But we also find *lawine* in German, meaning avalanche, and the word *lavish* in English, meaning overflowing abundance. Thus the words appear to be related to any movable or flowing mass.

A most similar series of words occurs in connection with blazing light. *Levo* in Latin means lift and is especially associated with the sunrise. In Sanskrit *lauha* is defined as glowing redness, while lightning is called *lohla.* In German we find the word *löhe,* meaning blaze or flame, while in Danish *lue* means to go up in flames. But it is perhaps in the English word *lava,* the German *lava* and the French *lave,* each meaning the blazing molten mass that pours from a volcanic mountain, that we may find the key to these two concepts, that which is light and flaming, while still pouring almost as a liquid at the same time.

The image of the god on the glowing mountain, the Indo-European image of their male deity, which also appears in the Hebrew imagery of the accounts of Mount Horeb, perhaps points to their ultimate connection as one-time worshipers of volcanic mountains. In the Exodus account of the "mountain of God" we read these descriptions: "On the third day when the morning came, there were peals of thunder and flashes of lightning, dense cloud on the mountain and a loud trumpet blast; the people in the camp were all terrified" (Exod. 19:16). And in Exod. 20:18–21: "When all the people saw how it thundered and the lightning flashed, when they heard the trumpet sound and saw the mountain smoking, they trembled and stood at a distance. 'Speak to us yourself,' they said to Moses, 'and we will listen; but if God speaks to us we shall die.' Moses answered, 'Do not be afraid. God has only come to test you, so that the fear of him may remain with you and keep you from sin.' So the people stood at a distance, while Moses approached the dark cloud where God was." Later, in Deuteronomy, when Moses was recounting the incidents that took place at "Horeb, mountain of God" he reminded the Hebrews, "Then you came near and stood at the foot of the mountain. The mountain was ablaze with fire to the very skies: there was darkness, cloud and thick mist. When the Lord spoke to you from the fire you heard a voice speaking, but you saw no figure; there was only a voice" (Deut. 4:11–13). Reminding them of the "pagan" calf that they had made during his absence, he recalls, "I took the calf, that sinful thing that you had made, and burnt it and pounded it, grinding it until it was as fine as dust; then I flung its dust into *the torrent that flowed down the mountain*" (Deut. 9:21, my italics).

Again looking through the Hebrew Psalms we find, "He shall rain down red-hot coals upon the wicked" (Ps. 11); "consuming fire runs before and wreathes Him closely round" (Ps. 50); "How long must thy wrath blaze like fire?" (Ps. 89); "the world is lit up beneath his lightning flash . . . the mountains melt like wax as the Lord approaches" (Ps. 97); "He spread a cloud as a screen and a fire to light up the night" (Ps. 39). Surely the most vivid description of Yahweh as a volcanic mountain occurs in Ps. 18. Here we read, "The earth heaved and quaked, the foundations of the mountain shook; they heaved, because He was angry. Smoke rose from his nostrils, devouring fire came out of His mouth, glowing coals and searing heat . . . Thick clouds came out of the radiance before Him, hailstones and glowing coals . . . He shot forth lightning shafts and sent them echoing." The imagery is difficult to ignore.

We may also find it significant that the mountain north of Lake Van, in the land once known as Urartu, known as Mount Suphan even today, is a volcanic mountain. In Cilicia, in the Kizzuwatna territory of the Luvians there are two volcanic mountains.* In the Caucasus region and just to the south, once again in the land of Urartu, there are no less than thirteen volcanic mountains, three still active today. One is located near Baku on the Caspian Sea, close to the mouth of the Araks River. It might also be pertinent that in the Greek legend of the battle between Zeus and the serpent Typhon, Typhon was born in a mountain cave in Cilicia where he was first attacked by Zeus, later battled with Zeus on Mount Casius (Saphon) and was finally killed by Zeus on the volcanic Mount Etna in Sicily. But it may be most significant that just to the east of Sinai in Arabia we find a string of volcanic mountains, now extinct, all along the western coast facing Egypt and that Mount Ararat itself is volcanic.

To gain a clearer picture of the times, it is important to realize that volcanic mountains often erupt many times over a relatively short period. Mount Kilauea on Hawaii has erupted over two dozen times during the last twenty years. (Incidentally, this volcano is worshiped as the Goddess Pele.) Even today the surviving Zoroastrians of Iran still pray to fire, while in the Kurdish territories, partially in the land that was once Urartu, fires are lit on the mountain tops at New Year's celebrations.

The worship of the Indo-European and Hebrew gods as volcanic mountains may explain the great importance of the fire rituals among both the Brahmins and the Levites. It may also explain the name of Yahweh, so long a puzzle to Bible scholars who have hunted for the meaning in Semitic texts and cultures, for the word *yahveh* in Sanskrit means everflowing, so suggestive of the lava of volcanic eruption; it may even be related to the word lava itself. It may also be significant that another group who spoke the Luvian language are thought to have lived in the area of another volcanic

---

*One of these, today known as Hasan Dag, has two volcanic peaks, perhaps explaining why the Hittite storm god and the Hittite king are often portrayed standing upon a double-crested mountain, a foot upon each summit.

mountain in Turkey; curiously enough these people were called the Ahhiyawa.

Connections between the Indo-Europeans and the Hebrews are too numerous to be lightly dismissed, but it is only as the Luvian texts are better understood, or new material in better condition is discovered, that we may eventually be able to affirm or reject the more direct relationship of the Luvians and the Levites.

THE LEVITES AND THE SONS OF LIGHT

The association of the Hebrew people and the Indo-Europeans, both worshiping a god of light, is even further suggested by the recent discoveries of old Hebrew texts, popularly known as the Dead Sea Scrolls. These scrolls, discovered at Qumran in Palestine, are the oldest extant Hebrew texts of the books of the Old Testament, dating from about the third century BC. Generally they are quite in keeping with the Greek version and even the later Hebrew one, with some variations. But there was an additional text which was completely new to Bible scholars. It is an account known as "The Scroll of the War of the Sons of Light Against the Sons of Darkness." The scroll consists of the plans for a battle that was about to be fought. The enemy was collectively known as the Sons of Darkness; the Hebrews, still led by the Levite priests, were the Sons of Light. It begins by stating that "The first engagement of the Sons of Light shall be to attack the lot of the Sons of Darkness . . . The Sons of Light are the lot of God."

Many authorities have once again attributed this surprising find to influence from Iran, where the worship of Ahura still prevailed. But when we consider that so many of the other texts discovered at Qumran were from the Old Testament, we may question why this particular account should have been included among them. Also, there is no specific mention of Ahura. As we have seen, the concept of the god of light was not a new one to the Hebrews. The Indo-European duality of light and dark may be seen underlying the earliest description of Yahweh's creation of the world. For in

Gen. 1:3 we read, "God said, 'Let there be light,' and there was light; and God saw that the light was *good* and he separated light from darkness."

Another significant factor in the scroll is that it reveals that the priestly Levites were still in control. The people at Qumran were from the tribes of Judah and Benjamin, the southern survivors after the other tribes of Israel in the north had been conquered and dispersed in 722 BC. Though the southern state of Judah had been conquered in 586 BC, many of the people had returned to the area to live under foreign rule. It is from these two tribes that the Hebrew people of today descend; the others probably dispersed into the populations of Syria, Lebanon, Turkey and Iraq, despite the aperiodic attempts to exhibit traces of them in Ireland or in the various Indian cultures of North America.

In the Qumran scroll, just as in the books of the Old Testament, the dress, the banners, the duties and the position of the Levites were separately and carefully described. The banners were to be decorated with the names of Aaron and his sons. Even more interesting is the fact that the Levites were once again, or still, in charge of the battle trumpets. Trumpet signals were as carefully explained in the scroll as in a war manual; various types of trumpet blasts commanded "get ready for battle," "advance," "approach," "start fighting" and "retreat." This account of the leadership of the Levites, written some ten centuries after the Levites of the time of Moses, may give us some idea of how strict the adherence to the old Mosaic position of the Levites must have been throughout those centuries.

This warlike aspect of the Hebrews, described from the time of Moses onward, will be further discussed in later chapters concerned with the Hebrew suppression of the worship of the Goddess. For the moment, it may explain the name of the Hebrews as Yehudi (Judah). The Sanskrit word for warrior is *Yuddha.*

SUMMARY

One comment must surely be made before I conclude this chapter. If this hypothesis bears up under further investigation, we must certainly view the events of the Second World War, and the atrocities enacted upon the Hebrew people of the twentieth century by the self-styled Aryans of Nazi Germany, not only as tragic but ironic. The researches and excavations of the Hittite culture have been carried on primarily by German archaeologists throughout this century. It was sometime before and directly after the First World War that *nasili* was slowly beginning to be accepted as the real name of the Hittite language and Nesa, or Nasa, their first capital. The original name of the Hittite invaders may have been Nesians or Nasians. Nuzi became the capital of the Indo-European nation of Mitanni. One cannot help but wonder how much Adolf Hitler was affected by the reports of these finds, which may have found their way into the popular media of the times. Was it these accounts that caused him to change his name from Schickelgrüber to Hitler, which in German would mean something like "teacher of Hit"? Strangely enough one more connection between the Hittites and the Hebrews is the Hebrew use of the word *nasi* for prince.

Over the last two centuries scholars of religion, archaeology, history and even science have had to revise many of the ideas that were held as fact prior to the advent of each archaeological discovery. We may yet find another revision which explains the origins of the god Yahweh, the god of the fire on the top of Mount Horeb, as the Luvian culture is better understood. If this occurs it may help to explain many of the patriarchal laws and attitudes of the Levite priests of the Hebrews in the Old Testament and their insistence upon the destruction of the Goddess religion.

With the knowledge that the worship of the Goddess was being affected by invading Indo-Europeans from at least 2400 BC onward, possibly, though less extensively, in Egypt from 3000 BC and in Sumer perhaps at the very earliest periods of Sumerian culture, 4000–3000 BC, we may better understand the transitions that occur in the myths, rituals and customs of the Goddess religion throughout the historic periods. In turn, we begin to understand the confrontations that took place as the patriarchal northerners began to suppress the ancient worship and all it represented.

One of the most controversial issues seems to have been the concept of divine right to royal privilege and the institution of hereditary kingship. The earliest laws and myths suggest that the people of the Goddess religion were communally oriented, though perhaps organized through the centralized shrines of the Goddess. We may then ask how the transition from the Goddess religion to the right of divine kingship, provided by a male deity—kingship as we still know it today—came to take place.

6

If the King Did Not Weep

Even in Neolithic and earliest historic periods, it seems that in many towns and settlements a person may have sat upon the throne by divine right, much as the remaining monarchies of the world claim to do even today. The major difference was that the divine right was probably provided originally not by a male god, but by the Goddess. And documentary and mythological evidence suggest that this right, rather than being bestowed upon a male, was originally held by a woman, the high priestess of the Goddess, who may have gained this position by the custom of matrilineal descent. In the role of high priestess of the Goddess, this woman may also have been regarded as queen or tribal ruler. This was certainly the case in Khyrim, where, according to Frazer, the high priestess automatically became the head of state.

The juxtaposition of these two roles, that of high priestess and that of queen, is repeatedly attested to in early historic times in tablets and texts of the Near East. Many writers, perhaps using our own male-oriented society as a pattern, reverse cause and effect, suggesting that when a woman became queen, she then also gained the title of high priestess, a position supposedly resulting from her marriage to the king. But, as I shall explain, evidence suggests that it was the other way around; that the highest and most sacred attendant of the female deity in the very earliest times was probably the origin of the concept of royalty.

As I mentioned earlier, the temples of the Goddess in Neolithic and Chalcolithic periods appear to have been the core of the community, apparently owning the land, the herds of animals and most material property. This was the situation even in the early historic times of E Anna, the House of Heaven, the temple of the Goddess Inanna in Erech.

A. Moortgat writes that "At about 3000 BC in Uruk (Erech), modern Warka, the sacred place of Inanna, the Sumerian Lady of Heaven, there arose a complex of buildings which even today would be numbered among the most splendid of architectural works, were they in a better state of preservation." Professor Albright goes on to explain, ". . . the discoveries in Erech in Babylonia have proved that the temple complex at Eanna was already, before 3000 BC the centre of an elaborate economic organization." According to Sidney Smith, Professor of Near Eastern Archaeology, in Sumer, ". . . the temple directed every essential activity, not only matters that might be considered religious business, but the urban activities of the craftsmen, the traders and the rural employment of farmers, shepherds, poultry keepers, fishermen and fruit gardeners."

In Neolithic and earliest historic times, the *Entu,* the name of the high priestess in Sumer, the *Tawawannas,* the name of the high priestess in Anatolia, and their counterparts in other areas would probably have been the nominal leaders of those temple communities. The priestly office of "Divine Lady," one of the gifts Enki complained had been taken by Inanna from Eridu to Erech, may have referred to just such a position.

But nominal leader does not infer monarchy. In fact, several documents and myths suggest that Neolithic and early historic Goddess-worshiping communities were governed by assemblies, probably composed of the elders of the community. One Mesopotamian tablet said that "Under the guidance of Inanna at Agade, its old women and its old men gave wise counsel." "Eldership" was another of the gifts of civilization that Inanna gave to Erech. Gurney writes that, before the arrival of the Hittites, the Hattians had "originally been loosely organized in a number of independent townships, each governed by a body of elders." Even in Hittite times, texts describe a group known as the Elderly Women, who held prophetic and advisory positions and were also associated with mental and physical healing.

Professor Thorkild Jacobsen of the University of Chicago has influenced many other archaeologists and historians on this subject. His theory, based on the fact that the earliest Sumerian myths included both female and male deities in the decision-making assemblies of heaven, suggests that such participation of women in leadership was very likely a reflection of the societies that wrote the legends, both women and men taking part in community government. We may even regard the concept of monotheism, so often presented as a more civilized or sophisticated type of religion, as reflecting the political ideology that places all power in a single dominant person, while polytheism, especially as represented in the image of divine assemblies, perhaps symbolized a more communal attitude in the societies that developed and followed this type of theological thought.

There is no definitive evidence of the relationship between the role of high priestess and these groups of elders, though "under the guidance of Inanna" may refer to the role played by Her high priestess. Judging from the mythological accounts of the Goddess (with the high priestess understood to be Her incarnation upon earth), we are presented with the image not of a celibate woman, nor of one who took a permanent husband, as queens did in historic periods, but of a woman who chose annual lovers or consorts, as she retained the more permanent position of highest rank for herself.

The symbolism of her yearly, youthful consorts, the dying son/

lover of the Goddess, occurs and recurs throughout the legends of the Goddess religion, probably recording Neolithic and earliest historic periods. It is found in the most ancient legends of both Sumer and Egypt and survives in all historic periods of the Near East until the first centuries of Christianity, in which it may have been retained in the annual mourning for the death of Jesus.

Sir James Frazer, author of *The Golden Bough,* explored this subject more extensively and thoroughly than any other scholar of comparative religion. Though some of his conclusions and theories have been questioned by later writers, the major body of material in his twelve extensive volumes even today holds a great deal of valuable information—and perhaps more pertinent, still raises some interesting points. The subject of the annual death of the son/lover of the Goddess interests us here because it appears to be a direct outgrowth of the original rituals and customs of the early female religion. It symbolizes one of the most ancient practices recorded—the ritual sacrifice of an annual "king," consort of the high priestess.

Several accounts of tribes in Africa describe queens who remained unmarried, while taking lovers of lesser rank. Records from Nigeria report that a male was the consort of the queen until she found herself pregnant, at which time he was strangled by a group of women—he had fulfilled his earthly task.

Numerous accounts, legends and fragments of texts and prayers suggest that there were similar practices in most of the Goddess-worshiping cultures throughout the Near East, slightly different adaptations depending on the location and the gradual transitions that took place over the years. It is pointless to make any firm generalization on what was done or why, since the information in each specific culture would not support such an overall statement. Yet there are pieces of evidence everywhere that suggest that in Neolithic and perhaps even in earliest historic periods the consort of the high priestess met a violent death, while she remained to grieve.

The material is derived from three separate lines of evidence.

The first includes the accounts of the actual ceremonies, which describe the marriage of the consort to the priestess, providing him with the position later defined as kingship; the second, the documents of rituals, which in historic times came to be used as a substitute for the original sacrifice: human substitutes, assault, effigies and animal sacrifice. The third, the most detailed descriptions, are provided by the legends, which probably accompanied these substitute rituals; these, at the proper ceremonial moment, offering the theological explanation of the symbolic action taken.

This material suggests that the high priestess, as the incarnation of the Goddess, chose a lover, probably much younger than herself, since he was so often referred to as the son of the Goddess. Numerous accounts tell of the sexual union that took place between them, often referred to as the *hieros gamos,* the sacred marriage. This sacred marriage or sexual union is attested to in the historic periods of Sumer, Egypt, Babylon and even in classical Greece. After the sexual ceremony the young man assumed the role as consort of the priestess. He was the "king."

"The inference that seems indisputable," writes Professor S. Smith, "is that the rite of the sacred marriage goes back to a remote antiquity, and that is the reason why it was included in the cults of distinctly different gods . . . Its annual nature seems to be connected with the annual reappointment of the king." Describing the status of the male who related to the high priestess in the Aegean, Butterworth tells us that "Access to the divine was through the queen."

The sacred sexual union with the high priestess gave the male consort a privileged position. According to Professor Saggs, in historic Sumer and Babylon, after the sacred marriage the Goddess "fixed the destiny" of the king for the coming year. But in earlier days this position of kingship was far from permanent. The male chosen held his royal rights for a specific period of time. At the end of this time (perhaps a year since the ceremony was celebrated annually, but other records seem to suggest possibly a longer period in certain areas), this youth was then ritually sacrificed.

In 1914 Stephen Langdon wrote that "The divine figures of Tammuz, Adonis and Osiris represent a theological principle, the incarnation of religious ideas which were once illustrated in a more tangible form. Not the divine son who perished in the waves, but a human king who was slain . . . ."

In 1952 Charles Seltman of the University of Cambridge described the situation in this way. "The Great Goddess was always supreme and the many names by which she was called were but a variety of titles given to her in diverse places. She had no regular 'husband' but her mate, her young lover, died or was killed every autumn and was glorified in resurrection every spring, coming back to the goddess; even as a new gallant may have been taken into favour every year to mate with an earthly queen."

In 1957 Robert Graves wrote of the ritual regicide as it appeared in pre-Indo-European Greece, explaining it as follows: "The Tribal Nymph, it seems, chose an annual lover from her entourage of young men, a king to be sacrificed when the year ended . . . the sacred king continued to hold his position only by the right of marriage to the Tribal Nymph . . . ." In his introduction to *The Greek Myths* he explains his theories on how kingship in the Aegean was made a permanent institution, as a gradual extension of the "year" into a "longer year" was introduced by the invading Indo-European Achaeans of the thirteenth century BC and later a permanent kingship instituted by the Indo-European Dorians at about 1100 BC.

Both Frazer and James offer the Shilluk groups of the Upper Nile as a possible analogy. Professor James, writing in 1937, says, "It was the custom in this tribe until recently to put the king to death whenever he showed signs of failing health and virility. Therefore as soon as he was unable to satisfy the sexual passions of his wives, it was their duty to acquaint the elders with the fact, and arrangements were made at once for his demise and the appointment of a vigorous successor to reign in his stead." Frazer listed Canaan, Cyprus and Carthage as places where in earliest historic times there was the most certain evidence of the slaying of the king. Frazer, Langdon, James, Seltman, Graves and many others agreed that the legend was enacted and that the male who was slain was the temporary king of the city, the youth who had previously played the role of the son/lover in the sacred sexual union.

Most authors who discuss the sacrifice of the "king" describe it primarily as a fertility rite, suggesting that his remains may even have been scattered over the newly sown fields. Though this perhaps became the custom in later periods, one of the earliest recorded legends (that of the Sumerian Goddess Inanna, written shortly after 2000 BC), probably a written record of even earlier myths and religious ideas, presented a different motive. In this legend the sacrifice of the consort occurred when he was no longer willing to defer to the wishes, commands and power of the Goddess. This most ancient account perhaps reveals the earliest origins and reasons for the death of the male consort. Later ideas of fertility or expiation of sins may have eventually been embroidered about the custom to ensure or explain its continuation.

The generally accepted explanation of the sacrifice of the king as a fertility rite was probably a result of the fact that all legends available until recently told only of the grief of the Goddess over the death of Her son/lover. It was only upon the discovery and decipherment of the last fragments of the Sumerian legend, which added the information that, although Inanna did grieve at the death, it had occurred as a result of Her own wrath at the youth's arrogance, that we are now in a position to question the actual meaning and reasons for this ancient ritual and revise those generally accepted explanations.

It may be helpful to examine the numerous accounts of the sacred marriage, or the son/lover as king and the position of the high priestess, in several of the cultures of the Near East; to gain a deeper comprehension of the custom as it may have originally been known by learning of its various adaptations in the historical periods following the Indo-European invasions.

SUMER—"THE BELOVED HUSBANDS OF INANNA"

In the Sumerian accounts of Inanna and Damuzi (defined as the true son) we learn that after he "proved himself" upon Her bed She then arranged his future for him, making him "shepherd of the land." Though this may symbolically sound like a very important post, we should remember that there were huge herds of animals owned and kept by the staff of the temples and the title may originally have been a description of his actual role. The son/lover as shepherd appears in many versions of the tale in various areas and epochs and once again suggests the relationship of the original son/lover to the later worship of Jesus.

But whatever the actual nature of the position, the Sumerian legend tells us that, when Inanna was looking for a replacement for Herself in the Land of the Dead, She passed over Her own servant because he had been most loyal and served Her well; She passed over a minor god because he had bowed down to Her as She requested; but eventually She chose Her own son, Her own lover, Damuzi, who had dared to climb joyfully upon Her throne during Her absence and had behaved in a most arrogant manner upon Her return. The death of the earliest Sumerian Damuzi was not an accident. He died at Inanna's command.

Sumerian documents reveal that the origins of kingship in Sumer began with the position of *En,* defined as both priest and consort of the Goddess. *En*ship was later replaced by *Ensi*ship, which appears to have provided greater and more secular powers. The office of *Ensi* was then supplanted by the title and position known as *Lugal,* which literally means "important man" but is usually translated as king. Another most ancient word, *Mukarrib,* is also often translated as king, though it literally means "bringer of offerings." Saggs explains that the Ensi was originally elected, probably in time of war, but near the end of the third millenium this position became hereditary. Professor Sidney Smith comments that the documents that describe the extensive use of oracular divination and prophecy reveal that, even after the role of king became more permanent, "no king acted according to his own judgement alone."

The position of king as leader seems to have been instituted in a period remembered by the time written records appear. In the early second-millenium legend of Etana we read, "At that time no tiara had been worn . . . there was at first no royal direction of the people of the Goddess, kingship then came down from heaven." But this kingship, as suggested by the accounts of the arrival of the Ubaid and Shemsu-Hor peoples of Sumer and Egypt, more likely arrived by sailboat than by spaceship.

Professor S. N. Kramer, eminent Sumeriologist, tells us that in the historical periods of Sumer,

> The most significant rite of the New Year was the *hieros gamos,* or holy marriage between the king, who represented the god Damuzi, and one of the priestesses, who represented the goddess Inanna . . . the idea arose that the King of Sumer, no matter who he was or from what city he originated, must become the husband of the life-giving goddess of love, that is, Inanna of Erech . . . the kings of Sumer are known as the "beloved husbands" of Inanna throughout the Sumerian documents from the time of Enmerkar [about 2600 BC] down to post-Sumerian days, since they seem to have been mystically identified with Damuzi.

Professor Kramer describes the role of the priestess of Inanna as that of the "dominant partner," explaining that She makes him king, not the other way about, that She brings Her lover to Her own house and that She is asked as the Queen of Heaven to allow him to enjoy long days at Her holy lap. Professor Henri Frankfort also pointed out that "In the sacred marriage the dependence of the god upon the goddess is strongly emphasized. Texts from Isin leave no doubt that the initiative was ascribed to her." All the kings of Isin, a city of Sumer that flourished between 2000 and 1800 BC, spoke of themselves as "the beloved consort of Nana."

Tablets from the reign of Shu Sin, about 1980 BC, also suggest the more aggressive role of Inanna at the sacred marriage. Her part reads, "Bridegroom, let me caress you. My precious caress is more savoury than honey; in the bed chamber let *us* enjoy *your* goodly beauty" (my italics).

When Enmerkar (an En in Erech) battled with the king of Aratta, Enmerkar won. The king of Aratta then said to him, "You are the beloved of Inanna, you alone are exalted. Inanna has truly chosen you for her holy lap." Another tablet tells us, "To Eannatum, the ensi of Lagash [about 2200 BC], Inanna, because she loved him, gave the kingship of Kish in addition to the Ensiship of Lagash."

Texts of Shulgi, a king of the third dynasty of Ur (about 2040 BC) read, "Goddess, I will perform for you the rites which constitute my royalty. I will accomplish for you the divine pattern." In these same tablets, which appear to be the written dialogue for the roles for the sacred ceremonial drama of the *hieros gamos,* the high priestess of Inanna then says of Shulgi, "When he has made love to me on the bed, then I in turn shall show my love for the lord, I shall make for him a good destiny, I shall make him shepherd of the land."

Two other names of the Goddess in Sumer, each (in different locations) describing her as the mother of Inanna, were also mentioned in connection with this custom. One inscription tells of the Goddess Ninmah (Lady Mother) "raising" Rim Sin to kingship, at about 1800 BC in Larsa. The accounts of four kings of Sumer recorded that the Goddess known as Ninlil brought the new young king into Her bower each time—presumably meaning that a sacred sexual union took place between the potential king and the high priestess of the Goddess. Professor Sidney Smith writes, "The records of the Ninlil festivals show that the occasions when a king of Sumer and Akkad was brought into the bower, marked the establishment of different dynasties."

At the beginning of the reign of Lipit-Ishtar, about 1930 BC, his "sister" was high priestess at Ur. But when another group of people conquered this city, her name was then associated with their king. Clearly by this time, and even from the time of Enmerkar, the ancient customs were being used to justify the results of battles and military conquests; marriage to the high priestess was being used to acquire legitimacy upon the throne in the eyes of the people.

Sidney Smith writes of "the exceptional political position of priestesses." He describes the situation of Lipit-Ishtar and the woman known as his sister saying, "The whole incident illustrates the political significance of these appointments . . . The sporadic appointment of princesses at Ur, when that city was compelled to acknowledge the rule of men not of southern origin was obviously due to political motives."

As I explained in the previous chapter, it seems that, as the followers of Enki and Enlil grew more powerful, the high priestess as representative of the Goddess lost a great deal of her earlier prerogatives, but was probably left with the role of bestowing kingship, matrilineal customs still being honored. The actual position of the high priestess at this period is open to question. We know from the records that many of them were daughters, sisters or mothers of the kings who were in power. The records of Hammurabi's time show that his sister was a *naditu* priestess, suggesting that the high priestess may have been connected with this group who seem to have managed the business affairs of the temples and community land.

BABYLON—"SHE WHO HOLDS THE REINS OF KINGS"

In Babylon of the eighteenth to the sixth centuries BC, which superseded Sumer as the major power in Mesopotamia, the Goddess was known as Ishtar. She was the Akkadian version of Inanna and revered as Ishtar even in the temple in Erech. Her dying son/lover, once known in Sumer as Damuzi, was now called Tammuz. Professor James comments on the relationship of Ishtar and Tammuz, writing, "In this alliance she was the dominant partner, as has been demonstrated, for when he was brought into close connection with Ishtar, in the Tammuz myth, he was her son as well as her husband and brother, and always subordinate to her as the Young-god."

The attributes and legends of Inanna and Ishtar are so similar that many writers speak of the Goddess as Inanna/Ishtar. But there were certain variations in the legends, transitions that perhaps reflect the change in attitudes over the centuries as the result of the more continual and successful invasions of the Indo-Europeans. In hardly any Babylonian literature do we learn that Ishtar actually caused the death of Tammuz, which is reported to have happened in a variety of accidental ways. Legends generally explain that Tammuz died and Ishtar grieved.

But in the Babylonian epic of Gilgamish, based on an earlier Sumerian saga known only from small fragments, the name of Tammuz was included in a long list of lovers whom Ishtar had in some way deeply injured. Gilgamish, historically listed as an early En of Erech, pointedly declined the honor of becoming the husband of Ishtar and thus being added to the list. The story probably represents one of the earlier refusals of a consort/king to follow the ancient customs and the attempt to institute a more permanent and powerful kingship. His quest for immortality in the same legend may also reveal this as its underlying message.

The story of Gilgamish takes place in Sumer. But once again we may suspect the influence or presence of the patrilineal northerners, perhaps from Aratta. The name Gilgamish may well be associated with the later Hurrian city of Carchemish, whose ancient name was Kar Gamish. The story of Gilgamish is found not only in Sumerian and Babylonian literature but in Hurrian and Hittite texts as well.

Gilgamish is listed as an En of Erech; therefore he gains the role of "king" as consort to the high priestess. His father is listed as Lugal Banda, who, though a previous En of Erech, is also described as a shepherd and a nomad. In the very beginning of the story we learn that Gilgamish is oppressing Erech, "taking the son from the father, taking the maiden from her lover." We next read that he is about to attend a feast at which he will "fertilize the woman of destiny," suggesting his role in the sacred marriage. Another figure appears at this time. He is known as Enkidu, a wild man of the woods. Enkidu is then treated to extravagant clothing, splendid food and drink and the company of a *qadishtu,* a holy woman of the temple, with whom he has his first sexual encounters.

Shortly afterward, Ishtar proposes marriage to Gilgamish, telling him that She has longingly gazed upon his beauty. But Gilgamish, acting not in accordance with the role he is supposed to play, spurns the proposal of the Goddess. In doing this, he lists all of Her past lovers who have met a tragic fate, ending with, "You would love me too and then make my fate like theirs." Among these past lovers, Tammuz is mentioned as a lover of Ishtar's younger days. The name Damuzi actually appears twice on the Sumerian king lists, once directly between Lugal Banda and Gilgamish, and once in an even earlier period, just a few names after Alalu, first king of Sumer at Eridu. The second Damuzi, and Gilgamish himself, appear to be from about 2500 BC.

After the marriage rejection a fight then ensues between Ishtar, Enkidu and Gilgamish, in which the two men insult the Goddess, kill Her heavenly bull and throw its thigh bone or genitals (depending upon the translation) in Her face. Gilgamish calls out, "If I could, I would do the same to you." As a result of this incident Enkidu, who probably symbolizes the substitute sacrifice, is put to death. Gilgamish is spared and at this point goes off on his search for immortality, which leads into the Sumerian account of the flood and its survivors.

Apart from the possible connections of the name Gilgamish with the later Hurrian city of Kar Gamish, the hints at the very beginning that Gilgamish is oppressing Erech, the general plot of the story and the existence of Hurrian and Hittite texts of the same epic, several other factors suggest that this epic may once again reflect northern attitudes. In it we may be witnessing a confrontation of the two cultures. In the Sumerian king lists Enmerkar directly precedes Lugal Banda, the father of Gilgamish. Several cuneiform tablets reveal that both Enmerkar and Lugal Banda were in close touch with the land of Aratta (possibly Urartu). One myth tells of Lugal Banda accompanying Enmerkar to that area, a trip brought to a halt by a rather mystical event at a place named Mount Hurum. Enmerkar also had very close connections with the

Enki temple at Eridu, demanding that the people of Aratta send tribute there. The king who preceded Enmerkar apparently founded the First Dynasty of Erech. The king lists tell us that he "entered the seas and climbed the mountains," perhaps suggesting his travels before reaching Erech, possibly from the mountain lands of Aratta. The account of the rebellion against Ishtar (probably as represented by the high priestess) may well have actually occurred at the time of the institution of kingship in Erech and the story later added to the Babylonian accounts of Gilgamish, who seems to have become something of a legendary hero in many other tales as a result of his military exploits.

Whenever it actually occurred, this account may symbolize an incident much like the one Diodorus Siculus reported among the Nubians of the Upper Nile. He wrote that a king, who rebelled against being sacrificed, murdered all the presiding clergy, thus proclaiming a permanent kingship for himself.

By Babylonian times the king was certainly no longer put to death. Yet Ishtar was still described as the one who appointed the king; "She who endowed him with prestige." In one inscription She was titled, "Counsellor of All Rulers, She Who Holds the Reins of Kings." In another She was known as "She who gives the sceptre, the throne, the year of reign to all kings." Sargon of Akkad, one of the earliest kings of central Mesopotamia (at about 2300 BC), wrote that his mother was a high priestess, his father was unknown. Later, he says, Ishtar came to love him ". . . and then for years I exercised kingship."

In *The Childhood of Man,* L. Frobenius, discussing the ritual of the sacrifice of the king, explained, "Already in ancient Babylon it had been weakened, in as much as the king at the New Year Festival in the temple was only stripped of his garments, humiliated and struck, while in the marketplace a substitute, who had been ceremonially installed in all glory, was delivered to death by the noose."

Various accounts of the ceremonies that took place during Babylonian periods tell of the king going to the temple to be struck in the face, his clothing and royal insignia temporarily removed. Other texts tell us that his hair was shorn, his girdle removed and in this state he was thrown into the river. When he emerged he was made to walk about in sackcloth for several days as a symbol of mourning. Saggs observes that "There is some evidence, even from the first millenium that the king at his death may have been assimilated to the (supposedly) dying god Tammuz."

These were symbolic reminders of the days when the consort/king would have met his death. But just as Gilgamish continued to live, while Enkidu died, the substitute lost his life as kingship in Sumer and Babylon became a permanent and hereditary institution. There are hints of expiation of sins and atonement in these rituals—the king is being punished. But for what? It seems that eventually the chastisement came to be for the sins of the people, but did this not originate from his earlier punishment for refusing to defer to the priestess-queen? The fact that good fortune was predicted if tears came to his eyes when he was struck perhaps reveals these origins. According to the Babylonian tablets, "If the king does not weep when struck, the omen is bad for the year."

EGYPT—ISIS MOURNS THE DEATH OF OSIRIS

Saggs, writing of the ritual regicide, states, "This latter practice certainly occurred in Egypt in prehistoric times, while some authorities argue that it survived into historical times." In the earliest records of Egypt, shortly after 3000 BC, men were sacrificed at the "grave of Osiris," brother/husband of the Goddess Isis. The records tell us that the sacrificed men had red hair, perhaps, as I mentioned before, a result of the invasion of the Shemsu-Hor.

In Egyptian theogyny Horus was the son of Isis. Upon his death he becomes *Osiris.* Though it is the death of Osiris that is commemorated, it is actually Horus, the son, who has died. At the death of Osiris the new Horus was then installed upon the throne. Thus in the cumulative myths of Egypt, where each new idea seems to have been added and little if anything eliminated, both Horus and Osiris engaged in a battle against Set, but it is Osiris who is killed by Set. The stories of the death of Osiris were not only remembered and ceremonially re-enacted in Egypt but were also closely connected with Canaan, especially at the most ancient port of Byblos. Byblos, a city slightly north of Beirut in Lebanon, was an Egyptian colony or commercial seaport as early as the Second Dynasty of Egypt, which occurs at about 2850–2600 BC. But even as late as about AD 150, Lucian speaks of the death of the lover of the Goddess, then known as Adonis, taking place at Aphaca, near Byblos. Lucian then reveals that the secret rites of Adonis are actually those of Osiris. Some accounts claimed that the body of Adonis was buried at Aphaca, just a few miles from Byblos, while Egyptian myth tells us that Isis brought the body back to Egypt for burial, describing in detail all the various problems She encountered in doing this.

CRETE—"THE GOD (WHO USUALLY DIES SHORTLY AFTER HIS WEDDING)"

Hawkes, describing the Goddess and the dying youth on the island of Crete, where worship of the female deity flourished from before 3000 BC until the arrival of the Indo-European Dorians in about 1100 BC, stated: "She is accompanied by a youthful male deity, a Year Spirit who is her consort and offspring, who dies and is born again—the Cretan version of Adonis. In Minoan Crete this young god was always subject to the goddess—he was the instrument of her fertility and is shown in humble and worshipful attitudes."

Stylianos Alexiou suggests that in Crete "The sacred marriage, the union of the goddess and the god (who usually dies shortly after his wedding) symbolizes the fertility of the earth."

Even in classical times the Indo-European Zeus was worshiped by the people of Crete as an infant and revered primarily as the son of his mother, Rhea. Greek theogyny tells us that the Goddess Rhea hid the infant Zeus from his father in a Cretan cave. In one legend Rhea was described as being "sexually attacked" by Her son Zeus, possibly a remnant of an earlier account of the sacred sexual union that took place between them. On Crete, Zeus was thought of as the dying son, a concept deeply resented by the Indo-European Greeks of the mainland, who insisted that Zeus was immortal.

NORTHERN CANAAN—"MISTRESS OF KINGSHIP"

In the texts of Ugarit of the fourteenth century BC many of the accounts appear to be the result of the assimilation of the religion of the Goddess with newer Indo-European concepts, possibly derived from the great number of Hurrians living there at the time. The texts tell the story of the death of Baal, Lord of Mount Saphon. They record that Baal's death was as a result of a battle with Mot, a name otherwise unknown, though the legends reveal that Mot was an enemy greatly feared by Baal. After his death the Goddess Anath carried Baal's body on Her shoulders to find a burial place. As soon as this was done She avenged the death of Baal by killing Mot, an event described in rather gruesome detail. But the revenge killing seems to be the reason that Baal was then allowed to re-enter the world of the living. According to the legend he then joined Anath in a field, fell down before Her in grateful appreciation, "admiring Her horns of strength." She taking the form of the sacred heifer, he of a bull, they united in sacred sexual union. Even at this period, Anath was still known as the "Mistress of the Heavens, Mistress of Kingship."

ANATOLIA—"SHE WHO CONTROLS KINGSHIP . . ."

There are no records among the Hittite texts of Anatolia that suggest that the king was put to death, possibly because the earliest written material that has so far been found seems to have been produced by the Indo-European Hittites themselves. Yet the Sun Goddess of Arinna, the Hattian deity who appears to have been adopted by the invading Hittites, was still known in prayer as "She who controls kingship in heaven and on earth." Texts of the Hittites describe a ritual that a queen performs in front of eight statues of the Sun Goddess, each bearing the name of a previous high priestess-queen.

Gurney writes that "The great national deity of the Hittites was the sun-goddess of Arinna, 'who directs kingship and queenship,' and it is therefore no surprise to find that her 'regular festivals' were among those for which the presence of the king was essential." Though the evidence is scanty, it seems to point to much the same relationship between the priestess of the Goddess and the king in pre-Hittite days. Possibly adopted into Hittite custom to ensure royal legitimacy, early Indo-European leaders may have at one time taken part in the sacred marriage with Hattian priestesses.

After about 1000 BC stories of the Goddess, then known as Cybele, and the youth, then known as the shepherd Attis, predominate in Anatolia, legends once again probably surviving from the earlier religion of the Goddess people. Various versions of the death of Attis, at times associated with his castration, retell the story of the dying son/lover. An interesting factor in the accounts of Cybele and Attis is that this version of the religion of the Goddess was eventually brought from Anatolia to Rome. It was celebrated there in great processions and festivals until AD 268 and embraced by such emperors as Claudius and Augustus. We can only guess at the influence this had upon the Christian religion that was developing there at that time. Roman reports of the rituals of Cybele record that the son, this time as an effigy, was first tied to a tree and then buried. Three days later a light was said to appear in the burial tomb, whereupon Attis rose from the dead, bringing salvation with him in his rebirth. Cybele was always closely identified with the Goddess Rhea, who was known as the mother of Zeus, and it is quite possible in pre-Christian Rome that the mother of the dying god was known as Ma Rhea.

CYPRUS AND GREECE—THE RITES FOR THE DEAD SHEPHERD

On the island of Cyprus the death of Adonis was recalled in the worship of Aphrodite. Greek tales explained that the Goddess had taken a shepherd youth as a lover, having fallen in love with this youth when She first saw him as an infant. After living with him for a year in the wooded hills of Cyprus, according to the legend She left to visit Corinth, one of the major centers of Aphrodite worship in classical Greece. Upon Her absence Adonis was killed by a wild boar, a description of the death which also appeared in some of the legends of Osiris and Attis. Through the worship of Aphrodite, which on the island of Cyprus was closely associated with the Canaanite Astarte, the rites for the dead shepherd youth Adonis survived in classical Greece, though frowned upon by Indo-European government officials.

ISRAEL—A DYING GOD NAMED TAMMUZ

In biblical accounts the rituals of the death of the son/lover were once again described, this time taking place among the Hebrew women who prayed at the temple in Jerusalem in about 620 BC. In the book of Ezekiel we read, "Then he brought me to the gateway of the Lord's house which faces north; and there I saw the women sitting and wailing for Tammuz" (Ezek. 8:14). There they were at the temple wall, still performing the mourning ceremonies, weeping for Tammuz.

In 1933 Professor T. H. Robinson wrote of the ceremonial death of Tammuz occurring in Israel, claiming, "This subject has been closely studied in recent years, and it is generally (although not universally) agreed that a ritual involving a dying god, a divine marriage and a ceremonial procession, was found in Israel."

In 1958 Professor Widengren stated that "We are thus able to assert that there was just such a ritual mourning in Israel as there was in Mesopotamia after the death of Tammuz, and that this lamentation festival was celebrated in connection with the Feast of Booths, after the jubilation ceremonies of the sacred marriage."

CASTRATED GODS AND EUNUCH PRIESTS

It is possible that in certain areas one of the substitute rituals that initially replaced the actual death of the temporary king was the act of castration, perhaps the actual origin of the Freudian fantasy fear. The severing of the male genitals appeared in several legends that announced the deposition of the ruling male. These accounts occur in the same general areas that also report the death of the male consort; and in some, such as Osiris and Attis, castration and death are closely intertwined.

Indo-European Hittite mythology related in the story of Kumarbi, who wrested the position of power from the previous reigning god Anu, that Kumarbi castrated Anu as Kumarbi ascended to the superior rank. Greek mythology, probably borrowing from these earlier Hittite stories, told of Cronus castrating his father Uranus and usurping his position at the suggestion of his mother, the Goddess Gaia. Cronus then feared that his son might do the same to him, thus setting off a series of Greek mythological events in which the son, Zeus, did eventually overthrow his father. Both the Hittite and the Greek stories are Indo-European. Castration may have been the original Indo-European solution to the ritual regicide.

The Anatolian myth of the Goddess Inara revealed that once a man slept with the Goddess (presumably the high priestess), he might never again sleep with another woman, for fear that he would transfer the sacred powers of the Goddess to her. One Attis legend explained his voluntary castration as a reaction to his fear of being unfaithful to the Goddess. If the consort was not allowed to have sexual relations with anyone after he had been with the high priestess, castration may have been the solution that at first allowed him to remain alive.

When the body of Osiris was cut into fourteen pieces by Set,

sometimes depicted as a wild boar, Isis repaired it, patiently rejoin-
ing all the mutilated sections. But according to the Egyptian myth
the genitals were irrevocably lost, eaten by the fish of the River
Nile. Uranus's genitals were, incidentally, also "cast into the waters." The Anatolian Attis appears to have castrated himself in a
feverish fit of love, religion, fear of infidelity, shame or self-punish-
ment, depending upon the version of the story. The loyal helpers
and attendants in the legends of Ishtar and Inanna were described
as eunuchs.

The element of castration appears in many ancient accounts of
the Goddess religion. Repeated references were made to the presence of eunuch priests in ancient Sumer, Babylon, Canaan and
most especially in Anatolia, where classical texts report that the
number of such men serving in the religion of the Goddess at that
time was as high as five thousand in certain cities. The eunuch
priests in Anatolia of classical times actually called themselves
Attis.

Suggestions have been put forth to explain the evident willingness of these men to castrate themselves, a custom we may find
somewhat astonishing today. These explanations are supported by
the appearance all through the Near East of representations of
priests in female clothing, the costume eunuch priests are said to
have worn.

Stylianos Alexiou writes, "The priests and musicians wearing
long feminine robes fall into a special category. This practice has
led to the surmise that, perhaps owing to Syrian influence, there
existed companies of eunuch priests in the Cretan palaces. During
a later period the eunuch priests of Cybele and Attis in Asia Minor
formed a similar class."

It seems quite possible that as men began to gain power, even
within the religion of the Goddess, they replaced priestesses. They
may have initially gained this right by identifying with and imitat-
ing the castrated state of the son/lover; or in an attempt to imi-
tate the female clergy, which originally held the power, they
may have tried to rid themselves of their maleness by adopt-

ing the ritual of castration and the wearing of women's clothing.

In Anatolia and even in Rome, after a young male devotee of the Goddess had taken the sacred knife to his own body he then ran through the streets, still holding the severed parts. He eventually flung these into a house along the way, custom decreeing that the inhabitants of that house should provide him with women's clothing, which he wore from that time on.

G. R. Taylor, in his abridgment of Briffault's *The Mothers,* commented on this custom. He observed that "The first step in the limitation of the status of women was to take over from them the monopoly of the religious function." Graves pointed out that the king was often privileged to deputize for the queen, but only if he wore her robes. He suggested that this was the system in Sumerian Lagash.

In some areas of Anatolia of classical times, eunuch priests appear to have totally gained control of the Goddess religion. A large group of eunuch priests accompanied the statue and rites of Cybele when these were first brought into Rome. We may only speculate as to the effect and influence this may have had upon the newly forming Christian religion and the custom of celibacy among the priests, still existent in the canons of the Catholic Church.

The laws of the early Hebrews stated that a man without a penis was not to be considered as a member of the congregation. "No man whose testicles have been crushed or whose organ has been severed shall become a member of the assembly of the Lord" (Deut. 23:1). It is perhaps significant that the Bible claims that the original covenant that Yahweh made with Abraham was so explicit about the practice of circumcision. It required that it be done to all Hebrew males shortly after birth. Though this has often been explained by writers in contemporary society as having been a preventive health measure against venereal diseases, could it actually have been a means of emphasizing the "maleness" of the male-worshiping Hebrews from the "femaleness" of those who had joined the Goddess?

SUMMARY

The castrated and/or dying youthful consort, a vestige of the times in which the high priestess held the divine right to the throne, is often ignored or misunderstood by writers who concentrate on one geographical area or one chronological period and fail to examine the gradual transition from the supremacy of the female deity and Her priestesses to the eventual suppression and obliteration of those beliefs.

At times the misunderstanding seems astonishingly disconnected from all documentary evidence. In 1964 A. Leo Oppenheim, who in less than two lines hastily whisked over the Goddess first worshiped in Sumer as the patron deity of written language, then proceeded to spend five full pages discussing his theory that the word *istaru* was simply a concept that implied fate or life destiny, later personified by *men* as the Goddess Ishtar. He asserted that this in turn explained why the Goddess was continually described as "the carrier, the fountainhead of the power and prestige of the king." But the mass of evidence makes it clear that Ishtar, as well as other versions of the Goddess throughout the Near and Middle East, was described as "the fountainhead of the power and prestige of the king" because it was actually required that the king become the sexual consort of the high priestess, incarnation of the Goddess on earth, who probably held the rights to the royal throne through matrilineal descent.

The custom of ritual regicide disappeared as the patrilineal tribes gained dominance. The numerous copies of the legend of Gilgamish, in various languages, may have been used to further this purpose. Permanent hereditary kingship became the rule and as the male deity gained supremacy, the role of the benefactor of the divine right to the throne was eventually shifted over to him, a concept of the rights of royalty that survives even today.

There can be little doubt that the original customs of ritual regicide, and the political position of the high priestess, presented a major obstacle to the desire of the northern conquerors for a permanent kingship and more total control of government. But a second, and perhaps equally vital, point of confrontation leads us in the following chapter to a more thorough explanation of the attitudes and cultural patterns that surrounded sex and reproduction in the religion of the Goddess, allowing and even encouraging a female kinship system to continue.

7

The Sacred Sexual Customs

The Canaanites are known throughout the Old Testament as the major element in the population of Palestine dispossessed by Israel in her occupation of the "land flowing with milk and honey." With great indignation and broad generalization "the abominations of the Canaanites" are stigmatized by Hebrew prophets, reformers and editors of the Old Testament. They roundly condemn their people for going "a whoring after the Baalim" and Ashteroth, the local manifestations of the deities of the Canaanite fertility-cult, which they caricature by referring to one element in it, sexual license . . .

So commented Professor John Gray in *The Canaanites,* written in 1964. This "sexual license" described among the Canaanites refers to the sacred sexual customs of the ancient religion, customs also found in many other areas of the Near and Middle East.

During biblical times it was still customary, as it had been for thousands of years before in Sumer, Babylon and Canaan, for many women to live within the temple complex, in earliest times the very core of the community. As we have seen, temples owned much of the arable land and herds of domesticated animals, kept the cultural and economic records and generally appear to have functioned as the central controlling offices of the society. Women who resided in the sacred precincts of the Divine Ancestress took their lovers from among the men of the community, making love to those who came to the temple to pay honor to the Goddess. Among these people the act of sex was considered to be sacred, so holy and precious that it was enacted within the house of the Creatress of heaven, earth and all life. As one of Her many aspects, the Goddess was revered as the patron deity of sexual love.

Some archaeologists assume that these sexual customs of the temples, so repeatedly attested to in the religion of the female deity throughout the early historic periods of the Near and Middle East, must have been viewed as a type of primitive symbolic magic to invoke fertility in cattle and vegetation as well as in humans. It is my opinion that they may have developed as a result of the earliest consciousness and comprehension of the relationship of sex to reproduction. Since this connection was probably initially observed by women, it may have been integrated into the religious structure as a means of ensuring procreation among the women who chose to live and raise children within the shrine complex, as well, possibly, as a method of regulating pregnancies.

The concept of reproduction was pictorially explained in a gray stone plaque discovered in the Neolithic shrine of the Goddess at Catal Hüyük, carved there some eight thousand years ago. One side of the relief depicts the bodies of two lovers in a close embrace, the other side, a woman holding an infant.

People today, raised and programmed on the "morality" of the contemporary male religions, may find the ancient sexual attitudes and customs disturbing, shocking or even sacrilegious. Yet we should consider the likelihood that such judgments or reactions are the result of the teaching and conditioning of religious attitudes present in our society, which are themselves based on the ideologies of those who initially and repetitively condemned the sexual customs of the Goddess.

In the worship of the female deity, sex was Her gift to humanity. It was sacred and holy. She was the Goddess of Sexual Love and

Procreation. But in the religions of today we find an almost totally reversed attitude. Sex, especially non-marital sex, is considered to be somewhat naughty, dirty, even sinful. Yet rather than calling the earliest religions, which embraced such an open acceptance of all human sexuality, "fertility-cults," we might consider the religions of today as strange in that they seem to associate shame and even sin with the very process of conceiving new human life. Perhaps centuries from now scholars and historians will be classifying them as "sterility-cults."

Documentary evidence from Sumer, Babylon, Canaan, Anatolia, Cyprus, Greece and even the Bible reveals that, despite the fact that the concept of marriage was known in the earliest written records, married women, as well as single, continued to live for periods of time within the temple complex and to follow the ancient sexual customs of the Goddess. The Bible itself reveals that these women were free to come and go as they pleased. Women of wealthy and royal families, as well as women of the community, participated in the sexual customs of the Goddess. These women were free to marry at any time, and Strabo tells us that even as late as the first century BC they were considered to be exceptionally good wives. In earliest historic times, never was the question or even the concept of respectability or propriety raised—it was later invented as the new *morality*.

> The Mediterranean Old World Religions, all save the Hebraic, agreed in regarding the processes of the propagation of life as divine, at least as something not alien and abhorrent to the godhead. But the early Christian propagandists, working here on Hebraic lines, intensified the isolation of God from the simple phenomena of birth, thereby engendering at times an anti-sexual bias, and preparing a discord between any possible biological view and the current religion's dogma, and modern ethical thought has not been wholly a gainer thereby.

So commented historian L. R. Farnell at Oxford in 1896. He was one of the few authors of that era, and of most since that time, who managed to deal with the ancient religious attitude toward sex in an objective manner, rather than causing the black type of the page to blush beet red with embarrassment or commenting upon them with righteous indignation.

In this chapter I intend to point out and try to explain the underlying reasons for this "anti-sexual" stance of the Hebrews, and subsequently the Christian religions, and the confrontations that ensued. This anti-sexual attitude was not the result of a more inherent purity or lesser sex drive among the adherents of the Judeo-Christian beliefs. As we shall see, it was probably developed and propagated for purely political motives, aiming at goals that would allow the invading patrilineal Hebrews greater access to land and governmental control by destroying the ancient matrilineal system.

From the time of the earliest Indo-European conquests, laws concerning the sacred women of the temples, the *qadishtu*—laws dealing with inheritance rights, property rights, business rights and their legal and economic relationship to their children—continually appear in the codes. Yet the Indo-Europeans, as we know them, do not appear to have taken an open position against the sexual customs themselves. At least none of the literature discovered and translated up until now suggests this, though the increasingly stricter laws concerning the infidelity of married women may have been aimed at them.

But among the Levite-led Hebrews we may observe the connections. The Levite laws of the Israelites, from the time of Moses onward, demanded virginity until marriage for all women, upon threat of death by stoning or burning, and, once married, total fidelity, only upon the part of the wife, also upon threat of death. Perhaps the penalty of death for a married or betrothed woman who had been raped most clearly exhibits the Levite insistence upon knowledge of paternity. Taking part in the sacred sexual customs of the temples would, of course, have broken these laws. Alongside the greater sexual restrictions for women, we find the Levite priests and prophets repeatedly condemning the sexual customs of the temple as well. I suggest that the point of the confrontation was as follows.

If, as *qadishtu*, sacred women of the Goddess, women made love to various men rather than being faithful to one husband, the children born to these women would be of questionable paternity. Sumerian and Babylonian documents reveal that these women, through their affiliations with the temple complex, owned land and other properties and engaged in extensive business activities. Various accounts report that they were often of wealthy families, well accepted in the society. Following the original kinship customs of the Goddess religion, children born to *qadishtu* would probably have inherited the names, titles and property of their mothers; matrilineal descent would have continued to exist as the inherent social structure of the community. Daughters may have become *qadishtu* themselves. One inscription from Tralles in western Anatolia, carved there as late as AD 200 by a woman named Aurelia Aemilias, proudly announced that she had served in the temple by taking part in the sexual customs, as had her mother and all their female ancestors before them.

The sacred sexual customs of the female religion offer us another of the apparent ties between the worship of the Divine Ancestress as it was known in Sumer, Babylon, Anatolia, Greece, Carthage, Sicily, Cyprus and even in Canaan. Women who made love in the temples were known in their own language as "sacred women," "the undefiled." Their Akkadian name of *qadishtu* is literally translated as "sanctified women" or "holy women." Yet the sexual customs in even the most academic studies of the past two centuries were nearly always described as "prostitution," the sacred women repeatedly referred to as "temple prostitutes" or "ritual prostitutes." The use of the word "prostitute" as a translation for *qadishtu* not only negates the sanctity of that which was held sacred, but suggests, by the inferences and social implications of the word, an ethnocentric subjectivity on the part of the writer. It leads the reader to a misinterpretation of the religious beliefs and social structure of the period. It seems to me that the word "prostitute" entirely distorts the very meaning of the ancient customs which the writer is supposedly explaining.

Professor Albright, who admired the lofty ideals of the Israelites, writes:

> Sacred prostitution was apparently an almost invariable concomitant
> of the cult of the Phoenician and Syrian goddess, whatever her personal
> name, as we know from many allusions in classical literature, especially
> in Herodotus, Strabo and Lucian. As sacred prostitute the goddess was,
> strangely enough from our point of view, called "the Holy One"
> . . . the practice was firmly implanted among the Canaanite aborigines
> of Palestine and was constantly being re-introduced from the countries
> which surrounded Israel as a "very sacred custom" to quote the words
> of Lucian, in discussing the same practice at Hierapolis in Syria, about
> a thousand years after Asa.

Professor James, somewhat less antagonistic, writes, "This is
borne out by the practice of ritual prostitution in connection with
Israelite shrines at Shiloh, condemned by Amos . . . As Hosea
makes it abundantly clear, these priestesses continued to exercise
their functions with undiminished zeal in his day (750–735 BC), in
spite of the efforts of Amos and other reformers like Asa to elimi-
nate them."

EVEN IN THE HEBREW LAND OF JUDAH

Yet despite the contemporary portrayals of the sexual customs,
archaeologists have found accounts of the sacred women in the
earliest records of Sumer. The legend of Inanna and Enki listed the
sacred sexual customs as another of the great gifts that Inanna
brought to civilize the people of Erech. The Queen of Heaven was
most reverently esteemed by the sacred women, who in turn were
especially protected by Her. At Erech the women of the temple
were known as *nu-gig,* the pure or spotless. One interesting
Sumerian fragment recorded the name of Lilith, described as a
young maiden, as the "hand of Inanna." We read on this ancient
tablet that Lilith was sent by Inanna to gather men from the street,
to bring them to the temple. This same name, Lilith, later appeared
in Hebrew mythology as the first wife of Adam, who refused to be

sexually submissive to him; and later as the name of the demon who hovered about, waiting to find spilled sperm, of which to make her "illegitimate demon children." Both these tales may well have developed in reaction to the original Lilith, so closely associated with the sexual customs of the worship of the Goddess.

In the eighteenth century BC in Babylonia, the Akkadian name of Ishtar began to replace the Sumerian name Inanna. One tablet referred to Erech, where Ishtar's worship eventually superseded that of Inanna, as the city of "courtesans and prostitutes" (a contemporary translation of the words). This same tablet mentioned priestesses who made love with strangers, claiming that they were incarnations of the holy spirit. The women of Ishtar were also known by the Akkadian word *qadishtu,* while at the important temple in Babylon they were known as *ishtaritu,* which simply means "women of Ishtar."

Remnants of these earlier sexual customs were described by Herodotus, who reported that in his era, about 450 BC, women of Babylon made love to a stranger only once in their life, as their initial sexual experience, later marrying and having sex only with their husbands from that time on.

Strabo, born in Anatolia shortly before the birth of Christ, recorded that the sexual customs were followed in the worship of the Goddess in many areas of Anatolia at that time. These were in the names of either Cybele or Anaitis. He reported that these customs were an integral aspect of the worship at Comana and in Lydia as well, which the inscription from Tralles, Lydia, certainly supports. He wrote that in his travels he had witnessed that the children who were born in this way were considered to be legitimate and respectable and simply given the name and social status of the mother. He added that the name and title were then proudly used in all official inscriptions and commented that in Anatolia of his period, "the unmarried mother seems to be worshipped."

Sacred women served at the temple of Aphrodite in Corinth during the classical period of Greece. Lucian later spoke of the customs in his day, AD 150. He explained that women of that time took strangers as lovers only on the feast day of Adonis. Even when the worship of the Egyptian Isis was brought into Rome, sacred women followed the ancient sexual customs there, at the temple of Isis.

There are no records known at this time that suggest that the women of ancient Egypt followed the sexual customs, but in chapter 23 of the book of the reformer-priest Ezekiel, he angrily accused a group of Hebrew women of debauchery and lewdness, insisting that they had learned their "evil" sexual ways from the Egyptians. In one passage he warned, "I will put an end to your lewdness and harlotry brought from the land of Egypt" (Ezek. 23:27). In his allegorical tale of the two young girls, who symbolized the two separate nations of the Hebrew people, Judah and Israel, he complained that the girls, because they had been so sexually free in Egypt, were now evil and fallen women in Canaan.

The worship of the Goddess as Ashtoreth (Astarte) was widespread throughout the Mediterranean area. Canaanites from Tyre and Sidon (Phoenicians) founded temples of Ashtoreth at Carthage, Eryx in Sicily and at several sites on Cyprus; at each of these places the sacred sexual customs were followed. Sozomenos reported the sexual customs of the temples of Ashtoreth at Aphaca and Baalbec in the area now known as Lebanon. Farnell explained many of the connections in the Mediterranean area.

In the religion of Ashtoreth, just as in the worship of the Goddess elsewhere in the Near and Middle East, women continued to follow the sacred sexual customs. The Bible relates that *qadishtu* in Jerusalem wove veils or cloths for the *asherim* (images of the Goddess Asherah) in what Roland de Vaux referred to as the "house of the sacred prostitutes." He too asserted that the sexual customs were quite typical of Canaanite temples and that the women of Israel followed this practice despite the condemnation of Hebrew leaders.

Most vital in achieving a total comprehension of the antagonism of the Hebrews toward this custom is the realization that the sacred women continued to serve the female divinity in the ancient sexual ways—even in the Hebrew land of Judah. The sexual customs had remained as an aspect of the religious worship at the temple in Jerusalem, the temple that had been claimed for Yahweh, the same temple where the women had been seen weeping for Tammuz.

Professor James and several other scholars wrote of the worship of Ashtoreth existing side by side with that of Yahweh in Jerusalem. James also described the sexual customs in Jerusalem and at the Hebrew temple at Shiloh.

In the Old Testament book of Hosea we learn that a woman, in this case Gomer (Hosea's wife), was free to marry, raise children and continue to make love to other men at the temple, dressing in all her finery to do so. Even in these biblical accounts, which were obviously written to demean and debase her actions, the description revealed that she took part in the sexual customs of her own free will and that she viewed them not as an obligatory or compulsory duty but as pleasant occasions, rather like festive parties. This situation was clearly unacceptable to the men who espoused the patrilineal Hebrew system, as Hosea did, but it does reveal that for those who belonged to other religious systems it was quite typical behavior.

For thousands of years these sexual customs had been accepted as natural among the people of the Near and Middle East. They may have permitted and even encouraged matrilineal descent patterns to continue and a female-kinship system to survive. Inherent within the very practice of the sexual customs was the lack of concern for the *paternity* of children—and it is only with a certain knowledge of paternity that a patrilineal system can be maintained.

I suggest that it was upon the attempt to establish this certain knowledge of paternity, which would then make patrilineal reckoning possible, that these ancient sexual customs were finally denounced as wicked and depraved and that it was for this reason that the Levite priests devised the concept of sexual "morality": premarital virginity for *women*, marital fidelity for *women*, in other words total control over the knowledge of paternity.

Where you stand obviously determines what you see. From the

point of view of those who followed the religion of the Goddess, they were simply carrying out the ancient ways. From the point of view of the invading Hebrew tribes, this older religion was now to be regarded as an orgiastic, evil, lustful, shameful, disgraceful, sinful, base fertility-cult. But may we suspect that underlying this *moral* stance was the political maneuvering for power over land and property accessible to them only upon the institution of a patrilineal system, perhaps a system long known to them in the northern lands of the Indo-Europeans? Was it perhaps for these reasons that the Levite laws declared that any sexual activities of women that did not take place within the confines of the marriage bed were to be considered as sinful, i.e., against the decrees of Yahweh? According to the Bible these laws were first instituted at the time of Moses, shortly before the Hebrew tribes invaded Canaan. The territorial and social confrontations took place side by side. It was a long and ugly battle, starting with the arrival of the Hebrews in Canaan and continuing well into the Roman and early Christian eras, much of it recorded in the Bible.

To fully comprehend the extent of the "anti-sexual" stance of the Hebrews and the attempt of the Levite priests to change the sexual behavior and attitudes of the Hebrew women, we should examine to what extent the religion of the Goddess directly affected the Hebrew people. Were the customs of the Goddess religion a rare diversion, encountered upon aperiodic occasions, or was the religion, despite the inroads of the Indo-Europeans and Levites, still a major factor in the life of those who lived in Canaan?

8

They Offered Incense to the Queen of Heaven

Though buried deep beneath the sands of what was once Canaan, statues of the female deity have been continually unearthed in archaeological excavations. These images of the Goddess, some dating back as far as 7000 BC, offer silent testimony to the most ancient worship of the Queen of Heaven in the land that is today most often remembered as the birthplace of both Judaism and Christianity.

Yigael Yadin, Professor of Archaeology at the Hebrew University of Jerusalem and Director of the Institute of Archaeology there, recently published his account of the excavation of the city of Hazor in biblical Canaan. Somewhat evasively, he describes the evidence of the worship of the Goddess there in this way:

> Although the official religion of northern Israel was that of Yahweh—the god of Israel—we know from both biblical verses and archaeological discoveries that the cult of Ba'al and Astarte strongly influenced the local population in the form of folk or popular beliefs—for double insurance as it were. Indeed we discovered quite a number of clay figurines representing Astarte, the fertility goddess, and of what may be called the holy prostitutes connected with the Ba'al and Astarte cult.

Discussing the Late Bronze Age in Canaan (about 1500–1300
BC) Professor Albright tells us that

> One of the commonest classes of religious objects found in Late Bronze
> levels is constituted by the so-called "Astarte" plaques. These are
> pottery plaques, generally oval in shape, on which were impressed
> (from a pottery or metal mould) a figure of the nude goddess Asherah,
> *en face* with her arms upraised, grasping lily stalks or serpents, or both,
> in her hands. The goddess's head is adorned with two long spiral
> ringlets identical with the Egyptian Hathor ringlets. These plaques
> were borrowed from Mesopotamia, where they have a long prehistory
> in the Early Bronze Age [about 3200–2100 BC].

Kathleen Kenyon, former Director of the British School of Archaeology at Jerusalem, discussing biblical Canaan, writes of:

> . . . the Astarte plaques which are the most common cult object on
> almost all sites of the period [Late Bronze Age]. That such plaques,
> with their association with Phoenician religion, are found cannot, how-
> ever, be taken on any particular site as evidence that it had not yet come
> under Israelite control, for Tell Beit Mersim itself provides clear evi-
> dence for the occurrence of such plaques or similar figurines right down
> to the 7th century BC. The denunciations by the prophets are enough
> to show that Yahwehism had continuously to struggle with the ancient
> religion of the land.

In exploring the influence and importance of the worship of the
Goddess in Canaan in biblical times, we find that as Ashtoreth,
Asherah, Astarte, Attoret, Anath or simply Elat or Baalat (both
defined as Goddess) She was the principal deity of such great
Canaanite cities as Tyre, Sidon, Ascalon, Beth Anath, Aphaca,
Byblos and Ashtoreth Karnaim.

In 1894 Robertson Smith conjectured that Astarte had already
become the less important wife of Baal by biblical times, yet we
read inscriptions to the Goddess in Canaan as Celestial Ruler,
Mistress of Kingship, Mother of all Deities. She is certainly associated with Baal, or a Baal or many Baalim, but upon careful
observation we find that the ritual and form of the religious practices are those of the ancient Goddess religion.

According to Seton Lloyd, Professor of Western Asiatic Archaeology, the word *baal,* which is usually translated as lord, originally implied a temporary position or temporary ownership of property. It may have been used much like the Indo-European word *pati,* also used as lord, owner, master and husband, and as I mentioned before may even be related to the Sanskrit word *bala.* In the legends of Ugarit in northern Canaan, Baal of Mount Saphon asked the Goddess, known there as Anath, to help secure a temple for him when he had none. In these same legends of the fourteenth century BC, Anath easily slew the enemy who had been powerful enough to first frighten and then murder Baal. Though the name Baal may have been introduced centuries earlier as the storm god of Mount Saphon by the Hurrians in Ugarit, by the time of the writing of these legends the name was also identified with the consort of the Goddess and in Ugarit, Baal held the dual role as storm god of the mountain and the dying consort, much like Damuzi, Tammuz, Attis, Osiris and Adonis. Upon his death, we are told, Anath's grief for him was like that of a cow for her calf.

Even Thor-El, an older male deity, described by some writers as the head of the deities at Ugarit, was recorded to have hidden in the innermost sanctuary of his eight chambers, trembling in fear at the approach of the mighty Anath. In these same texts, Anath was known as "Mistress of Kingship, Mistress of Dominion, Mistress of the High Heavens." In light of the tablets of northern Canaan, one can hardly defend the idea that either of these male deities was portrayed as all powerful or omnipotent, unless one simply insists upon assuming that all male deities always are. Though this conclusion is left unspoken by most writers, it is the Goddess Anath who emerges from these Canaanite legends as the deity of greatest valor and strength.

In his *Dictionary of the Bible* of 1900, J. Hastings asserted that Ashtoreth was supreme, saying of Her, "This Goddess was the chief divinity of the Semites in their primitive matriarchal stage of organization. She was the analogue of the human matriarch, free in her love, the fruitful mother of the clan, and its leader in peace and war."

In the pages of the Old Testament however, Ashtoreth, the name used most often in southern Canaan where most of the Hebrew people had settled, seldom appears alone. Her name was nearly always joined with Baal, much as many of the serpent demons of the Indo-European legends were the sons or husbands of the Goddess; at times the religion is even designated as Baalism. Though it is certainly possible that the Canaanite religion in the south, where Aryan princes had by now made deep inroads, may have elevated Baal to a higher status by later biblical times, the worship, the rituals, the sexual customs, the eunuch priests, the grieving for Tammuz or Baal as the dying consort, the abundance of the Astarte statues and plaques, the symbolic pillars and poles (actually called *asherah*, though always in lower case), all reveal that it was the symbolism and customs of the religion of the Goddess that were actually the target of Hebrew aggression. It appears more than likely that the Levite priests, just as they purposely misspelled and mispronounced Her name (reciting it as *boseth*, meaning shame), and referring to Her only in the masculine gender, refused to even recognize the position of the Goddess, doing this by continually linking Her name with that of Her male consort.

As we read before, the Bible and other religious literature may well be partially the result of intentional political aims as much as a record of some longstanding belief or lore. In discussing the Paradise myth of the Bible, Joseph Campbell wrote of "conspicuously contrived, counterfeit mythologies." Professor Chiera wrote that the Marduk myth was probably propagated with the help of the Babylonian armies and pointed out that the Ashur legend of supremacy was simply a reworked version of the Marduk myth. He also wrote that the myth of Adam and Eve had been "evidently produced in scholarly circles," and further explained that the Bible was subject to the censorship of priests who had the power of decision over "what was fit to be incorporated into the history of the founders of the race . . ." Professor Widengren also commented that the Bible as we know it ". . . has in many passages quite obviously been exposed to censorship and correspondingly purged."

Though many accounts of the Bible are probably based on actual historical events, confirmed in various ways by documents and evidence produced by archaeological excavation, it seems quite likely that the biblical Levite reports of the "pagan" religion in Canaan were presented from the point of view that was most advantageous and acceptable to the Levite theology, rather than as a totally objective historical record. Despite the various methods used to confuse the identity and gender of the Goddess as Ashtoreth or Asherah, even in the Bible as we know it today, passages and symbolism betray the influential and prevailing presence of the ancient worship of the female deity, while other Canaanite and Near Eastern artifacts confirm it.

In Egypt the Hebrews had known the worship of the Goddess as Isis or Hathor. For four generations they had been living in a land where women held a very high status and the matrilineal descent system continued to function at most periods. Judging from the numbers of the Hebrews who emerged from Egypt, as compared with the family of the twelve sons who supposedly entered it four generations earlier, it seems likely that a great number of those Hebrew people known as Israelites may actually have been Egyptians, Canaanites, Semitic nomads and other Goddess-worshiping people who had joined together in Egypt. Just to the east of Canaan, in Babylon, stood the temples of Ishtar. And in the land of Canaan, the land that the Hebrews invaded and made their own after their departure from Egypt, archaeological records and artifacts reveal that the religion of the Goddess as Ashtoreth, Astarte, Asherah, Anath, Elat or Baalat still flourished in many of the great cities.

"YE SHALL DESTROY THEIR ALTARS, BREAK THEIR IMAGES"

The Levite writers of the Old Testament claimed that their deity had presented them with the land of Canaan as the "promised land." Yet it is clear, even in their own accounts, that Canaan was not an empty land, even in the time of Abraham. In Num. 13:17–19 it was recorded that, upon the arrival of the Hebrew tribes, as they approached from the deserts of Sinai, they sent an advance envoy into the cities of Canaan. This was their report of the situation at about 1300–1250 BC: "We went into the land to which you sent us. It does indeed flow with milk and honey, this is its produce. At the same time its inhabitants are a very powerful people, the towns are fortified and very big" (Num. 13:28).

The Bible account admits that Canaan was already inhabited and that many of the people lived in great fortified towns. Despite this, we read of the intention of the arriving Hebrews not only to continue into the land of Canaan, but to purposely and violently destroy the existing religion and replace it with their own. This intention was presented by the Levites as the command of Yahweh, supposedly ordered before the Israelites entered Canaan:

> Observe thou that which I command thee this day: Behold I drive out before thee the Amorite, and the Hittite and the Perizite and the Hivite and the Jebusite. Take heed to thyself lest thou make a covenant with the inhabitants of the land whither thou goest, lest it be for a snare in the midst of thee; But ye shall destroy their altars, break their images and cut down their groves, for thou shalt worship no other god, for the Lord whose name is jealous is a jealous God [Exod. 34:11–16].

With this order the Hebrew invasion of Canaan began. Though the Hebrew entrance into the "promised land" of Canaan is often imagined to be the arrival into a haven of peace after centuries of slavery in Egypt, according to the Bible its occupation took the form of a series of bloody sieges, perhaps much like those of the earlier Indo-European invasions.

In Deut. 2:33 we read that, under the leadership of Moses and Aaron, the Israelites met a king named Sihon at the town of Jahaz. The Levite accounts tell us, "The Lord our God delivered him into our hands; we killed him with his sons and all his people. We captured all his cities at that time and put to death every one in the cities, men, women and dependants; we left no survivor." When they met Og, king of Bashan, we are told in Deut. 3:3–7 that "So the Lord our God also delivered Og king of Bashan into our hands, with all his people. We slaughtered them and left no survivor . . . in all we took sixty cities . . . Thus we put to death all the men, women and dependants in every city."

Both Aaron and Moses died in the desert. Joshua assumed command and the Israelites entered Jericho. We learn in Josh. 6:21 that "Under the ban they destroyed everything in the city; they put everyone to the sword, men and women, young and old . . ." But in this same siege we are told that "All the silver and gold, all the vessels of copper and iron, shall be holy; they belong to the Lord and they must go into the Lord's treasury" (Josh. 6:19). And in Josh. 6:24 we learn that these orders were carried out as "They set fire to the city and everything in it, except that they deposited the silver and gold and the vessels of copper and iron in the treasury of the Lord's house." In the battle of Ai we are told "the number who were killed that day, men and women, was twelve thousand, the whole population of Ai" (Josh. 8:25). And in Josh. 8:29 it claims that Joshua "hanged the king of Ai on a tree and left him there till sunset." Since in an earlier passage Joshua was told by Yahweh to do with the king of Ai as he had done with the king of Jericho, we may assume that this was the king of Jericho's fate as well, though the account of the event is no longer recorded.

We read in Joshua 10 that:

> Joshua captured Makkedah and put both king and people to the sword, destroying both them and every living thing in the city. He left no survivor, and he dealt with the king of Makkedah as he had dealt with the king of Jericho. Then Joshua and all the Israelites marched on from Makkedah to Libnah and attacked it. The Lord delivered its king and the city to the Israelites, and they put its people and every living thing in it to the sword; they left no survivor there, and dealt with its king as they had dealt with the king of Jericho. From Libnah, Joshua and all the Israelites marched on Lachish, took up their positions and attacked it. The Lord delivered Lachish into their hands: they took it on the second day and put every living thing in it to the sword, as they had done at Libnah.

Map 4 Southern Canaan – Old Testament

Meanwhile Horam, king of Gezer had advanced to the relief of Lachish; but Joshua struck them down, both king and people, and not a man of them survived. Then Joshua and all the Israelites marched on from Lachish to Eglon, took up their positions and attacked it; that same day they captured it and put its inhabitants to the sword, destroying every living thing in it as they had done at Lachish. From Eglon, Joshua and all the Israelites advanced to Hebron and attacked it. They captured it and put its king to the sword with every living thing in it and in all its villages; as at Eglon, he left no survivor, destroying it and every living thing in it. Then Joshua and all the Israelites wheeled round towards Debir and attacked it. They captured the city with its king, and all its villages, put them to the sword and destroyed every living thing; they left no survivor. They dealt with Debir and its king as they had dealt with Hebron and with Libnah and its king.

So Joshua massacred the population of the whole region—the hill country, the Negeb, the Shepelah, the watersheds—and all their kings. He left no survivor, destroying everything that drew breath, as the Lord the God of Israel had commanded [Josh. 10: 28–40].

In similarly described sieges, Joshua and the Israelites destroyed the cities of Gibeon, Hazor and as far as Baal Gad in the Vale of the Lebanon under Mount Hermon. At the risk of being repetitive, I cannot help thinking of Professor Albright's comment that the "orgiastic nature worship" of Canaan "was replaced by Israel with its pastoral simplicity and purity of life, its lofty monotheism and its severe code of ethics." Rather than the image of poor downtrodden slaves with lofty ideals, entering the "promised land" to rest their weary bones and build a new and better life, we are more likely to be reminded of the description Professor Lloyd gave of the Luvian entrance into Anatolia and the pathway that was made as "their progress was marked by signs of widespread destruction."

As if in further refutation of this supposed "purity of life" or "severe code of ethics" we read that, although all the accounts state that the Israelites left no survivors, this may not have been the total truth. For in the book of Numbers (31:17) we read that after a battle against the Midianites, while still under the leadership of Moses and Aaron, the Israelites were told: "Kill every male dependant, and kill every woman who has had intercourse with a man, but spare for yourselves every woman among them who has not had intercourse." In Num. 31:32–35, we read a list of the spoils and war booty taken by the Israelites at this same battle. In this order, they list sheep, cattle, asses and "thirty-two thousand girls who had no intercourse with a man."

In the book of Deuteronomy, also preceding the command of Joshua, we find:

> When you wage war against your enemy and the Lord your God delivers them into your hands and you take some of them captive, then if you see a comely woman among the captives and take a liking to her, you may marry her. You shall bring her into your house, where she shall shave her head, pare her nails, and discard the clothes she had when she was captured. Then she shall stay in your house and mourn her father and mother for a full month. After that you may have intercourse with her; you shall be her husband and she your wife. But if you no longer find her pleasing let her go free. You must not sell her, nor treat her harshly, since you have had your will with her [Deut. 21:10–14].

Though once again the numbers may have been somewhat exaggerated, these passages suggest that many of the women who were later known as the wives of the Israelites may well have been the girls who witnessed the murders of all their families and friends and the destruction of their homes and towns. The combination of the fear and trauma they must have felt, having been taken into the Hebrew tribes in this way, along with their memories of their childhood customs and religions must have made their attitude and position in Hebrew life a most difficult one. Though the number of women in the Hebrew tribes is never listed, these passages also suggest that when the Hebrews first left Egypt there may have been a much greater percentage of men. Each of these factors may help to explain the Hebrew women's "acceptance" of the new patriarchal laws.

"AND THEY FORSOOK THE LORD AND WORSHIPED BAAL AND ASHTORETH"

Though according to biblical records the entire population of many towns and cities had been massacred, several great cities had not been touched, cities where Ashtoreth was still worshiped with great reverence. Once in Canaan, the captured lands were divided among the tribes, the Levites to live among each of them. From this point on we observe the lengthy and violent attack the Hebrews launched upon the Queen of Heaven and Her Baal. Despite all the warnings, the religion of the Goddess was a great temptation to the Hebrews who had invaded Canaan; to many of them it may have been the religion of their ancestors. References to the Hebrew people worshiping in the ancient religion repeatedly appear in the pages of the Bible, once again the accounts of the Levite priests:

Judges 2:13—"And they forsook the Lord and worshiped Baal and Ashtoreth."

Judges 3:7—"And the people did what was evil in the sight of the Lord, forgetting the Lord their God, and served the Baals and the Ashtoreth."

Samuel 7:3, 4—"Samuel spake unto the house of Israel, saying, if ye do return unto the Lord with all your hearts, then put away the strange gods and Ashtoreth from among you and prepare your hearts unto the Lord and serve him only and he will deliver you out of the hands of the Philistines."

The period of Samuel took place in the time of Saul, the first Hebrew king, about 1050 BC. Judges takes place before that time. According to the Bible, King Solomon, at about 960–922 BC, worshiped Ashtoreth as well as other local deities. He was eventually threatened with the loss of his kingdom for having forsaken Yahweh and revering the Queen of Heaven, Ashtoreth of the Sidonians. In I Kings 15:13 we find the report of the dethroning of Queen Maacah by her son (or grandson) Asa at about 910 BC—the crime, worshiping Asherah. The name Asherah was also used in the texts of northern Canaan, at times alongside Anath. They may have been worshiped as mother and daughter at that time. But Asherah is also identified with Ashtoreth, who was deeply revered in Tyre and Sidon under that name. One text of northern Canaan describes Asherah as follows: "He arrived at the shrine of Asherah of the Tyrians, Yea, of the Goddess of the Sidonians." In the texts of Ugarit, Asherah was known as the "Creator of all Deities."

The defection from Yahweh, as described above, continued throughout the biblical accounts, as we shall see. But a most revealing passage is in the book of Jeremiah. This incident took place in a Hebrew colony in Egypt at about 600 BC. Here the religion of the Goddess and the reverence paid to Her, even by the Hebrews of that time, was described not as a new religion that they had recently adopted, but one that these Hebrews had followed before—in Jerusalem. It also strongly hints that this was a religion of women, though the Levite writer carefully depicted the husbands as having authority and exhibits an obvious insistence upon male lineage in the answer given even by the worshipers of the Queen of Heaven:

> At this time all the men who knew their wives offered incense to alien gods and all the women who were standing there, a large assembly with all the people living in Pathros in the land of Egypt, answered Jeremiah as follows, we have no intention listening to this word you have spoken to us in Yahweh's name but intend to go on doing all that we have vowed to do, offering incense to the queen of heaven and pouring libations in her honor as we used to do, we and our fathers, our kings and our leaders in the town of Judah and in the streets of Jerusalem. We had plenty of food then, we lived well, we suffered no disasters. But since we have given up offering incense to the queen of heaven and pouring libations in her honor we have been destitute and have perished either by sword or by famine. The women added, when we offer incense to the queen of heaven and pour libations in her honor, do you think we make cakes for her with her features on them and pour libations to her without our husband's knowledge? [Jeremiah 44:15–19]

Professor Hooke asked, "What are we to say when we find in the record the gardens of Adonis, Ezekiel's chambers of imagery, women declaring that since they ceased baking cakes for the Queen of heaven nothing has gone well with them, the masseboth, the asheras, the divinations . . . and the numerous other practices?" and answered, "It is surely impossible to deny that these are foreign elements, some Canaanite, some presumably Assyro-Babylonian, and some possibly Egyptian and that all these enter into the picture of the religion of Israel as it appears in the Old Testament."

Professor Widengren, as if in additional answer, observed, "Now this Queen of Heaven(s) cannot possibly be any other goddess than Astart, who accordingly as late as c. 600 enjoyed official worship in the kingdom of Judah."

Many Bible passages report that idols of the female deity, referred to as *asherah* (in lower case), were to be found on every high hill, under every green tree and alongside altars in the temples. They were a symbol identified with the worship of the Goddess as Asherah and may have been a pole or a living tree, perhaps carved as a statue. Arthur Evans wrote that "the biblical records again and again attest the cult of the asherah either as a living tree or its substitute, the dead post or pole before which the Canaanite altars were set."

I suspect that the *asherim* (plural) were actually fig trees, the sycamore fig, the tree that was in Egypt considered to be the "Body of the Goddess on Earth." There are many reasons to believe that this is so, evidence that we shall examine more thoroughly in unraveling the myth of Adam and Eve—evidence that perhaps explains the symbolism of the tree in the Paradise myth.

Continuing our exploration of the presence of the Goddess in Canaan, biblical accounts tell us that the *asherim,* though their association with Asherah as the Goddess is never explained, were to be found everywhere. "And the people of Israel did secretly against the Lord their God things that were not right. They built high places, set up pillars and asherim on every high hill and under every green tree, they served idols, made molten images of two calves, they made an asherah and sold themselves to do evil in the sight of the Lord" (II Kings 17:9).

As the Levites declared that it was the Hebrew mission to destroy these symbols of the religion they so often refer to as "their gods," wherever they were found, this is exactly what they did. The Levite priests wrote that the destruction had been commanded by Yahweh: "You shall surely destroy all the places where the nations whom you shall dispossess served their gods, upon the high mountains and upon the hills and under every green tree you shall tear down their pillars and burn their asherim with fire" (Deut. 12:2, 3); "You shall not plant any tree as an asherah beside the altar of the Lord" (Deut. 16:21).

But despite the warnings of the Levite priests, the *asherim* were continually erected and worshiped. In I Kings 16:13 we read that at about 850 BC the Hebrew king Ahab, husband of Jezebel, made an *asherah.* Isaiah, sometime in the eighth century BC, spoke of *asherim* in the city of Damascus. Gideon, in the period of Judges, destroyed the *asherah* of one temple, using its wood as a burnt offering to Yahweh.

It was threatened that "The Lord will smite Israel because they have made their asherim." King Hezekiah, who reigned about 715–690 BC, "did what was right in the eyes of the Lord." He broke the pillars and cut down the *asherah.* It was this same Hezekiah who destroyed a bronze serpent which had been kept at the temple in Jerusalem from the time of the arrival of the Hebrews in Canaan. After Hezekiah, his son Manassah, who ruled for fifty-five years, once again erected the *asherim* as did his son Amon who succeeded him.

In II Kings 23:4–15 the Levite priest Hilkiah, who served King Josiah at about 630 BC, took the vessels made for Asherah and Baal out of this same temple in Jerusalem. He removed the *asherah.* "He defiled the high place which Solomon had built for Ashtoreth." "He broke in pieces the pillars and cut down the asherim and filled their places with the bones of men."

Though again the religion of the Goddess is never mentioned, further evidence of Her worship in Canaan during late biblical times was revealed by the presence of the mourners for Her son/lover Tammuz. In the book of Ezekiel we read of the women weeping for Tammuz at this same temple in Jerusalem at about 620 BC, continuing to practice the mourning ceremonies of the religion of the Goddess, known so well from the Babylonian accounts of Ishtar. As previously quoted, Professor Widengren asserted that a ritual mourning took place in Israel, commemorating the death of Tammuz, just as it did in Mesopotamia.

I. Epstein, in his history of Judaism written in 1959, wrote of the influx of "pagan" ideas, especially at the time of Solomon, blaming Solomon's wives for his idolatrous ways. There is a strong possibility that Solomon's habit of collecting foreign princesses for his harem (seven hundred of them, according to the Bible) may have been a politically motivated system of securing the ultimate right to rule over the conquered lands by marrying the heiresses. The relationship of the rights to many a throne in the Near East to the matrilineal descent pattern of the Goddess-worshiping people may explain the great number of royal foreign women—all listed as legal wives of Solomon—and the accepted presence of the religions which they brought with them.

After Solomon's reign, when the Hebrew tribes divided into two separate nations, the worship of the Goddess continually appeared. This is evident in Samaria, the capital of the northern kingdom, Israel, during the period of Ahab and Jezebel (about 869–850 BC); the worship of Ashtoreth and Her Baal was apparently flourishing there at that time. The marriage of the Hebrew Ahab to Jezebel, the daughter of the queen and king of Sidon, who also served as high priestess and priest to Ashtoreth and Baal, may also have brought to him a more legitimate right to the throne. But even King Jeroboam, before that time (about 922–901 BC), had made golden calves, symbols of the Goddess religion.

In Judah, the southern Hebrew kingdom whose capital was Jerusalem, Rehoboam, at about 922–915 BC, and his son Abijam, both perhaps reigning as husbands of Queen Maacah, were said to have practiced "pagan idolatries." As we know, Queen Maacah worshiped Asherah and was eventually dethroned for having made an idol of Her. At about 842 BC Queen Athaliah ruled in Jerusalem and with her reign the "pagan" religion continued to flourish. As Jezebel's daughter, we may once again question if, in the eyes of many of the people of Canaan, Athaliah held the right to rule as the granddaughter of the high priestess and priest of Ashtoreth in Sidon. At about 735–727 BC King Ahaz also followed the ancient religion, committing "evil in the eyes of the Lord." At about 620 BC the women of Ezekiel's time were seen weeping for Tammuz at the temple in Jerusalem, while in Jeremiah's day, about 600 BC, rebellious women openly announced their intention of continuing to revere the Queen of Heaven.

SUMMARY

As a result of archaeological evidence, which helps to explain many of the obscure references, despite the evasive wording and lack of explanation in the Bible, there is no question that in biblical periods of Canaan the Levite priests of the Hebrews were in continual contact with the religion of the Goddess. Though the commanded destruction of artifacts has probably resulted in fewer archaeological finds in southern Canaan than the rest of the Near East, masses of evidence of the extensive worship of the Goddess have been unearthed in all the other lands in which the Hebrews either lived or were in close contact, lands such as Egypt, Babylon, Sinai and northern Canaan. Surrounding the Hebrews in southern Canaan were the original inhabitants of Canaan, people who lived in the cities that had not been destroyed and who had revered the female divinity from the most ancient times.

As revealed by the Bible itself, the adoration of the Goddess, even in the Hebrew capitals of Samaria and Jerusalem, even by those who were considered to be members of the tribes that followed the new religion of Yahweh (most especially their royalty and rulers, who do not seem to have been chosen from the Levite tribe), appears to be one of the major influential factors in the development of the Judaic and later the Christian attitudes. The possibility that the Levites may originally have been related to the Indo-European Luvians, while the other tribes may have been descendants of the Mediterranean Goddess-worshiping peoples, may help to explain this division between the Levite priests and prophets and the continual "waywardness and defection" of the Israelite people who appear to have drifted toward the ancient religion time and again.

The Levite priests declared, "There shall be no cult prostitutes of the daughters of Israel." Yet, as we have already seen, the ancient sexual customs continued. It seems to have been the very nature of the sexual customs, so inherent and integral a part of the female religion, allowing for and possibly encouraging matrilineal descent patterns to continue, that aroused the most violent reactions among the Levite patrilinealists.

Once aware of the continual presence of the Goddess religion, a careful reading of the accounts in the Old Testament (in which the Hebrew woman was initially assigned to the secondary status of obedient assistant), reveals extensive passages spent in continuous threat, at times veiled or hidden in symbolism, against the worship of the Goddess. But some of the threats were more open. They were aimed at those who continued to practice the ancient religion, revealing even within the records of the Bible accounts of slaughter and massacre of those who dared to pray to "other gods."

As we shall see in the following chapter, the insistent and repetitious sexual imagery allows us to observe the Levite attitudes toward the sexual customs of the Goddess religion and the sexual autonomy of women generally, autonomy that had for thousands of years helped to allow women to retain their independence economically, socially and legally. Thus into the laws of the Levites was written the destruction of the worship of the Divine Ancestress, and with it the final destruction of the matrilineal system.

9

And the Men of the City Shall Stone Her with Stones

So antagonistic were the Levite priests toward the religion of the Goddess in Canaan (though the term "other gods" is evasively used in each passage) that laws were written prohibiting the worship of these "other gods." The laws were so severe that they commanded the members of the Hebrew religion to murder even their own children if they did not worship Yahweh. The Levite laws of the Bible ordered: "If your brother or son or daughter or wife or friend suggest serving other gods, you must kill him, your hand must be the first raised in putting him to death and all the people shall follow you" (Deut. 13:6).

This order was obviously directed only toward men, for the one relative it did not suggest killing was the husband. Not only relatives were to be kept under watchful surveillance, for the Levites also wrote, "If the inhabitants of a town that once served the Lord your God, now serve other gods, you must kill all the inhabitants of that town" (Deut. 13:15).

Once aware of the identity of the Queen of Heaven and the extent of Her worship as it existed in Canaan, even among the

Hebrew royalty, we may gain a deeper insight into the political motivations of the Levites by becoming more familiar with the imagery of women in the Bible and the specific laws concerning them.

The Hebrew prophets and priests, the Levites, wrote with open and scornful contempt of any woman who was neither virgin nor married. They insisted that all women must be publicly designated as the private property of some man, father or husband. Thus they developed and instituted the concept of sexual *morality*—for women.

In a forword written by Bible historian I. Epstein in 1935, which prefaces a version of the Hebrew Talmud, he suggests that this was the major reason for the Hebrews being so threatened by the surrounding religions:

> Experience soon proved how great was the temptation to imitate the religious practices of surrounding nations, even at a time when the Israelites inhabited a land of their own. The difficulty of resisting alien influence grew much more severe in periods of dispersion when Jews were living in a heathen environment and the rabbis had to give serious attention to the problem of how to counteract the forces of assimilation which threatened to submerge the Jewish communities settled in countries where idol worship was the state religion.
>
> It is important to understand that the vehement opposition to idolatry which distinguishes the legislation of the Bible and later of the Talmud was not merely the antagonism of one theological system to another. Fundamentally it was a conflict of ethical standards. Heathen people practised abominations against which the scriptures earnestly warned Israel. Idolatry was identified with immoral conduct, an identification which was too often verified by experience.

This "conflict of ethical standards" and "immoral conduct" appears to be primarily the Levite perception of the sexual customs, known to have existed at all periods of biblical history. The lack of concern for the paternity of children among the Hebrew people who continued to revere the Queen of Heaven, thus allowing matrilineal descent patterns to continue as a result of the sexual customs, appears to have been the crux of the persecution of the ancient beliefs by the priests of the Hebrew tribes. It was surely apparent to Levite leaders that if a religion existed alongside their own, a religion in which women owned their own property, were endowed with a legal identity and were free to relate sexually to various men, it would be much more difficult for the Hebrew men to convince their women that they must accept the position of being their husband's property. Hebrew women had to be taught to accept the idea that for a woman to sleep with more than one man was evil. They had to be taught that it would bring disaster, wrath and shame from the almighty—while it was simultaneously acceptable for their husbands to have sexual relationships with two, three or fifty women. Thus premarital virginity and marital fidelity were proclaimed by Levite law as divinely essential for all Hebrew women, the antithesis of the attitudes toward female sexuality held in the religion of the Goddess.

Yet the influence and prestige of the ancient religion was ever present. As we have seen, there are continual biblical reports of "paganism" in every era; it loomed as a constant problem, described throughout the Old Testament. The prophet-priests of Yahweh threatened. They scolded. The Levite writers labeled any sexually autonomous women, including the sacred women of the temple, as whores and harlots and demanded the enforcement of their own patriarchal attitudes concerning the sexual ownership of women. Once having invented this concept of "morality," they flung accusations of "immorality" at the women whose behavior and lives, in accordance with their own most ancient beliefs, were of the highest and most sacred nature.

"BUT THOU HAST PLAYED THE HARLOT WITH MANY LOVERS"

Most revealing was the symbolic analogy they drew between any women who refused to abide by the laws of the new morality—

continually referred to as harlots and adulteresses—and the way-wardness and defection of the entire Hebrew people in their constant lack of fidelity to Yahweh. The use of female sexual infidelity as the ultimate sin—so serious that it was regarded as analogous to the betrayal of Yahweh—affords us some insight into the Levite attitude toward the sexually autonomous woman. The two parts of the analogy are often tightly intertwined, sometimes in a rather obscure fashion, but as the prophets of Yahweh railed at the Hebrews who dared to worship "other gods," the attack upon any woman who refused to be the property of a specific man was made simultaneously and automatically. As we have seen, despite the constant threats, Hebrew women and men alike, even their royalty, did indeed continue to worship the Queen of Heaven. In doing this they were symbolized by the priests as the "Daughter of Zion" and as this daughter denounced as an unfaithful harlot.

Jeremiah, Isaiah, Ezekiel, Hosea and Nahum all used the sexual metaphor extensively. Jeremiah, a Levite priest, put it this way: "They say if a man put away his wife and she goes from him and becomes another man's shall he return to her again? Shall not that land be greatly polluted? But thou hast played the harlot with many lovers; yet return again to me saith the Lord." In another passage he again compared the defection of the Hebrews to an unfaithful woman, saying, "Surely as a wife treacherously departeth from her husband, so have ye dealt treacherously with me, O House of Israel, saith the Lord." In yet another tirade he accused the Hebrews of "playing the harlot on every high mountain or under every green tree."

Angrily he spoke as Yahweh, asking, "How can I forgive you for all this? Your sons have forsaken me and sworn by gods that are no gods. I gave them all they needed, yet they preferred adultery and haunted the brothels" (Jer. 5:7). And once again the analogy was used as in Jer. 3:6–10 we read, "In the reign of King Josiah, the Lord said to me, Do you see what apostate Israel did? She went up to every hill top and under every spreading tree and there she played the whore. Even after she had done all this, I said to her,

Come back to me, but she would not. That faithless woman, her sister Judah, saw it all; she saw too that I had put apostate Israel away and given her a note of divorce because she had committed adultery. Yet that faithless woman, her sister Judah, was not afraid; she too has gone and played the whore. She defiled the land with her thoughtless harlotry and her adulterous worship of stone and wood." (Jeremiah's words were spoken about a century after the defeat of the northern kingdom, Israel, by Sargon II of Assyria in 722 BC.)

The Levite priest-prophet Ezekiel told his congregation, "The word of the Lord came to me: Man, he said, there were once two women, daughters of the same mother. They played the whore in Egypt, played the whore while they were still girls; for there they let their breasts be fondled and their virgin bosoms pressed. The elder was named Oholah, her sister Oholibah. They became mine and bore me sons and daughters. Oholah is Samaria; Oholibah is Jerusalem." The entire section of Ezek. 23 describes the "lewd" sexual behavior of these two sisters, symbolizing the two Hebrew capitals, during which Ezekiel says, "So I will put a stop to your lewdness and the way in which you learnt to play the whore in Egypt." He finally summarizes with "Thus I will put an end to lewdness in the land, and other women shall be taught not to be as lewd as they. You shall pay the penalty for your lewd conduct and shall be punished for your idolatries, and you will know that I am the Lord God." In still another passage Ezekiel warned, "And they shall burn thy houses with fire and execute judgments upon thee to cease from playing the harlot and thou shalt give no hire anymore."

Nahum, speaking of the city of Nineveh, a religious center of the Babylonian Goddess Ishtar, struck out against the Goddess and her sexuality in this way: "Because of the multitudes of the whoredom of the well favored harlot, the mistress of witchcrafts, that selleth nations through her whoredoms and families through her witchcrafts; Behold I am against thee, saith the Lord of Hosts, and I will discover thy skirts upon thy face, and I will show the nations thy nakedness and the kingdoms thy shame."

But the first few sections of the book of Hosea most clearly depict the outrage of the Hebrew man with the wife who refused to be his private property. First we read that Yahweh told Hosea, "Take yourself a wife of harlotry and have children of harlotry, for the land commits great harlotry by forsaking the Lord." Hosea then spoke to his daughter of the "whoredom" and "lewdness" of her mother Gomer, who was apparently a sacred woman of the temple. Later Gomer was told to put away her harlotry and adultery, to which she defiantly replied, "I will go after my lovers." In response to this rebellion the male deity threatened to thwart her activities until such time as she would finally say in desperation, "I will go and return to my first husband."

It is not clear whether these were intended to be the words of Hosea or Yahweh, for they are initially presented as the words of Hosea to his wife, but we read, "I will put an end to all her rejoicing, her feasts, her new moons, her sabbaths and all her solemn festivals. I mean to make her pay for all the days when she offered burnt offerings to the baals and decked herself with rings and necklaces to court her lovers, forgetting me. It is Yahweh who is speaking." Hosea then goes on to say: "Your daughters play the harlot and your brides commit adultery for the men go aside with harlots and sacrifice with cult prostitutes.

"AND THEY WENT FORTH AND THEY SLEW IN THE CITY"

Not only were those women insulted, but violent threats were also made. In the book of Jeremiah, that prophet angrily threatened the "daughter of Egypt, Tyre, Sidon and Ascalon," a symbolic reference, judging by the cities mentioned, to the Goddess. In another passage he warned the women who openly announced their intention to continue their worship of the Queen of Heaven that they would meet with famine, violence and total destruction as a result of their religious beliefs.

The prophet Isaiah, distraught with the situation, moaned, "As for my people, children are their oppressors and women rule over them." Exploding with derisive accusations at "the daughter of Babylon," again a reference to Ishtar, he insulted Her for Her self-assurance and Her sexuality, as well as Her magical powers and spells. Over what appears to be the independence of the Hebrew women, apparently influenced by the freedom of the women all about them, Isaiah listed all their jewelry and seductive apparel with the greatest contempt and then threatened, "The men shall fall by the sword and thy mighty in war and she being desolate shall sit upon the ground. And in that day seven women shall take hold of one man and say, only let us be called by thy name, to take away our reproach."

Thus the Hebrew prophet looked forward to the day of male glory when all independent women would choose to be the property of a man, as they may have been forced to be in the desert, or as their towns were burnt and their families killed and the earliest Israelite wives were taken as prisoners of war by the Hebrew tribes. In the struggle for male kinship, Isaiah dreamed of the day that women would say, "only let us be called by thy name."

In section eight of the book of Ezekiel we again find the religion of the Goddess under attack, as Ezekiel recalls this event: "Entering at the temple gate, I broke through a wall, there was a door. A mysterious figure was leading, apparently a messenger from the male deity. The figure said, 'Go in and look at the filthy things they are doing inside.' I went in and looked: all sorts of images and snakes and repulsive animals and all the idols of the House of Israel drawn on the walls all around." According to Ezekiel, the "filthy" things the worshipers inside this temple were doing were facing to the east, bowing to the sun and raising a branch to their nostrils. This was probably a branch of the sacred tree known as the *asherah*. Ezekiel continues, "He next took me to the north gate of the temple of Yahweh, where women were sitting, weeping for Tammuz." This remark, more clearly than any other, reveals that he was observing the religion of Ashtoreth/Ishtar—still in practice at the temple in Jerusalem.

The mysterious figure then said, "Son of man, do you see that?" This appellation, "Son of man," was used repeatedly throughout the book of Ezekiel, perhaps to remind its readers that Levite priests, such as Ezekiel, no longer considered themselves as the sons of women. Later, turning on the women who prayed in this manner, the figure ordered, "And you, son of man, turn to the daughters of your own people who make up prophecies out of their own head [unlike the Levite prophets of Yahweh, who apparently had a direct line with the proper source], prophesy against them."

Threats and insults to the native inhabitants of Canaan and the Hebrews who had joined in their customs were not all that was used to frighten and discourage people from following the religion of the Queen of Heaven. For next we read of accounts of cold-blooded massacres, merciless slaughters of those who still refused to accept Yahweh. The Bible itself records that any Hebrew who dared to worship in the ancient religion of the Queen of Heaven and Her Baal were the victims of a violent religious persecution.

The words and threats of Ezekiel, as well as the other prophets, were translated into murder and destruction, explained as having been commanded by Yahweh. They are recorded in this way in the pages of the Old Testament:

> And the Lord said unto him, "Go through the midst of Jerusalem and set a mark upon the foreheads of the men that sigh and that cry for all the abominations that are done in the midst thereof." And to the others he said in mine hearing, "go ye after him through the city and smite. Slay utterly, both old and young, both maids and little children and women, but come not near any man upon whom is the mark; and begin at my sanctuary." Then they began at the ancient men who were before the house. And he said unto them, "defile the house and fill the courts with the slain; go ye forth." And they went forth and they slew in the city [Ezek. 9:4–7].

An earlier account of a callous slaughter in the name of Yahweh aimed at the religion of the Goddess occurred during the reign of Ahab. Elijah exhibited the same self-righteous attitude that throughout history has allowed the commission of mass murder in the name of a principle, whether political, religious or a combination of the two. Referring to four hundred people who worshiped in the ancient religion, the passage states, "And Elijah said unto them, take the prophets of Baal, let not one of them escape. And they took them and Elijah brought them down to the Brook Kishon and slew them there."

This particular passage is the version given in the Revised Standard Version of the Old Testament. But in the New English Bible, published in 1970 by the Bible Societies of Scotland and England, which retranslated many of the old texts from the original Hebrew and Greek, we read the story in a slightly different way. In fact, in this version of the Old Testament, many of the references to Asherah, Ashtoreth and the *asherim* are more explicitly explained. In the New English Bible we read that Elijah confronts the ancient religion as that of Asherah. It tells us in I Kings 18:19 that these four hundred people were "four hundred prophets of the goddess Asherah, who are Jezebel's pensioners."

It is most evident in the story of Jezebel, who has long been presented as the epitome and symbol of the treacherously evil woman, that her real crime was her refusal to accept the worship of Yahweh, choosing instead the religion of her own parents, that of the Queen of Heaven and Her Baal. Her parents, as queen and king of Sidon (some say Tyre), held high positions in the ancient religion as high priestess and priest. Not only did Jezebel herself follow the ancient religion, but according to the Bible, as a result of her influence her husband Ahab, a Hebrew king of Israel, adopted the pagan ways as well, erecting *asherim* in the temple. Jezebel's supposed crime, that of starting a rumor that resulted in the death of a man, becomes questionable when we realize that it was her husband who actually desired the dead man's property and it was with letters signed with Ahab's name that she was accused.

Jezebel was murdered in the most gruesome manner, described in morbid detail in the Bible, surely intended as a warning to all other "treacherous" women. The execution was carried out by the avenging Hebrew hero Jehu. But Jehu's motives become frighteningly clear when, after the death of the "pagan" queen, he arranged a massacre of those who "ate at her royal table" and then later claimed the throne of Israel as his own.

Shortly after the murder of Jezebel, Jehu called for a solemn assembly of the people who paid homage to Ashtoreth and Baal, tricking them in this way into gathering together at their own temple at an appointed time. The holy shrine was described as being full from one end to the other. It was then reported in the Bible, "And when they went to offer sacrifices and burnt offerings, Jehu appointed four score men without and said, if any of the men that I have brought into your hands escape, he that letteth him go, his life shall be for the life of him." So it was recorded in the book of II Kings that Jehu and his men murdered every member of the congregation and then finally made a "latrine" of the building itself. And when the massacre and desecration was completed, Jehu is recorded to have heard Yahweh say, "Thou hast done well that which is right in mine eyes" (II Kings 10:18–31).

"THEN LET HIM WRITE HER A BILL OF DIVORCEMENT"

The evidence is abundant. The religion of Ashtoreth, Asherah or Anath and Her Baal—and the accompanying female sexual autonomy—were the enemies. No method was considered too violent to bring about the desired goals. To clarify even further the underlying goals of the Levites, alongside these massacres we confront the rules that the Levite priests declared for all Hebrew women. Upon reading the Levite laws it becomes apparent that the sexual autonomy of women in the religion of the Goddess posed a continual threat. It undermined the far-reaching goals of the men, perhaps led or influenced by Indo-European peoples, who viewed women as property and aimed at a society in which male kinship was the rule, as it had long been in the Indo-European nations. This in turn required that each woman be retained as the possession of one man, leaving no doubt as to the identity of the father of the children she might bear, especially of her sons. But male kinship lines remained impossible as long as women were allowed to function as sexually independent people, continuing to bear children whose paternity was not known or considered to be of any importance.

Laws, speeches and even the divine word had apparently been insufficient when freedom had been known so long. Thus severe punishments were designed and meted out to bring about the total sexual control of Hebrew women. Any deviation was sin, in many cases punishable by disgraceful and agonizing death. (Though these laws appear in the books of Leviticus and Deuteronomy, said to have been written at the time of Moses, Bible scholars generally date their writings to between 1000 and 600 BC.) According to the Levite laws, all women were to remain virgins until marriage. Once legally married, a woman was to relate sexually only to the one man who was designated as her husband, probably a man chosen by her father. This husband may already have possessed, or could acquire in the future, any number of other wives or concubines and was free to add a new one at any time.

In Lev. 20:10 we read that if a woman committed adultery, both she and her lover were to be put to death. In Deuteronomy the Levites wrote of the Israelite bride: "But if this thing be true and tokens of virginity not found for the damsel: then they shall bring out the damsel to the door of her father's house and the men of the city shall stone her with stones that she die because she hath wrought folly in Israel to play the whore in her father's house, so shall thou put away evil from among you" (Deut. 22:20–22). Thus a young Hebrew girl might be dragged from the house and brutally stoned to death—for having made love, or even for having lost her virginity through some other activity or accident, while her Canaanite contemporaries would have been considered holy for taking part in the sacred sexual customs.

So determined were the Levites that a reverent regard for the paternity of children be developed that among them even violent rape was equated with marriage, much as it was among the Indo-European-controlled Assyrians. In Levite law, the rape of a virgin was honored as a declaration of ownership and brought about a forced marriage. As the victim of rape, a woman automatically lost the right to continue her life as a single woman or to become a wife in a more carefully arranged and probably more desirable marriage. The law reads, "If a man find a damsel that is a virgin which is not betrothed and lay hold on her and they be found, then the man that lay with her shall give unto the damsel's father fifty shekels of silver and she shall be his wife" (Deut. 22:28, 29).

For Levite daughters it was decreed, "And the daughter of any priest, if she profane herself by playing the whore, she profaneth her father and shall be burnt with fire" (Lev. 21:9). Since it was the Levite priests who wrote the laws, this willingness to burn their own daughters to death perhaps most clearly reveals the intensity of the Levite attitude toward the sexual autonomy of women.

Perhaps just as astonishing is the law that tells us that if the victim of a rape was a married or betrothed woman she was to be killed—for having been raped. The law states that, if a betrothed woman or a married woman was sexually violated, she and the man were both to be stoned to death (Deut. 22:23–25). The rape was regarded as an affront to the male who owned her. Only in the deserted countryside might a woman be "excused" for having been raped, since perhaps she had called for help and had not been heard.

Though the Bible repeatedly announced that a woman who dared to make love to a man other than her husband was a shameful and profane degradation to the entire faith, Hebrew men went about honorably collecting as many women as they could economically afford. The records of the Hebrew kings reveal that they kept large harems and most Hebrew men appear to have taken several wives; yet each of these women was expected to be totally faithful to the fragment of the husband to whom she was assigned. A lack of fidelity on the part of the male appears to have been taken for granted, unless the other woman was already married or betrothed. This was regarded as sinful because it was a legal infringement upon the property of some other man. It was hardly a romantic fidelity for both partners of the marriage that was deemed as important or sacred, but only for the woman that premarital virginity and sexual fidelity became "moral" issues, attitudes we see reflected even today.

But the position of a married woman who had been faithful was also precarious. In Deut. 24:1 the plight of the married woman was made clear. "When a man hath taken a wife and it come to pass that she find no favor in his eyes because he hath found some uncleanness in her; then let him write her a bill of divorcement and give it in her hand and send her out of *his* house." As we read previously, under the Levite law only the husband could ask for or demand divorce; in fact, all he had to do was write a note. We may see this as a very different society from that of the Sumerian Eshnunna, where if a man took a second woman after the first had borne children, he was to be put out of the house without any possessions.

Here the advantages of male kinship and male inheritance lines, not only for royalty or the priesthood but even for the average male, become clear. A woman who had lived in the house with her husband, probably given birth to children, performed domestic services, perhaps added to or enhanced the value of the house, property and land by her efforts, no matter what her age or state of health, had no legal rights or claims to any of it. She could simply be handed a notice and sent on her way. The husband then assumed ownership of all the products of her time and efforts, and if he had not already done so, probably soon afterward replaced her with another wife or two. Having lost her virginity, she was probably nearly worthless as marriage material.

Such divorces may not have happened frequently, though we have no records with which to judge, but the laws allowing such divorce probably resulted in the woman, fearful at the possibility of being dismissed, becoming a submissive servant, the archetype of the "good wife" who obediently, smilingly caters to her husband's slightest whim or desire.

"I HAVE COME TO DESTROY THE WORKS OF THE FEMALE"

Over the centuries the suppression and persecution of the religion of the female deity continued. In the Abodah Zarah, a book of the Hebrew Talmud compiled in about the fifth century AD, directions were given to the pious worshiper so that he might understand how to destroy the powers of an "idol." This could be done by knocking off the tip of its ear or nose (which may account for the missing noses of so many statues). The entire book was filled with specific laws and regulations describing the relationship the Hebrews were to have with the "idolators."

The civilizations that worshiped the Goddess, which had flourished for thousands of years, bringing with them in earliest times inventions in methods of agriculture, medicine, architecture, metallurgy, wheeled vehicles, ceramics, textiles and written language, were gradually stamped out. Though the Indo-Europeans had initiated a great many changes, it was later the duty of every Hebrew and then of every Christian to suppress and destroy the worship of the female deity wherever it still existed.

If the Hebrews followed the commands in Deuteronomy, the massacres described in the Old Testament may have been only a symbolic portion of the murder and destruction that was actually committed. As the literature and tenets of the Levite-Hebrew religion were incorporated into the new faith, which eventually developed as Christianity, the persecution of the religion of the Goddess continued. The power and influence of the new Church grew, Levite law now juxtaposed to a revised image of the familiar legend of the mother and the dying son—and with it came the even more extreme suppression of the female religion.

In 1971 R. E. Witt wrote *Isis in the Graeco-Roman World.* In it he points out that the worship of the Goddess as Isis and Artemis, names that had become widely used by the time of Christ, was the target of the apostle Paul. He explains that

> Both in Palestine and in Syria, as in Asia Minor on which so much of Paul's apostolic zeal was concentrated, the cult of the female deities was deep rooted and very old . . . the sermon attacking the idolatry shown by the Ephesians towards the Great Goddess Artemis has not survived in detail. We need not doubt that Paul had taken the measure of the female deities of whose influence he had had long experience, especially Artemis and Isis . . . Paul could tell that here was a dangerous rival . . . Clearly the Pauline view of Isiacism [the worship of Isis] was penetratingly critical. Paul's world was a patriarchy, his religion was Christological and monotheistic, and God was found in fashion as a man. Isis was female . . . The obvious foe of the Church in its early ecumenical struggles was the cult of Isis and her temple companions. This is made clear even before the death blow which paganism received from Theodosius.

Witt also quotes perhaps the most revealing line in the story of the destruction of the Goddess religion, telling us that "Clement of Alexandria reproduces a saying from *The Gospel according to the Egyptians.* Christ's words are interesting and in such a context they are almost certainly directed against the current worship of Isis: 'I have come to destroy the works of the female.' "

In about AD 300 the Emperor Constantine brought an end to the ancient sanctuary of Ashtoreth at Aphaca and generally suppressed the worship of Ashtoreth throughout Canaan, claiming that it was "immoral." He is said to have seen a vision of Christ during a battle and to have heard the words. "In this sign, conquer." Strange words for the Prince of Peace.

In AD 380 the Emperor Theodosius closed down the temple of the Goddess at Eleusis, the temples of the Goddess in Rome and the "seventh wonder of the world," the temple of the Goddess then known as Artemis or Diana at Ephesus in western Anatolia. It was said that he despised the religion of women. This great Christian emperor may be better remembered for his massacre of seven thousand people in Thessalonica.

In Athens, the Parthenon of the Acropolis, a sacred site of the Goddess since the Mycenaean times of 1300 BC, was converted into a Christian church in AD 450. In the fifth century the Emperor Justinian converted the remaining temples of Isis into Christian churches.

In Arabia of the seventh century, Mohammed brought an end to the national worship of the Sun Goddess, Al Lat, and the Goddess known as Al Uzza, whose name might have been related to the ancient Ua Zit. Professor J. B. Pritchard writes that Al Lat was originally much the same deity as Asherah in Arabic religion. Mohammed brought about the worship of Allah as the supreme god. Allah actually means god, as Al Lat means Goddess. Though it is not always realized in western society, Mohammed incorporated many of the legends and attitudes of the Old and New Testaments into the Muslim Koran, the bible of Islam. In the Koran, Sura 4:31 tells us, "Men have authority over women because God has made the one superior to the other and because they spend their wealth to maintain them. So good women are obedient, guarding the unseen parts as God has guarded them."

As late as the sixteenth century AD, Hebrew scholars compiled a text known as the Kabbalah. The name of Lilith, once described in a Sumerian tablet as "the hand of Inanna" who brought men into the temple, a name also found in some Hebrew literature as the first wife of Adam who refused to lie beneath him and to obey his commands, appeared once again. In the Hebrew Kabbalah, Lilith was presented as the symbol of evil, the female devil. G. Scholem wrote that in the Zohar, a part of the Kabbalah, it was stated that "Lilith, Queen of the demons, or the demons of her retinue, do their best to provoke men to sexual acts without benefit of a woman, their aim being to make themselves bodies from the lost seed."

It gave the warning that Lilith hovered about, just waiting for available sperm from which she created demons and illegitimate children. The Kabbalah cautioned that, with the help of Lilith, the illegitimate children come. Was this a remote reference to the ancient *qadishtu*, their image now embodied in the wicked demon Lilith? The major factor in avoiding the dangerous Lilith was once again a matter of inheritance. This is apparent in the description of the actions of the illegitimate children, once their father has died.

Scholem tells us that

Wishing along with the other children to have a part in the deceased as their father, they tug and pluck at him, so that he feels the pain, and God himself when he sees this noxious offspring by the corpse, is reminded of the dead man's sins . . . All the illegitimate children that a man has begotten with demons in the course of his life appear after his death to take part in the mourning for him and in his funeral . . . the demons claim their inheritance on this occasion along with the other sons of the deceased and try to harm the legitimate children.

SUMMARY

We have seen that the orders for the destruction of the religion of the Goddess were built into the very canons and laws of the male religions that replaced it. It is clear that the ancient reverence for the female deity did not simply cease to be but that its disappearance was gradually brought about, initially by the Indo-European invaders, later by the Hebrews, eventually by the Christians and even further by the Mohammedans. Along with the ultimate acceptance of the male religions throughout a large part of the world, the precepts of sexual "morality," that is, premarital virginity and marital fidelity for women, were incorporated into the attitudes and laws of the societies which embraced them.

There is no question about the antagonism expressed by the Levite patriarchs toward the religion of the female deity. Accounts, perhaps originally remembered in oral form, taken from other Hebrew scripts or even some other language, became part of the biblical texts which are assumed to have first been written as we know them in about 1000 BC. From the time of Moses onward, the Levites appear to have made the decision to destroy the shrines and sanctuaries of the earlier worship. From that time on until the fall of the two Hebrew nations in 722 and 586 BC, we read in the Bible of the actual massacres and desecrations, claimed to be executed at the command of the male deity. We cannot avoid observing the continual emphasis upon female sexuality as acceptable only when women were safely designated as the property of one specific male and that any deviation from that rule was denounced as harlotry or adultery and subject to punishment by death, making the sexual customs of the older religion rather difficult to follow.

It is then, perhaps, not overly speculative to suggest that the myth of Adam and Eve, the myth which Professor Chiera tells us shows evidence of having been "produced in scholarly circles," may have been intentionally written and included in the creation story of the Bible as yet another assault upon the Goddess religion.

Within the legend of the creation of all existence and life by Yahweh, the story which supposedly explained what happened at the very beginning of time, the image of woman as the dangerously seductive temptress, who brought about the fall of all humanity, may have been inserted. Knowing all that we do about the sacred sexual customs in the religion of the Goddess, the continual presence of these customs among the Hebrews even in Jerusalem, the use of dragon or serpent myths, often in conjunction with creation stories, by the Indo-Europeans and the vestiges of the Leviathan myth in the Old Testament, we may gain a most clarifying and enlightening insight into the symbolism and message contained in the biblical myth of Adam and Eve.

The examination of the symbolic imagery of the Goddess religion and that of the Genesis tale of creation in the following chapter provides some surprising information. We may begin to understand what it means when the Bible tells us that Eve defied the male deity and instead accepted the word and advice of the serpent. We may indeed find that the seemingly innocent myth of Paradise and how the world began was actually carefully constructed and propagated to "keep women in their place," the place assigned to them by the Levite tribe of biblical Canaan.

10

Unraveling the Myth of Adam and Eve

When first I started upon my investigation of the worship of the female deity, it was to a great extent motivated by the image of woman presented by Judaism and Christianity—the woman known as Eve. The further I explored the rites and symbolism of those who revered the Divine Ancestress, the more convinced I became that the Adam and Eve myth, most certainly a tale with a point of view, and with a most biased proclamation for its ending, had actually been designed to be used in the continuous Levite battle to suppress the female religion. It was, perhaps, a more updated version of the dragon or serpent myth whose vestiges are found in the biblical Psalms and the book of Job.

The female faith was a most complex theological structure, affecting many aspects of the lives of those who paid Her homage. It had developed over thousands of years and its symbolism was rich and intricate. Symbols such as serpents, sacred fruit trees and sexually tempting women who took advice from serpents may once have been understood by people of biblical times to symbolize the then familiar presence of the female deity. In the Paradise myth, these images may have explained allegorically that listening to women who revered the Goddess had once caused the expulsion of all humankind from the original home of bliss in Eden.

SACRED SNAKES AND PROPHETIC VISION

Let's begin with the serpent. It seems that in some lands all existence began with a serpent. Despite the insistent, perhaps hopeful, assumption that the serpent must have been regarded as a phallic symbol, it appears to have been primarily revered as a female in the Near and Middle East and generally linked to wisdom and prophetic counsel rather than fertility and growth as is so often suggested.

The Goddess Nidaba, the scribe of the Sumerian heaven, the Learned One of the Holy Chambers, who was worshiped as the first patron deity of writing, was at times depicted as a serpent. At the Sumerian town of Dir the Goddess was referred to as the Divine Serpent Lady. The Goddess as Ninlil, who at times is said to have brought the gift of agriculture and thus civilization to Her people, was said to have the tail of a serpent. In several Sumerian tablets the Goddess was simply called Great Mother Serpent of Heaven.

Stephen Langdon, the archaeologist who led some of the earliest excavations of Sumer and later taught at Oxford, asserted that Inanna, then known as Ininni, was closely connected with serpent worship. He also described Her as the Divine Mother who Reveals the Laws. He wrote that the Goddess known as Nina, another form of the name Inanna, perhaps an earlier one, was a serpent goddess in the most ancient Sumerian periods. He explained that, as Nina, She was esteemed as an oracular deity and an interpreter of dreams, recording this prayer from a Sumerian tablet: "O Nina of priestly rites, Lady of precious decrees, Prophetess of Deities art Thou," and commenting that, "The evidence points to an original serpent goddess as the interpreter of dreams of the unrevealed future." Several sculptures unearthed in Sumer, which date from about 4000 BC, portray a female figure with the head of a snake.

Writing of Elam, just east of Sumer, where in earliest times the Goddess reigned supreme, Dr. Walther Hinz tells us: ". . . part of this individuality [in Elam] consists of an uncommon reverence and respect for eternal womanhood and in a worship of snakes that has its roots in magic . . . Even the pottery of the third and fourth millenia swarms with snakes . . ."

Ishtar of Babylon, successor to Inanna, was identified with the planet known as Venus. In some Babylonian texts this planet was called Masat, literally defined as prophetess. Ishtar was depicted sitting upon the royal throne of heaven, holding a staff around which coiled two snakes. One seal from Babylon, which shows Ishtar holding the serpent-entwined scepter, was inscribed, "Lady of Vision of Kisurru." Ishtar was elsewhere recorded as "She who Directs the Oracles" and "Prophetess of Kua." Babylonian tablets offer numerous accounts of priestesses who offered prophetic advice at the shrines of Ishtar, some of these very significant in the records of political events.

Even in the Babylonian-Kassite myth, Tiamat was recorded as the first divine being. According to this legend, Tiamat originally possessed the Tablets of Destiny, which, after Her murder, were claimed as the property of Marduk. Tiamat was described in this myth as a dragon or serpent. The actual association of the serpent with the female deity, all through the texts and inscriptions of Sumer and Babylon, was probably the very reason this symbolism was used in the Indo-European myths.

On the island of Crete the snake appears in the worship of the female deity more repeatedly than anywhere else in the Mediterranean area. All over the island, artifacts have been unearthed that portray the Goddess or Her priestesses holding snakes in their hands or with them coiled about their bodies, revealing that they were an integral part of the religious rituals. Along with the statues of serpent-entwined priestesses, cylindrical clay objects, also wrapped about with serpents, have been discovered on Crete. Arthur Evans, the archaeologist who excavated the Cretan palace at Knossos, described them as "snake tubes" and suggested that they were used to feed the sacred serpents that were kept at the sanctuaries of the Cretan Goddess. The abundant evidence of the sacred nature of the serpent, along with the Goddess, has in fact appeared to such an extent on Crete that many archaeologists refer to the female deity there as the Serpent Goddess.

Evans, offering supportive evidence, asserted that the Lady of the Serpents on Crete was originally derived from the worship of the Cobra Goddess of the predynastic people of Egypt. He suggested that the worship of the Serpent Lady may have been brought to Crete in about 3000 BC. This is much the same time that the First Dynasty of Egypt was forming, and he further suggested that Egyptian people may have fled to Crete as a result of the invasions at that time.

The use of the cobra in the religion of the Goddess in Egypt was so ancient that the sign that preceded the name of any Goddess was the cobra (i.e., a picture of a cobra was the hieroglyphic sign for the word Goddess). In predynastic Egypt the female deity of Lower Egypt (north) was the Cobra Goddess known as Ua Zit. Not a great deal is known about this most ancient Cobra Goddess, but we later see Her as the *uraeus* cobra worn upon the foreheads of other deities and Egyptian royalty. The cobra was known as the Eye, *uzait,* a symbol of mystic insight and wisdom. Later derivations of the Cobra Goddess, such as Hathor and Maat, were both known as the Eye. This term, in any context it is used, is always written in feminine form. The position of the Eye and its eventual association with male deities was explained in Chapter Four. The Goddess as Hathor was also associated with the male deity Horus; Her name actually means House of Hor. But one text preserved the story that Hathor had been the serpent who had existed before anything else had been created. She then made the heavens, the earth and all life that existed on it. In this account She was angry, though the text is not clear about the reason; She threatened to destroy all of creation and once more resume Her original form as a serpent.

A prophetic sanctuary stood in the Egyptian city of Buto, once the foremost religious center of the Cobra Goddess. The town was actually known as Per Uto in Egyptian, but the Greeks called it Buto, also applying this name to the Cobra Goddess Herself. This shrine was credited in classical Greek times to the Goddess known as Lato, but it is likely that the same site had once been the shrine of oracular advice of the Goddess Ua Zit Herself. Herodotus reported that he saw enormous numbers of snake skeletons lying in a pass in that city.

In Greece, we are afforded the closest look at the derivatives of the Egyptian and Cretan Serpent Goddess. Though the nature of the religion had undergone some major transformations after the invasions of the Achaeans and Dorians, who brought with them the worship of Zeus, many vestiges of the earlier images and symbolism still survived. This was especially manifested in the heroic figure of Athena. Her serpent continually appeared in legends, drawings and sculptures. In some statues it peered out from beneath Her great bronze shield or stood by Her side. A special building known as the Erechtheum stood on the Acropolis alongside Her temple, the Parthenon. This Erechtheum was considered to be the home of Athena's snake. But the snake of the Greek Goddess of Wisdom, who was revered on the majestic heights of the Athenian Acropolis, was not a creation of the classical Greek period. Despite the Indo-European Greek legend that suggests that Athena was born from the head of Zeus, the worship of the Goddess had arrived on the Acropolis long before—with the Cretan Goddess of the Mycenaean settlements. The classical temples of the Acropolis, consecrated to the Greek Athena, were actually built on Mycenaean foundations.

The connections begin to take form. As we read before, the Mycenaeans were the people who had lived on Crete at the palace of Knossos at about 1400 BC. They had integrated the earlier Minoan-Cretan culture into their own to such an extent that the worship is often described as the Minoan-Mycenaean religion. Clothing styles, signet rings, murals, seals and artifacts of all kinds reveal the great similarity of the Mycenaean religious beliefs to those of the Cretans. Once understanding these connections, we realize the significance of the fact that, beneath the ruins of the classical Greek temples of Athens and Delphi, as well as many other Greek shrines where the Goddess was most reverently associated with Her serpent, lay these older Mycenaean remains.

The shrine that perhaps offers the deepest insight into the connections of the female deity of Greece to the Serpent Goddess of Crete is Delphi. Under the classical temple and buildings of Delphi, Mycenaean artifacts and ruins of earlier shrines have been unearthed. In the earliest times, the Goddess at Delphi was held sacred as the one who supplied the divine revelations spoken by the priestesses who served Her. The woman who brought forth the oracles of divine wisdom was called the Pythia. Coiled about the tripod stool upon which she sat was a snake known as Python. Though in later Greek writings Python was male, in the earliest accounts Python was described as female. The serpent Python was of such importance that this city had once been known as Pytho. According to Pausanius the earliest temple at this site had been built by women, while Aeschylus recorded that at this holiest of shrines the Goddess was extolled as the Primeval Prophetess. In later times the priests of the male Apollo took over this shrine, and Greek legend tells us of the murder of Python by Apollo. The many sculptures and reliefs of women, generally described as "the Amazons," fighting against men at this shrine may actually depict the initial seizure.

Reports of Python, as well as the legend of Cassandra of Troy, reveal that snakes were familiar inhabitants of the oracular shrine at Delphi. Sacred snakes were also kept at a temple of the Goddess known as Hera, who was closely associated with Gaia of Delphi, the Primeval Prophetess. The sites of divination at Delphi, Olympia and Dodona were initially identified with the Goddess but were later confiscated by the priests of Zeus and Apollo (both of whom are described as having killed the serpent of the Goddess Gaia). Yet, even under the name of the male deities, it was still priestesses who most often supplied the respected counsel.

So far we have seen that the female deity, as She was known in Babylon, Egypt, Crete and Greece, was identified as or with serpents and closely associated with wisdom and prophecy. But it was not only in these lands that the Serpent Goddess was known. Again, when we look over to Canaan, which bordered on the Mediterranean Sea (as do Egypt, Crete and Greece), we discover evidence of the esteem paid to the Goddess as the Serpent Lady.

The manner in which the connections occur are intriguing. They are really deserving of an entire book rather than the few paragraphs we have room for here. From Neolithic times onward, people were quite mobile, trading and warring in areas many miles from their original homes. Distant colonies were founded and settled where timber, gold, spices and other valuable materials were found. Phoenician ships traversed not only the entire Mediterranean Sea and the inland rivers but made their way well around the coast of Spain as far as Cadiz, and possibly even up to the British Isles, many centuries before the birth of Christ and the Roman invasions. Even before the Phoenicians, who were actually the Canaanites of Tyre and Sidon, there were groups of people who sailed the Mediterranean waters freely and who were known simply as the Sea Peoples. They appear to have traveled widely, often leaving behind them the evident remains of their visit or settlement.

One such people were known as the Philistines. This name has been made familiar to us through the Bible, where they are continuously described as a treacherously evil people, obviously the archenemies of the Hebrews. But as Professor R. K. Harrison wrote, "Archaeological excavations in Philistine territory have shown that it is clearly a mistake to regard the Philistines as synonymous with barbarity or cultural deficiency, as is so frequently done in common speech."

The Philistine people present one of the most significant links between the worship of the Serpent Goddess of Crete and the female deity as She was revered in Canaan. The Philistines are recorded in the Old Testament to have come from the isle of Caphtor—which is generally believed to be Crete; the Egyptians called it Keftiu. The Bible described them as coming from Caphtor and Egypt. Though their major migrations to Canaan appear to have taken place about 1200 BC, Philistines are mentioned in Canaan in the time of Abraham. Several writers have suggested that the Philistines were actually a branch of the Mycenaeans, who were culturally active upon Crete and Greece at the same time. Some writers associate their name with the Pelasgians, the people who lived in Greece before the Indo-European invasions. During the periods of the greatest Philistine migrations into Canaan, they settled primarily in the southwest. This area came to be known as Philistia, the origin of the name Palestine. Evidence suggests that along with the Philistine people came the religion of the Serpent Goddess.

Some of the most revealing evidence of the connections of the worship of the Serpent Goddess of Crete to the female deity of Canaan, as well as the nearby island of Cyprus, has been the discovery in both places of "snake tubes"—nearly identical to those found on Crete. Of even greater significance is the fact that a snake tube was unearthed in a Philistine temple devoted to the worship of Ashtoreth.

Archaeologist R. W. Hutchinson pointed out some of the connections:

> The snake tubes of Gournia [a town on Crete] have interesting parallels outside Crete and Evans collated a convincing series of examples of clay tubes connected with the household snake cult, some with modelled snakes crawling up them . . . Some of the more interesting examples of snake tubes, however, come not from Crete at all but from Late Bronze Age sites in Cyprus and Philistia. One tube found at Kition on Cyprus shows the snake tube converted into a dove cot . . . Another tube found in the House of Ashtoreth on the Philistine site of Beth Shan [Canaan] dated to the reign of Ramses II of Egypt (c. 1292–1225 BC) shows two snakes crawling round and into the tube . . .

Another piece found at Beth Shan portrayed the Goddess leaning from the window of a shrine, while a serpent emerged from a lower level. At this same site quite a few "Astarte plaques" were found, along with the statue of a woman, probably intended to represent a priestess—with a serpent coiled about her neck. Another interesting discovery made in this temple was a terra cotta serpent with female breasts. According to the Bible it was this House of Ashtoreth in Beth Shan where the armor of the defeated Hebrew King Saul was victoriously displayed by the Philistines (I Sam. 31:10).

On the nearby island of Cyprus, at another temple of Ashtoreth located in the town of Kition, near present-day Larnaca, not only a snake tube most similar to those found on Crete was discovered but also a small clay figure holding a snake. Recent excavations at Kition have unearthed another figure of Ashtoreth. We may not be too surprised to learn that the Ashtoreth temple at Kition was built on what are thought to be Mycenaean or Cretan foundations.

Though the presence of the Philistines alone might be sufficient to attest and explain the appearance of the Serpent Goddess in Canaan, Her worship gained entrance into the "promised land" through other channels as well. The Goddess Isis-Hathor, whose worship assimilated that of Ua Zit, the Cobra Goddess of Egypt, was well known in certain sections of Sinai and Canaan. Even as early as the Second Dynasty, some of these places are believed to have been seaports or even colonies of Egypt.

Some of the connections of the Goddess in Canaan with the female deity as She was known in Egypt are revealed through their names. In Egypt the Canaanite Ashtoreth was known as Asit, again much like Ua Zit and Au Set. The name Umm Attar, Mother Attar, was known in parts of Arabia, probably related to the name Hathor but also to another Canaanite name for Ashtoreth—Attoret.

Several ancient temples offer evidence of the connections between Isis-Hathor and the Goddess in Canaan. In both She appears as the Serpent Goddess. At the first, Serabit el Khadim, a shrine on the Sinai Peninsula close to the great Egyptian turquoise mines, bilingual Egyptian and Semitic inscriptions have been discovered.

The inscriptions named the deity once worshiped at the shrine as the Goddess Hathor. In these bilingual inscriptions Hathor was also referred to as Baalat, meaning Lady or Goddess, as the word was then known in Canaan. J. R. Harris wrote of the temple on Sinai and discussed the relationship between the two names of the Goddess as She was known there. He explained, "Here she [Baalat] was evidently identified with the Egyptian Goddess Hathor at whose temple all the inscriptions were found." But perhaps most significant is the fact that, on the walls of this shrine, two prayers had been carved into the stone. In both of these the Goddess was invoked—as the Serpent Lady.

Sir Flinders Petrie wrote of probable oracles at the enclosures of the Serabit complex. This shrine on the Sinai Peninsula, which lies between Egypt and Canaan, is particularly worth noting since many scholars have suggested that it may have been on the route the Hebrew tribes took upon their exodus from Egypt. The Bible records that it was during this period in the desert that Moses came to possess the "brazen serpent," which appeared seven hundred years later in the shrine in Jerusalem. It was eventually destroyed by the Hebrew reformer Hezekiah as a "pagan abomination," but it is not inconceivable that it may have come into the possession of the Hebrews at Serabit and even have been accepted temporarily by Moses as a means of placating the Hebrew people.

Yet this bronze serpent seems to have been identified with the Goddess religion, for the Bible reveals that it was kept in the same temple in Jerusalem where in 700 BC we find vessels for Ashtoreth and Baal, the *asherah,* the house of the sacred women and the women who wept for Tammuz.

The title of Baalat as another name for Hathor leads to yet another shrine of the Goddess, the one at the Canaanite port of Byblos, a site first settled as long ago as 6000 BC. As late as the fourth century BC, writings from Berytus (Beirut) stated that the Baalat was still the principal deity of Byblos. Overlooking the Mediterranean waters, on this coastal site of what is now Lebanon in what had once been Canaan, temple foundations date back to at least 2800 BC. Many records of Byblos tell us that it was, during most periods, closely aligned with Egypt.

At this temple in Byblos the Goddess was revered both as Baalat and as Isis-Hathor. Many symbols of the Goddess and Her cobra were found amid the ruins. One headband, adorned with the rising cobra, was constructed so that the snake would emerge from the forehead of the person who wore it, as the Eye of Wisdom. At this same site two golden cobras and an offering bowl decorated with snakes were also unearthed. According to Egyptian legend, it was to this city of Byblos in Canaan that Isis had once traveled to retrieve the body of Her dead brother/husband Osiris.

Elsewhere in Canaan evidence of snakes appears alongside the worship of the Goddess. It seems likely that the majority of the sculptures and artifacts associated with the female deity and Her serpent in Canaan may have met destruction at the time of the occupation of the Levite-led Hebrews; yet scattered remains offer silent testimony to Her one-time existence even in the cities of southern Canaan.

At Taanach a number of serpent heads were discovered, as well as a small figure holding a serpent. Here too was found a bronze figure of Ashtoreth along with an inscription that the Goddess gave the oracles by the pointing of Her finger.

At Beth Shemesh, jugs with serpents and a figure of the Goddess with a snake falling over Her shoulder and into Her lap were unearthed in excavations. At Tell Beit Mersim, another Philistine stronghold, there were many "Astarte plaques," as well as a plaque that Albright refers to as the Goddess, a serpent coiled about the lower half of the body. The piece is very badly mutilated and I would hesitate to say who the figure actually represents, though the snake is certainly clear enough.

Hutchinson draws a connection between this particular figure and the Serpent Goddess of Minoan Crete, writing, "A similar snake goddess seems to have been worshipped during the Bronze Age in Palestine where a stele was found at Tell Beit Mersim in a deposit dated about 1600 BC, carved with a representation of a goddess with her snake curling round her body. This stele was practically contemporary with the faience figure of the Snake Goddess found in the temple repositories at Knossos."

Another bronze serpent was found at Shushan, while at Shechem archaeologists unearthed a figure with a snake coiled about its body. At the town of Gezer, eighteen miles northwest of Jerusalem, a bronze serpent was found near a cave which had been used as a religious sanctuary. There was also a plaque of the Goddess with a cobra. Serpents also appear to have been depicted in the margins of the plaque. It has been suggested that in Her outstretched arms She once held serpents, as in so many of the other plaques of this type which combine the aspects of both Ashtoreth and Hathor, clay reliefs simply marked Qadesh—Holy. A bronze figure of Ashtoreth was also discovered at this same site.

Archaeologist R. A. S. Macalister described the excavation at Gezer in this way: "In an enclosure close to the standing stones was found a bronze model of a cobra which may have been a votive offering. It recalls the story of the brazen serpent of Moses to whose worship Hezekiah put an end in II Kings. Possibly this object was similar in appearance. Another remarkable find made within the precincts of the high place was the unique figure of the two horned Astarte."

Gezer had two large underground caverns; the cobra was found at a nearby circular structure. Again, several writers have suggested that oracular divination may have been practiced in the underground chambers where libation bowls decorated with snakes were discovered.

And in Jerusalem itself was the serpent of bronze, said to date back to the time of Moses and treasured as a sacred idol in the temple there until about 700 BC.

The symbol of the serpent entwined about accounts of oracular revelation appears throughout the Near and Middle East. To summarize, connections are drawn between the Cobra Goddess of Egypt and the Serpent Goddess of Crete. The Mycenaeans appear to have brought the oracular serpent with them from Crete to the shrines of pre-Greece, observed most clearly at the sites of Athens and Delphi. Other people, known as the Philistines, probably from Crete, brought the Serpent Goddess to Cyprus and Canaan, while the Egyptians carried the worship of the Serpent Lady across the Mediterranean Sea to Byblos and across the sands of Sinai to Serabit. Both in Babylon and Sumer we find the Goddess associated with snakes and with oracular prophecy. There is hardly an area in the Near and Middle East where we do not find accounts of the serpent and/or the shrines of divine wisdom as separate elements; yet both of these occur together often enough to suggest that the relationship between these two separate elements be recognized.

In questioning the nature and purpose of the oracular shrines and the priestesses who gave advice, historical records, especially in Babylon and Greece, explain that they were primarily utilized for vital political, governmental and military matters. It was not only the belief that the priestesses could see into the future that made oracular divination so popular but the idea that these women were understood to be in direct communication with the deity who possessed the wisdom of the universe. It is evident from the accounts of the people who believed in prophetic revelation that they did not view the future as totally predestined and determined by uncontrollable fates but rather as something that could be acted upon, as long as one knew the most advantageous action to take. The oracular priestesses were not consulted for a firm prediction of the future but for counsel as to the best strategy, considering the situation. This advice was available at shrines all the way from Greece to Mesopotamia.

Evidence of the Goddess in Sumer, under the names such as Nina, Ininni or Inanna, suggests that divine revelation was an aspect of the religion from the most ancient times. In later Babylon, records of Queens Sibtu and Nakia revealed the importance and influence of the oracular priestesses in the political affairs of Babylon and the city of Mari. Babylonian prophetesses were known as *appiltu* or *muhhtu*. It is rather interesting that the Hebrew word *zonah* is at times defined as "prostitute" and at times as "prophetess."

J. Hastings wrote that in Egypt, "In the Old and Middle Kingdoms, women of important families often bear the title 'prophetess.' It was nearly always the goddesses Hathor and Neith that they served in this capacity."

D. S. Russell wrote of the prophetesses who came to be known as the Sibyls. The Sibyls were often identified with a prophetess of Anatolia, named as Sybella, whom we may suspect has some connection with the Goddess known there as Cybele. It was, in fact, the Sibyls of Rome who were responsible for having the worship of the Anatolian Cybele brought into Rome. According to Russell,

> These Sibylline oracles were written during the latter half of the second century BC in Alexandria. They are imitative of the Greek Sibyls who exercised a considerable influence upon pagan thought both before and after this time. The pagan Sibyl was a prophetess who, under the inspiration of the god, was able to impart wisdom to men and to reveal to them the divine will. There were many varieties of such oracles in different countries and in Egypt in particular they came to have an increasing interest and significance.

At the temple in Jerusalem in about 620 BC, Ezekiel spoke of the women who dared to prophesy "out of their own heads." Even the much later canons of St. Patrick, who is said to have brought Christianity to "pagan" Ireland, warned against "pythonesses." Pythoness is still defined in most contemporary English dictionaries as a prophetess or witch.

"MY MIND HAD EXTRAORDINARY POWERS"

This continual appearance of the serpent with the Goddess, in association with prophecy and divine revelation, raises the question of the purpose and meaning of its repeated presence. The manner in which the serpent was used in oracular divination has never been made clear, but there are some clues hinting at the possible explanation.

One of these is from the story of Cassandra, a tale that may have survived from the period of the Achaeans and the Trojan War. The legend related that Cassandra was left overnight at the shrine of Delphi as a very young child. When her mother, the Trojan Queen Hecuba, arrived there in the morning, she is said to have found the child surrounded by the sacred snakes that were kept in the shrine. They were licking Cassandra's ears. This experience was offered as the explanation of how Cassandra gained the gift of prophecy.

A Greek prophet named Melampus was also recorded to have had his ears licked clean by serpents, thus allowing him to understand the language of birds. In the writings of Philostratus, he claimed that it was quite common for Arabians to understand divine revelations, especially the sounds of birds, explaining that they had acquired this ability by feeding themselves the heart or liver of serpents. The sounds of birds were very often associated with the oracular shrines of Greece, while on Crete and in Ascalon, Canaan, statues often included one or more doves perching on the head of the Goddess or priestess.

In both Hebrew and Arabic the terms for magic are derived from the words meaning serpent. In Brittany supernatural powers were said to be acquired by drinking broth prepared from serpents. Among the Sioux Indians in North America the word *wakan* means both wizard and serpent. Indians in the southwest United States had an initiation ritual in which a brave who had been chosen as eligible for the honor performed a dance in which he allowed himself to be bitten several times by a snake. As a result of this experience, provided he did not die, he was said to gain great wisdom and insight into the workings of the universe and the meaning of all things.

In addition to these connections between serpents and oracular revelation, contemporary science has perhaps provided the deepest insight into the possible relationship between the two elements. Normally, when a person receives a venomous snake bite, and subsequently the venom is introduced into the system, there are various reactions, depending upon the species of snake, including swelling, internal bleeding, difficulty in breathing and paralysis. These effects often prove fatal. But there are recent records of people who have been immunized, thus preventing the venom of a snake bite from causing death. When bitten after the immunization, especially by krait, cobra or other elapids, the subject experiences an emotional and mental state that has been compared to the effects of hallucinogenic drugs.

In an account kept by his wife, William Haast of the Florida Serpentarium (where venom is extracted for various medicinal uses) described his reaction to a krait bite, received after he had been repeatedly immunized for his work. The account was later recalled in H. Kursh's *Cobras in the Garden*. Kursh writes:

> Suddenly he began to feel pleasantly light and weirdly buoyant, almost gay, as though he were slightly intoxicated . . . he had developed an acute sense of hearing, almost painfully acute. The air about him was a charivari, a veritable jungle of discordant noises. It was as if he was under the influence of a strange narcotic . . . He had one inexplicable sensation. It was a peculiar emotional reaction which he could not control. As he lay with his eyes involuntarily closed, he could "see" things. There were visions in front of him.

In another report on this same incident, Marshall Smith of *Life* magazine quoted Haast as saying, "I found myself making up the most wonderful verses. My mind had extraordinary powers." It may or may not be related, but the oracles of the shrines in Greece were said to be given in verse.

Much like mescaline (a product of the peyote cactus) or psilocybin (found in certain types of mushrooms), both used as sacraments in some North American Indian religions, the chemical makeup of certain types of snake venom, may have caused a person, especially someone in the expectant frame of mind, to feel in touch with the very forces of existence and a sensation of perceiving the events and meaning of the past, present and future with great clarity and comprehension. This type of sensation is certainly often reported by people using mescaline, psilocybin and lysergic acid diethylamide (LSD). The sacred serpents, apparently kept and fed at the oracular shrines of the Goddess, were perhaps not merely the symbols but actually the instruments through which the experiences of divine revelation were reached. This may explain the title of the Egyptian Cobra Goddess, who was at times known as the Lady of Spells.

According to an old Talmudic tradition, the venom of the serpent, which had corrupted Eve and all humanity, lost its strength through the revelation of Mount Sinai but regained it when Israel began to worship the golden calf.

THE FLESH AND FLUID OF THE GODDESS

But the serpent is not the only link between the story of Adam and Eve and the worship of the Goddess. Another most important symbol in the story is that of the tree, the tree of knowledge of good and evil, from which hung the forbidden fruit. There are legends known from classical Greece about the golden apple tree of the Goddess Hera, about which the serpent Ladon coiled. The tree, incidentally, was said to be given to Hera by the Goddess Gaia, the Primeval Prophetess of the shrine at Delphi. Though legends of apple trees were known in classical Greece, I suggest that the tree of knowledge of good and evil in earliest times was not an apple but a fig.

A particular species of tree was continually mentioned as sacred in various ancient records, but deceptively under three different names, so that its singular identity has been overlooked. At times it was called the sycamore, at times the fig and sometimes the mulberry. This tree is actually the Near Eastern *ficus sicomorus,* the sycamore fig, sometimes denoted as the black mulberry. It differs from the common fig tree in that its reddish colored fruit grows in large clumps, something like a cluster of grapes.

References to this sacred tree are found in the writings of Egypt, while representations of it appear on Egyptian murals. The Goddess Hathor of Egypt, revered both as the Eye of Wisdom and the

Serpent Lady, was also known by another title—the Lady of the Sycamore. This tree was known as the Living Body of Hathor on Earth. To eat of its fruit was to eat of the flesh and fluid of the Goddess. Some Egyptian murals depicted the Goddess within this tree, passing out its sacred fruit to the dead as the food of eternity, immortality and continued life, even after death.

The type of tree represented on the signet rings of Crete was perhaps the same one, though depicted in a more symbolic form, simply showing the clusters of fruit. Evans suggested that the fig was sacred to the Cretans and described a section of a mural at Knossos where the tree alongside the altar was a fig. He also mentioned a group of sacred trees portrayed within the walls of a Cretan sanctuary, whose foliage showed them to be fig trees. Cretan seals and rings repeatedly depicted the Goddess or Her attendants alongside small fruit trees, caring for them, almost caressing them, as if in sacred devotion. In India, where the fig is known as the "pipal tree," it is still considered sacred.

Some of the most explanatory evidence of the symbolic meaning of this tree is the knowledge we have of the memorial rituals celebrated at the "annual death" of Osiris, brother/husband of Isis, a death closely related to the sacrifice of the annual king. According to Egyptian records, Osiris was first buried in a mulberry coffin. This coffin was later placed inside a living sycamore tree, symbolic of Isis-Hathor as his mother/wife. In this way She was to provide him with the food of eternity. This custom was closely linked with the legend that Isis went to Canaan to retrieve the tree in which Osiris had been buried, cut the coffin of Osiris from that tree and left the remainder of it as a sacred relic in Her temple at Byblos; this was the Canaanite shrine at which Isis-Hathor and Baalat were synonymous.

The sacred symbolism of this coffin tree of Hathor makes it likely that this was the tree repeatedly referred to in the Bible as the *asherah*. Ezekiel spoke harshly of the "idolators" in the temple at Jerusalem passing around the sacred branch of a tree, as if it were a great sin. Passages in Ezekiel threaten, "Never again will they defile my name with their prostitutions and with their funeral pillars of their kings," and "The House of Israel shall no more defile my holy name, neither they nor their kings, by their harlotry or by their dead bodies of their kings." Isaiah referred to the planting of small trees for Adonis, warning that "the sprigs of foreign gods" would bring a harvest of grief and desperate sorrow.

Evans mentioned gold fig leaves found at Mycenaean tombs in connection with a "funeral cult" there. The fig tree was regarded as a gift given by the Goddess, as She was worshiped at the Greek shrine of Eleusis, a temple also built on Mycenaean foundations. It was against a tree that Adonis and Attis both met their legendary deaths and on a tree that the annual effigy of Attis was displayed in Rome. Dionysus, a figure quite similar to Attis and Adonis, associated with the worship of the Goddess both at Delphi and Eleusis, was symbolically associated with the fig tree.

As I mentioned previously, the *asherah* or *asherim* of the Bible were planted or stood alongside the altar at the shrines of the Goddess. They were the despised pillars and poles which the Hebrews were continually ordered to destroy. Though we have no certain proof that these were sycamore fig trees, the evidence suggests that this was so. The fruit of this tree, described in Egyptian texts as "the flesh and fluid of Hathor," may even have been eaten as a type of "communion" with the Goddess, perhaps giving rise to the custom of the communion of the "flesh and the blood" of Jesus, taken in the form of wafers and wine even today. Most intriguing is the line in the Bible that relates that, when Adam and Eve realized their nakedness as a result of having eaten the forbidden fruit of the tree, they then made aprons to cover their sexual parts—with fig leaves.

SERPENTS, SYCAMORES AND SEXUALITY

It is here that our understanding of the sacred sexual customs and matrilineal descent patterns enters the matter, further clarifying the symbolism of the forbidden fruit. In each area in which the

Goddess was known and revered, She was extolled not only as the prophetess of great wisdom, closely identified with the serpent, but as the original Creatress, and the patroness of sexual pleasures and reproduction as well. The Divine Ancestress was identified as She who brought life as well as She who decreed the destinies and directions of those lives, a not unnatural combination. Hathor was credited with having taught people how to procreate. Ishtar, Ashtoreth and Inanna were each esteemed as the tutelary deity of sexuality and new life. The sacred women celebrated this aspect of Her being by making love in the temples.

Considering the hatred the Hebrews felt toward the *asherim*, a major symbol of the female religion, it would not be too surprising if the symbolism of the tree of forbidden fruit, said to offer the knowledge of good and evil, yet clearly represented in the myth as the provider of sexual consciousness, was included in the creation story to warn that eating the fruit of this tree had caused the downfall of all humanity. Eating of the tree of the Goddess, which stood by each altar, was as dangerously "pagan" as were Her sexual customs and Her oracular serpents.

So into the myth of how the world began, the story that the Levites offered as the explanation of the creation of all existence, they place the advisory serpent and the woman who accepted its counsel, eating of the tree that gave her the understanding of what "only the gods knew"—the secret of sex—*how* to create life.

As the advocates of Yahweh destroyed the shrines of the female deity wherever they could, murdering when they could not convert, the Levite priesthood wrote the tale of creation. They announced that male supremacy was not a new idea, but in fact had been divinely decreed by the male deity at the very dawn of existence. The domination of the male over the female, as Hebrew women found themselves without the rights of their neighbors, rights that they too may have once held, was not simply added as another Hebrew law but written into the Bible as one of the first major acts and proclamations of the male creator. With blatant disregard for actual history, the Levite leaders announced that woman must be ruled by man, declaring that it was in agreement with the original decree of Yahweh, who, according to these new legends, had first created the world and people. The myth of Adam and Eve, in which male domination was explained and justified, informed women and men alike that male ownership and control of submissively obedient women was to be regarded as the divine and natural state of the human species.

But in order to achieve their position, the priests of the male deity had been forced to convince themselves and to try to convince their congregations that sex, the very means of procreating new life, was immoral, the "original sin." Thus, in the attempt to institute a male kinship system, Judaism, and following it Christianity, developed as religions that regarded the process of conception as somewhat shameful or sinful. They evolved a code of philosophical and theological ideas that inherently espoused discomfort or guilt about being human beings—who do, at least at the present time, conceive new life by the act of sexual intercourse—whether it is considered immoral or not.

This then was the unfortunate, unnatural and uncomfortable trap of its own making into which the patriarchal religion fell. Even today we may read in the Common Prayer Book of Westminster Abbey under the Solemnization of Matrimony, "Secondly it was ordained for a remedy against sin, and to avoid fornication; that such persons that have not the *gift of continency* might marry, and keep themselves undefiled members of Christ's body" (my italics).

The picture takes form before us, each tiny piece falling into place. Without virginity for the unmarried female and strict sexual restraints upon married women, male ownership of name and property and male control of the divine right to the throne could not exist. Wandering further into the Garden of Eden, where the oracular cobra curled about the sycamore fig, we soon discover that the various events of the Paradise myth, one by one, betray the political intentions of those who first invented the myth.

A LEVITE ACCOUNT OF CREATION—THEOLOGY OR POLITICS?

Let us take a closer look at the tale of creation and the subsequent loss of Paradise as related by the Hebrew leaders and later adopted and cherished by the advocates of Christianity. As we compare the Levite creation story with accounts of the Goddess religion, we notice how at each turn, in each sentence of the biblical myth, the original tenets of the Goddess religion were attacked.

Stephen Langdon wrote, "Thus beyond all doubt the Nippurian school of Sumerian theology originally regarded man as having been created from clay by the great mother goddess." Professor Kramer tells us, "In a tablet which gives a list of Sumerian gods the goddess Nammu, written with the ideogram for 'sea' is described as 'the mother who gave birth to heaven and earth.' " One Sumerian prayer goes as follows: "Hear O ye regions, the praise of Queen Nana, Magnify the Creatress, exalt the dignified, Exalt the glorious One, draw nigh unto the Mighty Lady." The Egyptians wrote, "In the beginning there was Isis, Oldest of the Old. She was the Goddess from whom all becoming arose." Even in Babylonian periods there were prayers to Mami or Aruru as the creator of human life. Yet the worshipers of Yahweh, perhaps one thousand years later, asserted that it was a male who initially created the world. It was the first claim to male kinship—maleness was primal.

According to legends of Sumer and Babylon, women and men had been created simultaneously, in pairs—by the Goddess. But in the male religion it was of ultimate importance that the male was made first, and in the image of his creator—the second and third claims to male kinship rights. We are next told that from a small rather insignificant part of man, his rib, woman was formed. Despite all that we know about the biological facts of birth, facts the Levites certainly knew as well, we are assured that the male does not come from the female, but the female from the male. We may be reminded of the Indo-European Greek story of Athena being born from the head of Zeus.

Any unpleasant remnant or reminder of being born of woman had to be denied and changed. Just as in the myth of the creation through an act of masturbation by the Egyptian Ptah, the Divine Ancestress was written out of reality. We are then informed that the woman made in this manner was presented as a gift to the man, declaring and assuring her status—among those who accepted the myth—as the property of the male. It tells us that she was given to him to keep him from being lonely, as "a helper fit for him." Thus we are expected to understand that the sole and divine purpose of women's existence is to help or serve men in some way.

The couple so designed was placed in the Garden of Eden—paradise—where the male deity warned them not to eat any of the fruit of the tree of knowledge of good and evil. To the ancient Hebrews this tree was probably understood to represent the sacred sycamore fig of the Goddess, the familiar *asherah* which stood beside the altars of the temples of the Goddess and Her Baal. The sacred branch being passed around in the temple, as described by Ezekiel, may have been the manner in which the fruit was taken as "communion." According to Egyptian texts, to eat of this fruit was to eat of the flesh and the fluid of the Goddess, the patroness of sexual pleasure and reproduction. According to the Bible story, the forbidden fruit caused the couple's conscious comprehension of sexuality. Upon eating the fruit, Adam and Eve became aware of the sexual nature of their own bodies, "And they knew that they were naked." So it was that when the male deity found them, they had modestly covered their genitals with aprons of fig leaves.

But it was vitally important to the construction of the Levite myth that they did not both decide to eat the forbidden fruit together, which would have been a more logical turn for the tale to take since the fruit symbolized sexual consciousness. No, the priestly scribes make it exceedingly clear that the woman Eve ate of the fruit first—upon the advice and counsel of the serpent.

It can hardly have been chance or coincidence that it was a serpent who offered Eve the advice. For people of that time knew that the serpent was the symbol, perhaps even the instrument, of divine counsel in the religion of the Goddess. It was surely intended in the Paradise myth, as in the Indo-European serpent and dragon myths, that the serpent, as the familiar counselor of women, be seen as a source of evil and be placed in such a menacing and villainous role that to listen to the prophetesses of the female deity would be to violate the religion of the male deity in a most dangerous manner.

The relationship between the woman and the serpent is shown to be an important factor, for the Old Testament related that the male deity spoke directly to the serpent, saying, "I will put enmity between you and the woman and between your seed and her seed." In this way the oracular priestesses, the prophetesses whose advice and counsel had been identified with the symbolism and use of the serpent for several millenia, were now to be regarded as the downfall of the whole human species. Woman, as sagacious advisor or wise counselor, human interpreter of the divine will of the Goddess, was no longer to be respected, but to be hated, feared or at best doubted or ignored. This demand for silence on the part of women, especially in the churches, is later reflected in the passages of Paul in the New Testament. According to the Judaic and Christian theology, woman's judgment had led to disaster for the whole human species.

We are told that, by eating the fruit first, woman possessed sexual consciousness before man and in turn tempted man to partake of the forbidden fruit, that is, to join her sinfully in sexual pleasures. This image of Eve as the sexually tempting but God-defying seductress was surely intended as a warning to all Hebrew men to stay away from the sacred women of the temples, for if they succumbed to the temptations of these women, they simultaneously accepted the female deity—Her fruit, Her sexuality and, perhaps most important, the resulting matrilineal identity for any children who might be conceived in this manner. It must also, perhaps even more pointedly, have been directed at Hebrew women, cautioning them not to take part in the ancient religion and its sexual customs, as they appear to have continued to do, despite the warnings and punishments meted out by the Levite priests.

The Hebrew creation myth, which blamed the female of the species for initial sexual consciousness in order to suppress the worship of the Queen of Heaven, Her sacred women and matrilineal customs, from that time on assigned to women the role of sexual temptress. It cast her as the cunning and contriving arouser of the physical desires of men, she who offers the appealing but dangerous fruit. In the male religions, sexual drive was not to be regarded as the natural biological desires of women and men that encouraged the species to reproduce itself but was to be viewed as woman's fault.

Not only was the blame for having eaten the fruit of sexuality, and for tempting Adam to do the same, laid heavily upon women, but the proof or admission of her guilt was supposedly made evident in the pain of childbirth, which women were assured was their eternal chastisement for teaching men such bad habits. Eve was to be severely punished as the male deity decreed: "I will greatly multiply your pain in childbearing; in pain you shall bring forth children, yet your desire shall be for your husband and he shall rule over you."

Making use of the natural occurrence of the pains of the pressure of a human child passing from the womb, through a narrow channel, into the outside world, the Levite writer pretended to prove the omnipotent power of his deity. Not only was woman to bear the guilt for sexual consciousness, but according to the male deity her pain in bearing a child was to be regarded as punishment, so that all women giving birth would thus be forced to identify with Eve.

But perhaps most significant was the fact that the story also stated that it was the will of the male deity that Eve would henceforth desire *only* her husband, redundantly reminding us that this whole fable was designed and propagated to provide "divine" sanction for male supremacy and a male kinship system, possible only with a certain knowledge of paternity.

We are perhaps all too familiar with the last line of the decree, which announced that from that time on, as a result of her sin and in eternal payment for the defiant crime which she had committed against the male deity, her husband was awarded the divine right to dominate her, to "rule over" her, to totally assert his authority. And in guilt for what she had supposedly done in the very beginning of time, as if in confession of her poor judgment, she was expected to submit obediently. We may consider here the more practical reality that, once the economic security of women had been undermined by the institution of male kinship, women were forced into the position of accepting this one stable male provider as the one who "ruled the roost."

Once these edicts had been issued, the couple was expelled from the Garden of Eden, the original paradise where life had been so easy. From that time on they were to labor for their livelihood, a most severe warning to any woman who might still have been tempted to defy the Levite Yahweh. For hadn't it been just such a woman, listening to the advice of the serpent, eating the forbidden fruit, suggesting that men try it too and join her in sexual consciousness, who had once caused the downfall and misery of all humankind?

11

The Daughters of Eve

Even today Hebrew males are taught to offer the daily prayer, "Blessed Art Thou O Lord our God, King of the Universe, who has not made me a woman."

Mohammed stated, "When Eve was created, Satan rejoiced."

As the Hebrew myth of the creation was later adopted into the sacred literature of Christianity, along with all the other writings of the Old Testament, the writers and religious leaders who followed Christ assumed the same pose of contempt for the female, continuing to use religion to lock women further into the role of passive and inferior beings, and thus the more easily controlled property of men. As the years went on and the position and status of women continued to lose ground, the Church held fast to its goals of creating and maintaining a male-dominated society. For hadn't it been one of the first decrees of the god who made the world and all life? Women were to be regarded as mindless, carnal creatures, both attitudes justified and "proved" by the Paradise myth.

In Paul's letter to the Ephesians we read, "Wives, submit yourselves unto your own husbands as unto the Lord. For the husband is the head of the wife even as Christ is the head of the Church and he is the savior of the body. Therefore as the Church is subject unto Christ, so let the wives be to their own husbands in everything" (Eph. 5:22–24).

This brings to mind the quote from Hosea in which the husband so totally identified himself with the male deity that his words became the words of Yahweh. In the new religion not only the priests, but all men, were to be considered as direct messengers of the Lord, not merely in Church but in the privacy of a woman's kitchen or even in her bed.

Using the now-familiar Eden myth, Paul asserted that this was the reason that women must be obedient, denying themselves even the faculty of their vocal chords, not to mention their minds. We read in I Tim. 2:11–14, "Let the woman learn in silence with all subjection. But I suffer not a woman to teach, nor to usurp authority over the man, but to be in silence. For Adam was first formed and then Eve and Adam was not deceived, but the woman being deceived was in the transgression."

And in Corinthians the word of the creation legend was brought home once again. "The head of every man is Christ; and the head of the woman is the man; and the head of Christ is God. For a man indeed ought not to cover his head for as much as he is the image and glory of God, but the woman is the glory of the man. For the man is not of the woman but the woman of the man. Neither was man created for the woman but the woman for the man" (I Cor. 11:3, 7, 9).

Statements carefully designed to suppress the earlier social structure continually presented the myth of Adam and Eve as divine proof that man must hold the ultimate authority. The status of the male deity was the status of the male mortal, and it was surely no accident that the Levite priests of Yahweh had fought so bitterly for his position. So intent was Paul on declaring maleness to be first that he was willing to blind himself to the biological truth of birth—"For the man is not of the woman but the woman of the man." Woman bears the pain but man takes the credit.

When the apostle Peter was in Anatolia, where the Goddess was still revered, he condemned the "pagans" for the "lust of defiling passion," much like the prophets of the Old Testament, angrily deriding those who "reveled in the daytime." He complained that these heathens still followed Baalim. Peter solemnly lectured, "Likewise ye wives, be in subjection to your own husbands, for after this manner in the old time, the holy women also, who trusted in God, adorned themselves, being in subjection to their own husbands" (I Pet. 3:1).

St. Clement, father of the Roman Church, denied women—in the name of the Lord—the pleasure and health and strength-building effects of such physical sports as wrestling and running, claiming that it was in greater accord with the Bible that women's activities be confined to spinning, weaving and cooking.

St. John Chrysostom, a Christian teacher of the fifth century, warned, "The woman taught once and ruined everything. On this account . . . let her not teach."

St. Augustine of the same period claimed that man, but not woman, was made in God's image and woman therefore is not complete without man, while he is complete alone.

Taking his cue from these same biblical ideas, Martin Luther asserted in his writings that it was quite natural for women to be secondary to men. In his "Vindication of Married Life" he wrote that men must continue to maintain their power over women, since man is higher and better than she, "for the regiment and dominion belong to the man as the head and master of the house."

Sixteenth-century Swiss reformer John Calvin also spoke out against political equality for women, stating that it would be a "deviation from the original and proper order of nature." He even spoke favorably of polygamy, suggesting that it would help to keep women from being unwed and childless.

In 1527, in a treatise on the freedom of will, Christian theologian Hubmaier wrote:

The reason that the fall of the soul is partially reparable, however, and not fatal, even here on earth, but the fall of the flesh is to a certain extent irreparable and deadly, is that Adam as a type of the soul (as is Eve, of the flesh) would have preferred not to eat of the forbidden tree. He was also not deceived by the serpent but Eve was (I Timothy 2:14). Adam knew very well that the words of the serpent were contrary to the words of God. Yet he willed to eat the fruit against his own conscience, so as not to vex or anger his rib, his flesh, Eve. He would have preferred not to do it.

Dr. Margaret Murray suggested in several of her books that witch hunts of the western world were actually a continuation of the suppression of the ancient "pagan" religions. Since women were the primary target and victims of those brutal massacres, and so many of the charges were in some way connected to sex, this is certainly a possibility. The Goddess Danu, the Divine Ancestress of the Tuatha de Danaan of Ireland, perhaps related to the Goddess Diana of the Romans, Dione of the Greeks and even Danu of India, may have been the basis of the worship labeled as the witch cult. We know that the worship of Isis was known in England during the Roman period; a Thames-side temple of Isis in London and an altar to Isis in Chester both attest to the existence of Her religion in the British Isles at that time.

Murray quoted a ninth-century statement concerning witches in which Diana was mentioned as their leader. "Certain wicked women, reverting to Satan, and reduced by the illusions and phantasms of demons, believe and profess that they ride at night with Diana on certain beasts, with an innumerable multitude of women, passing over immense distances, obeying her commands as their mistress, and evoked by her on certain nights."

In *A Cauldron of Witches,* Clifford Alderman relates that the story of Eve was once again put to use, this time to justify the murder of the many women who defied the Church. In a sixteenth-century Church report we read, "Woman is more carnal than man: there was a defect in the formation of the first woman, since she was formed with a bent rib. She is imperfect and thus always deceives. Witchcraft comes from carnal lust. Women are to be chaste and subservient to men."

Through the violent imposition and eventually forced acceptance of the male religions, women had finally been maneuvered
into a role far removed from the ancient status they once held in
the lands where the Queen of Heaven reigned. Most alarming was
the quality of the absolute in the decrees credited to the omnipotent
male deity. As time went on the long, powerful arm of the Church
reached everywhere and with it came the unquestionable "moral"
attitudes and the guilt-ridden, subservient role assigned to women.

Within the very structure of the contemporary male religions are
the laws and attitudes originally designed to annihilate the female
religions, female sexual autonomy and matrilineal descent. These
are the precepts that many of our own grandparents and parents
accepted as the sacred and divine word of God, making them such
an inherent part of family life that they now affect even those of
us who have lived far removed from the masses and sacraments of
organized religions. It is surely time to examine and question how
deeply these attitudes have been assimilated into even the most
secular spheres of society today, insistently remaining as oppressive
vestiges of a culture once thoroughly permeated and controlled by
the word of the Church.

We may find ourselves wondering to what degree the suppression of women's rites has actually been the suppression of women's
rights.

THE COURAGEOUS CHALLENGE OF THE
EIGHTEENTH AND NINETEENTH CENTURIES

The myth and the image of Eve penetrated far into that part of
women where her deepest feelings and ideas are stored, the presence of the story of the first woman in the Hebrew creation myth
repeatedly rankling in the hearts, minds and spirits of women who
resented being lorded over by men, despite the divine word of the
omnipotent male deity.

Many of the women who first dared to speak out about the ways in which females were oppressed and the flagrant inequality of their position in society still had to contend directly with the Bible story of the woman who had listened to the word of the serpent and had initially brought about the proclamation of male rule. In the eighteenth and nineteenth centuries the power and influence of the Church was an even greater obstacle to the quest for female autonomy than it is today. Yet the pioneers of the struggle for the equality of women courageously spoke out against that power, defying the Church and its teachings. The vindication of the rights of women was in a sense a vindication of the woman Eve.

Thoughts and memories of the unfair punishment of Eve still symbolically hovered over women who dared to demand equal rights. In the writing of Mary Wollstonecraft in 1792, the characters in the Garden of Eden once again became the topic of conversation. In one of the earliest attempts to expose the shameful treatment of half the people in the world, *A Vindication of the Rights of Woman,* Wollstonecraft wrote:

> Probably the prevailing opinion, that woman was created for man may have taken its rise from Moses' poetical story; as very few it is presumed, who have bestowed any serious thought on the subject, ever supposed that Eve was, seriously speaking, one of Adam's ribs, the deduction must be allowed to fall to the ground; or only be so far admitted as it proves that man, from the remotest antiquity, found it convenient to exert his strength to subjugate his companion, and his invention to show that she ought to have her neck bent under the yoke; because she as well as the brute creation was created to do his pleasure . . .

Bravely chancing accusations of atheism or even of being under the influence of "the devil," still potentially dangerous charges in 1792, she continued by publicly stating, ". . . though the cry of irreligion, or even atheism, be raised against me, I will simply declare, that were an angel from heaven to tell me that Moses' beautiful, poetical cosmogony, and the account of the fall of man, were literally true, I could not believe what my reason told me was derogatory to the character of the Supreme Being: and, having no fear of the devil before mine eyes, I venture to call this a suggestion of reason . . ."

Also included in this same book was her critical analysis of Jean Jacques Rousseau's *Emilius (Emile)*, the 1761 proposal for the education of children in a "free society." This treatise, along with Rousseau's *Social Contract*, played an extremely influential role in both the American and French revolutions. Along with many other male-oriented passages from Rousseau's writings, she quoted his prescribed rules for the religious educations of females in that liberated utopia of which he dreamed. Rousseau wrote:

> As the conduct of a woman is subservient to the public opinion, her faith in matters of religion should, for that very reason, be subject to authority. Every daughter ought to be of the same religion as her mother, and every wife to be of the same religion as her husband: for, though such religion should be false, that docility which induces the mother and daughter to submit to the order of nature, takes away, in the sight of God, the criminality of their error . . . they are not in a capacity to judge for themselves, they ought to abide by the decision of their fathers and husbands as confidently as that of the church.

Mary Wollstonecraft commented, "The rights of humanity have been thus confined to the male line from Adam downwards."

Though at the time of Rousseau's writing the French and American revolutions were yet to be fought, this man, who most ardently advocated freedom and independence and whose ideas deeply affected revolutionaries in both of these countries, proposed (presumably with clear conscience) that women, even in a "free society," should still "be subject to authority" and "abide by the decisions of their fathers and husbands," especially in matters of religion. A daughter was to follow her mother's religion, but her mother's religious beliefs were to be determined by her mother's husband. Other than in a family that had a long line of fatherless households, a rather unlikely occurrence, women, supposedly devoid of the "capacity to judge for themselves," were to simply reflect the theological doctrines of men. Rousseau's dramatic first line of his *Social Contract*, "Man is born free, yet everywhere he is in chains," a call for independence and freedom, still rings in our ears, perhaps especially in 1976. Yet, according to this same author, the religious institutions and beliefs that insisted that the male domination of the female was divinely ordained (religion being primarily Christian in France and the colonies of North America) were to continue to be accepted by women without question.

In 1838, sixty-two years after the American revolution, another staunch fighter, demanding equal rights for women, wrote once again of the mythological mother of all Jewish and Christian women, as Eve's sin and punishment continued universally to explain the right of men to oppress and subjugate women. Sarah Grimke, as if in a court of cosmic law, presented the argument that, even if the original account had been true, hadn't women surely served their time?

> Woman, I am aware, stands charged to the present day with having brought sin into the world. I shall not repel the charges by any counter assertions, although as was hinted, Adam's ready acquiescence with his wife's proposal does not savour much of that superiority in strength of mind that is arrogated by man. Even admitting that Eve was the greater sinner, it seems to me that man might be satisfied with the dominion he has claimed and exercised for nearly six thousand years, and that more true nobility would be manifested by endeavouring to raise the fallen and invigorate the weak, than by keeping women in subjection. I ask no favours for my sex. I surrender not our claim to equality. All I ask of our brethren is that they will take their feet from off our necks.

Lucy Komisar, former vice-president of the National Organization of Women (NOW) in America, in her informative study *The New Feminism,* described that early period of women's struggle for liberation and the opposition. She explains that women first became aware of their own problems of oppression when they tried to speak out in favor of the abolition of black slavery, relating that women's attempt to take part in politics aroused the ire of the Church, the official representatives of the word of the male deity:

When Sarah and Angelina Grimke toured New England to speak
against slavery in 1836 the Council of Congregational Ministers of
Massachusetts issued a statement attacking them and pointing out that,
"The power of a woman is her dependency flowing from the consciousness of that weakness which God has given her for her protection
... when she assumes the place and tone of man as a public reformer,
she yields the power which God has given her for her protection and
her character becomes *unnatural.*"

But Sarah Grimke was not afraid to fight back, even in times
when the Church had not long before emerged from its practice of
burning women at the stake for much less. In angry retort she
explained the advantage of the male religions—for men—and the
disadvantages for women by answering, "As they have determined
that Jehovah has placed women on a lower platform than man,
they of course wish to keep her there; and henceforth the noble
faculties of our minds are crushed and the noble reasoning powers
are almost wholly uncultivated."

Several women concerned with the abolition of slavery planned
to attend an international conference in London that had been
arranged to discuss the problem, only to find that a group of
American clergymen had taken it upon themselves to precede them
to London to warn the English clergymen that they were coming
and even intended to *speak.* This set off a lengthy debate among
the men about the admission of women, which resulted in the
decision that the women who attended would be allowed to be
present—but only if they sat silently behind a curtained enclosure.

It was the shock of this decision that eventually brought about
the first women's rights conference at Seneca Falls, New York. At
that meeting, in 1848, a Women's Declaration of Independence
was drawn up, and once again women spoke out against the lowly
position that the Church had assigned them. Into that Declaration,
some fifteen centuries after the major obliteration of the worship
of the Queen of Heaven and Her priestesses, it was written: "He
[man] allows her in Church, as well as State, but in a subordinate
position, claiming Apostolic authority for her exclusion from the

Ministry and with some exceptions, from any public participation in the affairs of the Church . . . He has usurped the prerogative of Jehovah himself, claiming as his right to assign for her a sphere of action, when that belongs to her conscience and her god."

Just as Hosea had once spoken as Jehovah himself, many men of 1848, making use of the authority of those same ideas, still identified themselves with the male deity, and through this authority decided, proclaimed and enforced their decisions upon women, self-righteously informing them what they might and might not do. The Bible was brought out over and over again to "prove" that their position was beyond question.

In 1848, feminist Emily Collins told of a man who habitually whipped his wife, the hard-working mother of his seven children. Not only did this woman care for all the children and her husband as well, but she milked the cows, spun and wove the cloth for all the family's clothing which she then sewed, and did all the cooking, cleaning, washing and mending for the entire brood. According to the husband, her crime was that she "scolded," that is, nagged, in other words spoke up and said what was on her mind. And this was accepted as reason enough for a Christian man to beat his wife. Emily Collins asked with a bitter and angry sarcasm: "And pray why should he not have chastised her? The laws made it his privilege—and the Bible, as interpreted, made it his duty. It is true, women repined at their hard lot; but it was thought to be fixed by a divine decree for 'The man shall rule over thee' and 'Wives submit yourselves unto your husbands as unto the Lord,' caused them to consider their fate inevitable."

Male domination and control were once again justified by those ancient words. The early feminists went so far as to compile their writings in a book titled *The Woman's Bible,* in which Elizabeth Cady Stanton wrote, "It is rather remarkable that young Hebrews should be told to honour their mothers when the whole drift of the teaching thus far has been to throw contempt on the whole sex. In what way could they show their mothers honour? All the laws and customs forbid it."

Religion, as it was known in the western world in the nineteenth century, was male religion. Judaism, Christianity and Islam, though they may have differed about what sacrament to take when or which day was actually the Sabbath, were in complete agreement on one subject—the status of women. Females were to be regarded as inferior creatures who were divinely intended to be obedient and silent vessels for the production of children and the pleasure and convenience of men. These attitudes not only thrived in the Church but found their way past those great arched doorways to install themselves in a more personal way into the thoughts, feelings and values of every Jewish, Christian or Mohammedan family.

In *The Victorian Woman*, Duncan Crow describes some of the laws of that time and their effects upon women. He explains that until 1857 a woman could not sue for divorce (except by an Act of Parliament, which was generally reserved for the aristocracy); that until 1881 the legal right of a husband using physical force to restrain his wife from leaving home had never been questioned; and that until 1884 a wife could be imprisoned for denying her husband "conjugal rights." He writes that, along with these laws, "The Christian religion, too, was a powerful force in proclaiming and maintaining women's inferior position. On its Judaic inheritance it had erected the myth that women's subordinate place was a punishment for the original sin of Eve. It worshipped the words of Paul that 'man is not of the woman but the woman of the man.'" Crow observes that during the Victorian period men and women were not only expected to attend church every Sunday but that Bible readings in the home, organized prayer meetings, listening to and reading sermons and very strict observance of the Sabbath were quite typical in many homes, and adds that ". . . the importance of religion can hardly be overstressed."

In 1876, when Annie Besant defended a pamphlet on the use of contraception, she met great resistance from the government and the Church. Her biographer, Arthur Nethercot, explaining the situation at that time, writes, "Physical preventives at any time were regarded as against the will of God; few people seemed to see any inconsistency between interfering with the course of nature by preventing or curing disease, or building houses against the elements, and yet refusing to interfere with the process of procreation." The courageous Annie Besant also wrote on the laws concerning the custody of children, suggesting that many of the attitudes of the times were not far from the Hebrew attitudes "when woman was still regarded as a chattel." Crusading against the power of the Christian Church, from the point of view of secularism as well as feminism, she gave a great many speeches throughout England and wrote numerous articles and pamphlets including one titled *Woman's Position According to the Bible,* exposing herself to a great deal of antagonism and resentment, at times expressed by threats of physical violence.

In the collection of articles and quotes entitled *Voices From Women's Liberation,* many excerpts of the speeches and writings of the early women's movement appear, many of which are found in a little-known book called *The History of Woman Suffrage,* published in 1881. One excerpt of a speech given in 1853 by a woman named Abby Foster claimed that the education and molding of young minds at that time were deeply influenced by the Church. Much of this, she claimed, was done through the power that the Church held over the mother, for in the long run it was the teachings and attitudes of the Church that the child received. She pointed out: "You may tell me that it is a woman who forms the mind of a child, but I charge it back again, that it is the minister, who forms the mind of the woman. It is he who makes the mother what she is, therefore her teaching of the child is only conveying the instructions of the pulpit at second hand."

Despite the accusations, men of the organized Church had no intention of re-examining or revising the lowly position that they had allotted to women. Clergymen continued to hold that males, according to the divine ancient word, were meant to rule over females, who were by nature spiritually weak and mentally somewhat deficient. So it was that in 1860, after some seventy years of continuous accusations against the Church's position on women, Susan B. Anthony was prompted to comment: "By law, public sentiment and religion, from the time of Moses down to the present day, woman has never been thought of as other than a piece of property, to be disposed of at the will and pleasure of man."

LOOKING BACK TO LOOK AHEAD—PARADISE IN PERSPECTIVE

As the struggle to obtain equal rights for women continued to gather force, the Church continued to exercise its power and influence with great zeal, carefully protecting the cherished and holy concept of male supremacy. Despite the arrogance of male comments, which were often little more than apparent admissions of the discomfort of the ruling class in fear of being deposed, scantily clad in what they tried to pass off as easy jest or humor, the antagonism at times broke out as vicious physical violence when the humor failed to work. Komisar explains that "the clergy were often in the forefront of the fight against suffrage, dredging up quotations from the Bible to prove that the natural order of things was female obedience to man."

Though women did eventually gain the right to vote, actually only a part of their initial overall goals, they found themselves with this incredibly hard-won vote still living in a totally male-controlled society in which women had been well conditioned to believe that the male creator had indeed actually made men wiser than women: women were now free to vote—for men.

Those in political control often spoke of State and God in one breath. The word of the Church was still powerful, and centuries of violence in the name of religion, fanatic and terrifying crusades, inquisitions and witchhunts hovered in threatening memory for any who dared to defy the authority of the Church.

Fear and terror had forced the precepts of the male religions into all aspects of society. And the institution that had so persistently annihilated the worship of the Queen of Heaven now offered in Her stead the guilty, sinful, painful, obedient role of Eve. Pat Whiting in *The Body Politic,* a recent collection of writings from the current women's liberation movement in Britain, observes that "our culture is impregnated with the mythology of the ancient Hebrews. The original sin of Eve is still with us." Barbara Cartland, in her study of women in today's society, refers to woman as "the eternal Eve." And the name chosen for an English magazine concerned with the position of women in contemporary society, is titled, with a humorous sarcasm, *Spare Rib.*

For thousands of years male supremacy has been suggested, declared, proven, explained, announced, proclaimed, affirmed, confirmed, and reaffirmed by the Bible and by those who believe in the Bible as the sacred word of the creator.

As recently as 1965, Cartland commented on the ego-building, heady effects of the Paradise story—for the male:

> In the concise record in the book of Genesis man can gain great satisfaction in learning that he is indeed, as of course he always thought, the most splendid of all God's creatures . . . It is comforting too, it leaves man in no doubt about the exclusive, solitary position of supreme perfection that he has in the world . . . Over nine-tenths of the world, the basis of the Genesis story, with its condemnation of the wickedness of woman, has found an echo in the hearts of men.

Simone de Beauvoir, in her classic study of the oppression of women, *The Second Sex,* pointed out with a sensitive sarcasm the convenience of the male religion—for males. According to de Beauvoir, "Man enjoys the great advantage of having a god endorse the code he writes; and since man exercises a sovereign authority over women it is especially fortunate that this authority has been vested in him by the Supreme Being. For the Jews, Mohammedans and Christians among others, man is master by divine right, the fear of God will therefore repress any impulse towards revolt in the downtrodden female."

Eva Figes, in *Patriarchal Attitudes,* reported the not-too-surprising reaction of an English archbishop in 1968, who observed with a blunt honesty, as he commented upon the ordination of women in the clergy of the English church, "If the church be thrown open to women, it will be the death knell of the appeal of the Church for men."

An Episcopalian bishop in San Francisco, when faced with the question of the ordination of women in the Church in 1971, gave the answer with which this book begins: "The sexuality of Christ is no accident nor is his masculinity incidental. This is the divine choice."

Komisar listed a series of events that have taken place since the women's movement has been gathering momentum in recent times, events that exhibit a serious questioning of the attitudes of the Church toward women. She included accounts of Catholic sisters who have openly accused the Church of being a male church, stating that it places women in much the same category as children, whom it then places in the same category as imbeciles.

The Church may have weakened in its effects upon individuals and communities, especially for those who live in large cities, where there is less community life or community pressure. Yet within the Church the emphasis upon male supremacy continues to exist. It is written into the very canons and sacred literature upon which the male religions were built. As Eva Figes so aptly comments, "The church may be dying on its feet, but it will cling to the last to the male exclusiveness which was its *raison d'être* in the first place."

Yet the memory of the ancient female religion—the Queen of Heaven, the priestesses, the sacred sexual customs—still lingers on in the memory of some of the men who control the Church even today. In *The Times* (London) on 23 May 1973, an article appeared, headed "Priestesses, a shift to pagan creeds." Once again the ordination of women in the male-controlled church set off the reaction. According to *The Times* religious affairs correspondent:

> A warning that the admission of women to the priesthood in the Church of England would be a subtle shift towards the old pagan

religions was given by the Bishop of Exeter, Dr. Mortimer, to the convocation of Canturbury yesterday.

In the old nature religions, he declared, priestesses were common— "and we all know the kinds of religions they were and are." The church has too often adapted to changing conditions in the past, and had to be doubly careful "in a sex obsessed culture."

Whatever the condition of the Church at this point in history, we cannot afford to ignore or dismiss lightly the far-reaching effects that centuries of Church power continue to have on each of us today, no matter how far removed we may be from the actual pulpit or altar. It is the rare family that can trace back beyond two or three generations and not find that their predecessors were deeply immersed in the attitudes and values of one of the male-oriented religions. It is for this reason that religious pressures are not as far from us as we might prefer to think.

For within the very structure of family life, in families that do or did embrace the male religions, are the almost invisibly accepted social customs and life patterns that reflect the one-time strict adherence to the biblical scriptures. Attitudes toward double-standard premarital virginity, double-standard marital fidelity, the sexual autonomy of women, illegitimacy, abortion, contraception, rape, childbirth, the importance of marriage and children to women, the responsibilities and role of women in marriage, women as sex objects, the sexual identification of passivity and aggressiveness, the roles of women and men in work or social situations, women who express their ideas, female leadership, the intellectual activities of women, the economic activities and needs of women and the automatic assumption of the male as breadwinner and protector have all become so deeply ingrained that feelings and values concerning these subjects are often regarded, by both women and men, as natural tendencies or even human instinct.

Biblical attitudes may no longer be justified to many contemporary women or men as being vital or absolute because the Lord has decreed that they were so, but centuries of having followed these religiously based precepts have provided the next argument—people have "always" accepted them as right; therefore they must be the natural, normal way of being.

The knowledge of the early female religions, so often revealing human behavior and attitudes that were the very antithesis of these so-called "natural" human tendencies, and which, as we have seen, were actually the underlying cause of so many of these later religious reactions and attitudes, rests almost totally forgotten or misunderstood. The accidental or intentional censorship in general education and popular literature denies the very reality of their importance or even their existence.

As recently as 1971, one extremely knowledgeable and educated woman began a book on the political struggles of women today by covering the ancient female religion in three lines. She wrote that pagan religions originally worshiped women, but that in an era we know little about, gods replaced goddesses and male supremacy in religion was established.

Another recent book on the status of women in history starts with Greece, the introduction vaguely hinting that the culture of Crete was the only major society to precede Greece, and that almost nothing is known of Crete or any of the other early cultures.

A woman anthropology professor from a well-known university in the United States assured a group of women at a women's studies conference in 1971 that all goddesses were simply obese, naked fertility figures, developed and worshiped by men.

It is time to bring the facts about the early female religions to light. They have been hidden away too long. With these facts we will be able to understand the earliest development of Judaism, Christianity and Islam and their reactions to the female religions and customs that preceded them. With these facts we will be able to understand how these reactions led to the political attitudes and historical events that occurred as these male-oriented religions were forming—attitudes and events that played such a major part in formulating the image of women during and since those times. With these facts we will be able to clear away the centuries of confusion, misunderstanding and suppression of information, so that we may gain the vantage point necessary for examining the image, status and roles still assigned to women today. With these facts we will gain the historical and political perspective that will enable us to refute the ideas of "natural or divinely ordained roles," finally opening the way for a more realistic recognition of the capabilities and potential of children and adults, whether female or male, as individual human beings. When the ancient sources of the gender stereotyping of today are better understood, the myth of the Garden of Eden will no longer be able to haunt us.

Killing off a defiant consort was not the answer, any more than silencing and debilitating women economically has been. Perhaps when women and men bite that apple—or fig—at the same time, learn to consider each other's ideas and opinions with respect, and regard the world and its riches as a place that belongs to every living being on it, we can begin to say we have become a truly civilized species.

Date Charts

It is important to remember that these dates are continually being revised as new evidence is discovered and that even with the present evidence archaeologists differ in assigning these dates. The dates are given here to provide a general idea of the various periods in each location, and they should be understood to be approximate rather than definitive.

GRAVETTIAN-AURIGNACIAN

(Upper Paleolithic sites)
25,000–15,000 BC

CANAAN

Early Bronze Age 3000–2000 BC

Middle Bronze Age 2000–1600 BC

Late Bronze Age 1600–1200 BC

Early Iron Age I 1200–900 BC

Early Iron Age II 900–600 BC

Early Iron Age III 600–300 BC

Biblical Figures in Canaan

Abraham sometime between 1800 and 1550 BC

Moses and Aaron 1300–1250 BC

Saul 1020–1000 BC (Samuel slightly earlier)

David 1000–960 BC

Solomon 960–922 BC

Hosea 735 BC

Ezekiel 620 BC

Jeremiah 600 BC

JUDAH (capital, Jerusalem)
Rehoboam 922–915 BC
Abijam 915–913 BC
Asa 913–873 BC
Jehosophat 873–849 BC
Jehoram 849–842 BC
Ahaziah 842 BC
Athaliah 842–837 BC
Hezekiah 715–687 BC
Fall of Jerusalem 586 BC
(first conquered by
Babylon, then Cyrus of
Persia [Iran])

ISRAEL (capital, Samaria)
Jeroboam 922–901 BC
Zimri 876 BC
Omri 876–869 BC
Jezebel and Ahab 869–850 BC
Ahaziah 850–849 BC
Joram 849–842 BC
Jehu 842–815 BC
From Joahaz to Hoshea 815–
724 BC
Fall of Samaria 722 BC
(conquered by Sargon of
Assyria)

MESOPOTAMIA

Jarmo 6800 BC
Hassuna Period 5500 BC
Halaf Period 5000 BC
Ubaid Period 4000–3500 BC
Uruk Period 3500–3200 BC
Jemdet Nasr Period 3200–2850
BC
Early Dynastic Period in Sumer
2850–2400 BC
Agade Dynasty (Sargon) 2370–
2320 BC
Guti invasion 2250–2100 BC
III Dynasty of Ur (including
Ur Nammu, Shulgi, Bur

Sin, Shu Sin, Ibbi Sin)
2060–1950 BC
Isin Dynasty of Sumer 2000–
1800 BC
Larsa Dynasty of Sumer 2000–
1800 BC
I Dynasty of Babylon 1830–
1600 BC (under Kassite con-
trol by 1600 BC)
Hammurabi 1792–1750 BC
Babylonia 1830–540 BC
Assyria 1900–600 BC (under
Hurrian control 1500–1300
BC)

EGYPT

Neolithic (Badarian, Amratian, Gerzean) 4000–3000 BC
I–V Dynasties 2900–2300 BC
VI–X Dynasties 2300–2000 BC
XI–XVI Dynasties 2000–1600 BC
XVII Dynasty 1600–1570 BC (Kamosis)
XVIII Dynasty 1570–1304 BC (Amosis, Amenophis I, Tutmosis I, Tutmosis II, Tutmosis III, Hatshepsut, Amenophis II, Tutmosis IV, Amenophis III, Amenophis IV (Ikhnaton), Semenkhere, Tutenkhamun, Ay, Haremhab)
XIX Dynasty 1304–1200 BC (Rameses I, Seti I, Rameses II, Merneptah)
XX Dynasty 1200–1065 BC (Rameses III, Rameses IV, Rameses XI)
XXII Dynasty 935–769 BC
XXIII–XXVII Dynasties 760–525 BC
XXVIII–XXX Dynasties 431–404 BC

ANATOLIA (Turkey)

Catal Hüyük 6500–5000 BC
Hacilar 6000–5000 BC
Early Bronze Age 3000–2000 BC
(Alaca Hüyük 2500–2300 BC)
Middle Bronze Age 2000–1700 BC
Late Bronze Age 1700–1200 BC

The Hittite Kings in Anatolia
Pitkhanas and Anittas early twentieth century BC
Labarnas 1700 BC
Hattusilis I 1650 BC
Mursilis I 1620 BC
Shuppiliuma 1375–1306 BC

CRETE

Neolithic Age 5000–3000 BC
Early Minoan 2900–2000 BC
Middle Minoan 2000–1500 BC

Late Minoan 1500–1350 BC
Mycenaeans 1350–1100 BC
Dorians invade Crete 1100 BC

550–525 BC Iranians (Persians) under Cyrus conquered most of Mesopotamia, Anatolia, Canaan, Northern Egypt and Northwestern Greece.

By about 330 BC the Greeks (under Alexander) had conquered most of the territories that had been under Persian control.

Bibliography

Akurgal, Ekrem. *Art of the Hittites.* London, Thames and Hudson, 1962.
Albright, Wm. *Recent Discoveries in Bible Lands.* New York, Funk and Wagnalls, 1936.
Albright, W.,F. In *The Bible and the Ancient Near East,* ed. by G.E. Wright. New York, Doubleday, 1961.
———. *From Stone Age to Christianity.* Baltimore, Johns Hopkins Press, 1941.
———. *Archaeology and the Religion of Israel.* Baltimore, Johns Hopkins Press, 1942.
———. "The Early Alphabetic Inscriptions from Sinai." *Bulletin of the School of Oriental Research.* vol. 110, April 1948, 6–22.
———. *The Archaeology of Palestine.* Harmondsworth, Penguin, 1949.
———. *Yahweh and the Gods of Canaan.* London, Athlone Press, 1968.
Alderman, Clifford. *A Cauldron of Witches.* New York, Julian Messner, 1971.
Alexiou, Stylianos. *Ancient Crete.* London, Thames and Hudson, 1967.
———. *Minoan Civilization.* Iraklion, Crete, The Archaeological Museum 1969.
Allegro, John. *The Dead Sea Scrolls.* Harmondsworth, Penguin, 1956.
Ames, D. *Greek Mythology.* Feltham, Hamlyn, 1963.
Anati, E. *Palestine Before the Hebrews.* London, Jonathan Cape, 1963.
Anthes, Rudolf. "Mythology in Ancient Egypt." In *Mythologies of the Ancient World,* ed. by S. N. Kramer. New York, Doubleday, 1961.

Astrom, L. *Studies of the Arts and Crafts of the Late Cypriot Bronze Age.* London, Lund, 1967.

Avery, C. *The New Century Classical Handbook.* New York, Appleton-Century-Crofts, 1962.

Bachofen, J. *The Mothers, Myth, Religion and Mother Right.* Stuttgart, 1861.

Bacon, E. *Vanished Civilizations.* London, Thames and Hudson, 1963.

Baramki, Dmitri. *Phoenicia and the Phoenicians.* Beirut, American University Press, 1961.

Barnett, R. D. *Catalogue of the Nimrud Ivories.* London, British Museum, 1957.

Baron, S. W. *A Social and Religious History of the Jews.* New York, Columbia University Press, 1937.

Bennett, Florence. *Religious Cults Associated with the Amazons.* New York, Columbia University Press, 1912.

Bertholet, A. *A History of Hebrew Civilization.* London, Harrap, 1926.

Bittel, Kurt. *Hattusha, Capital of the Hittites.* London, Oxford University Press, 1970.

Boscawen, W. *Egypt and Chaldea.* London, Harper, 1894.

Braidwood, R. J. *Prehistoric Men.* Chicago, University of Chicago Press, 1948.

Brandon, S. G. F. *Creation Legends of the Ancient Near East.* London, Hodder & Stoughton, 1963.

Briffault, Robert. *The Mothers.* London, Allen & Unwin, 1927.

Brown, Norman. "Mythology of India." In *Mythologies of the Ancient World,* ed. by S. N. Kramer. New York, Doubleday, 1961.

Bucke, E. *Interpreter's Dictionary of the Bible.* Nashville, Tenn., Abingdon Press, 1962.

Budge, E. A. W. *Egyptian Book of the Dead.* London, British Museum, 1895.

―――. *The Gods of the Egyptians.* London, Methuen, 1904.

―――. *The Babylonian Legends of Creation.* London, British Museum, 1921.

―――. *The Babylonian Story of the Deluge and the Epic of Gilgamish.* London, British Museum, 1920.

Bulfinch, Thomas. *Bulfinch's Mythology.* Boston, S. W. Tilton, 1881.

Butterworth, E. A. *Some Traces of the Pre-Olympian World.* Berlin and New York, De Gruyter, 1966.

Cadoux, C. J. *Ancient Smyrna.* Oxford, Basil Blackwell, 1938.

Campbell, Joseph. *The Masks of God: Primitive Mythology.* New York, Viking Press, 1959.

―――. *The Masks of God: Oriental Mythology.* London, Secker and Warburg, 1962.

―――. *The Masks of God: Occidental Mythology.* London, Secker and Warburg, 1965.

————. *The Masks of God, Creative Mythology*. London, Secker and Warburg, 1968.

Cartland, Barbara. *Woman, The Enigma*. London, Frewin, 1968.

Casson, S. *Essays in Aegean Archaeology*. London, Oxford University Press, 1927.

————. *Ancient Cyprus*. London, Methuen, 1937.

Cassuto, U. *Anath*. Jerusalem, 1951.

Catling, H. W. *Patterns of Settlement in Bronze Age Cyprus*. London, Lund, 1963.

Chiera, Edward. *They Wrote on Clay*. Chicago, University of Chicago Press, 1938.

Childe, Gordon. *New Light on the Most Ancient East*. London, Routledge & Kegan Paul, 1952.

Clayton, A. C. *The Rg Veda and Vedic Religion*. Madras, Christian Literature Society for India, 1913.

Cole, S. *The Neolithic Revolution*. London, British Museum, 1970.

Collins, Sheila. "A Feminist Reading of History." *Radical Religion Journal*. Berkeley, California, 1974, 12–17.

Contenau, G. *Everyday Life in Babylon and Assyria*. London, Edward Arnold, 1954.

Cook, Stanley. *The Religion of Ancient Palestine in the Second Millenium B.C.* London, Constable, 1908.

————. *The Religion of Ancient Palestine in the Light of Archaeology*. London, Oxford University Press, 1930.

Cottrell, Leonard. *The Bull of Minos*. London, Evans, 1953.

————. *Lost Worlds*. N.Y., American Heritage Publishing Co., 1962.

————. *The Lion Gate*. London, Evans, 1963.

Crawford, O. G. S. *The Eye Goddess*. London, Phoenix House, 1957.

Crossland, R. A. "Immigrants from the North," in *Cambridge Ancient History*, vol. 1. London, Cambridge University Press, 1970.

Crow, Duncan. *The Victorian Woman*. London, Allen & Unwin, 1971.

Daniels, Glyn. *Malta*. London, Thames and Hudson, 1957.

Dawson, Christopher. *Age of the Gods*. London, John Murray, 1928.

Dawson, D. *The Story of Prehistoric Civilizations*. New York, Franklin Watts, 1951.

Delaporte, L. *Mesopotamia*. London, Routledge & Kegan Paul, 1925.

Delougaz, P. *The Temple Oval at Khafajah*. Chicago, University of Chicago Press, 1940.

————. *Pre-Sargonic Temples in the Dyala Region*. Chicago, University of Chicago Press, 1942.

Dempsey, T. *Delphic Oracle*. London, Blackwell, 1918.

De Vaux, Roland. *Ancient Israel*. London, Darton, Longman & Todd, 1965.

Dhorme, E. P. *La Religione Assyro-Babylonienne*. Paris, Presses Universitaires de France, 1949.

Di Cesnola, L. P. *Cyprus, its Ancient Cities, Tombs and Temples.* London, John Murray, 1877.

Dikaios, P. *Khirokitia.* London, Oxford University Press, 1953.

Dossin, G. "Un Ritual du Culte d'Istar Provenant de Mari." *Revue d'Assyriologie,* vol. 35, 1938, 1–13.

Drees, Ludwig. *Olympia.* London, Pall Mall Press, 1971.

Dresden, M. J. "Mythology of Ancient Iran." In *Mythologies of the Ancient World,* ed. by S. N. Kramer. New York, Doubleday, 1961.

Driver, G. R. *Canaanite Myths and Legends.* Illinois, Allenson, 1950.

Ehrich, R. W. *Relative Chronologies on Old World Archaeology.* Chicago, University of Chicago Press, 1954.

Emery, Walter. *Archaic Egypt.* Harmondsworth, Penguin, 1961.

Epstein, I. *Judaism.* Harmondsworth, Penguin, 1959.

Evans, Arthur. *The Mycenaean Tree and Pillar Cult.* London, Macmillan, 1901.

_____. *The Early Nilotic, Libyan and Egyptian Relations with Minoan Crete.* London, Macmillan, 1925.

_____. *The Earlier Religions of Greece in Light of the Cretan Discoveries.* London, Macmillan, 1925.

_____. *The Palace of Minos at Knossos.* London, Macmillan, 1936.

Farnell, L. R. *The Cults of the Greek States.* Oxford, Clarendon Press, 1896.

_____. *Greece and Babylon.* Edinburgh, Clark, 1911.

Figes, Eva. *Patriarchal Attitudes.* London, Faber and Faber, 1970.

Finegan, J. *Light from the Ancient Past.* Princeton, Princeton University Press, 1946.

Flaceliere, R. *Greek Oracles.* London, Paul Elek, 1965.

Frank, C. *Kultleider aus dem Ischtar-Tammuz-Kreis.* Leipsig, Harrassowitz, 1939.

Frankfort, Henri. *Cylinder Seals.* London, Macmillan, 1939.

_____. *Kingship and the Gods.* Chicago, University of Chicago Press, 1948.

_____. *The Problems of Similarities in Ancient Near Eastern Religions.* Oxford, Clarendon Press, 1951.

_____. *The Art and Architecture of the Ancient Orient.* Harmondsworth, Penguin, 1954.

Frazer, James. *The Golden Bough.* London, Macmillan, 1907.

_____. *Attis, Adonis and Osiris.* London, Macmillan, 1920.

_____. *A Study in Magic and Religion.* London, Macmillan, 1924.

Frobenius, L. *The Childhood of Man.* London, Seeley, 1909.

Gadd, C. J. *Ideas of Divine Rule in the Ancient Near East* (Sweich Lectures). London, Oxford University Press, 1933.

_____. *The Stones of Assyria.* London, Chatto and Windus, 1936.

Garcia, L., Galloway, J., and Lommel, A. *Prehistoric and Primitive Art.* London, Thames and Hudson, 1969.

Gardiner, A. H. *The Astarte Papyrus*. Oxford, Griffiths Institute, 1936.

Gaster, T. *Thespis*. New York, Doubleday, 1950.

Gimbutas, M. *The Gods and Goddesses of Old Europe*. London, Thames and Hudson, 1974.

Gjerstad, E. *Studies of Prehistoric Cyprus*. Uppsala, Sweden, Uppsala Universitets Arsskrift, 1926.

Glotz, G. *The Aegean Civilization*. London, Routledge & Kegan Paul, 1925.

Glubb, J. B. *The Life and Times of Muhammed*. London, Hodder and Stoughton, 1970.

Godard, Andre. *The Art of Iran*. New York, Praeger, 1965.

Göetze, A. "Cilicians." *Journal of Cuneiform Studies*, vol. 16, 1962, 48–58.

Gordon, Cyrus. *Ugaritic Literature*. Rome, Pontifical Biblical Institute, 1949.

————. *Ugaritic Manual*. Rome, Pontifical Biblical Institute, 1955.

————. *The Ancient Near East*. New York, W. W. Norton, 1962.

————. *The Common Backgrounds of the Greek and Hebrew Civilizations*. New York, W. W. Norton, 1962.

————. *Ugarit and Minoan Crete*. New York, W. W. Norton, 1966.

————. *Forgotten Scripts*. Harmondsworth, Penguin, 1968.

Graves, Robert. *The White Goddess*. New York, A. A. Knopf, 1948.

————(translator). *The Golden Ass* by Apuleius, New York, Pocket Books, 1951.

————. *The Greek Myths I & II*. Harmondsworth, Penguin, 1955.

Gray, John. *The Legacy of Canaan*. Leiden, 1957.

————. *Archaeology of the Old Testament World*. London, Nelson, 1962.

————. *The Canaanites*. London, Thames and Hudson, 1964.

————. *Near Eastern Mythology*. Feltham, Hamlyn, 1969.

Graziozi, P. *Paleolithic Art*. London, Faber and Faber, 1960.

Grimke, Sarah. Quotes from *Voices from Women's Liberation*, ed. by L. Tanner. New York, Signet, 1970.

Guido, M. *Sardinia*. London, Thames and Hudson, 1963.

Guilliame, A. *Islam*. Harmondsworth, Penguin, 1954.

Gurney, O. R. *The Hittites*. Harmondsworth, Penguin, 1952.

Guterbock, Hans. "Hittite Mythology." In *Mythologies of the Ancient World*, ed. by S. N. Kramer. New York, Doubleday, 1961.

Guthrie, W. *The Greeks and their Gods*. London, Methuen, 1950.

Hall, H. R. *The Ancient History of the Near East*. London, Methuen, 1913.

Hamilton, Edith. *Mythology*. New York, Mentor, 1955.

Handcock, P. *Mesopotamian Archaeology*. London, Macmillan, 1912.

Harden, D. *The Phoenicians*. London, Thames and Hudson, 1962.

Harris, J. R. *The Legacy of Egypt*. London, Oxford University Press, 1971.

Harris, Rivkah. "Naditu Women of Sippar I & II." *Journal of Cuneiform Studies*, vol. 15, 117–120; vol. 16, 1–12, 1962.

Harrison, Jane. *Prologomena to the Study of Greek Religion.* Cambridge, 1903.

———. *Themis.* Cambridge, 1912.

Harrison, R. K. *Ancient World.* Edinburgh, English Universities Press, Ltd., 1971.

Hartland, E. S. *Primitive Paternity.* London, David Nutt, 1909.

———. *Primitive Society.* London, Methuen, 1921.

Haspels, C. H. *The Highlands of Phrygia.* Princeton, Princeton University Press, 1971.

Hastings, J. *A Dictionary of the Bible.* Edinburgh, T & T Clark, 1900.

Hawkes, Jacquetta. *Dawn of the Gods.* London, Chatto and Windus, 1958.

———. *Prehistory: History of Mankind, Cultural and Scientific Development,* vol. 1, part 1. New York, Mentor, 1965.

———. *The First Great Civilizations.* London, Hutchinson, 1973.

Hays, H. R. *The Dangerous Sex.* London, Methuen, 1966.

Heidel, A. *Babylonian Genesis.* Chicago, University of Chicago Press, 1951.

Higgins, R. *Minoan and Mycenaean Art.* New York, Praeger, 1967.

Hill, G. *The History of Cyprus.* London, Cambridge University Press, 1940.

Hinz, Walther. *The Lost World of Elam.* New York, New York University Press, 1973.

Hitti, P. *The History of Syria.* London, Macmillan, 1951.

Hood, Sinclair. *The Home of Heroes.* London, Thames and Hudson, 1967.

———. *The Minoans, Crete in the Bronze Age.* London, Thames and Hudson, 1971.

Hooke, S. H. *Myth and Ritual.* London, Oxford University Press, 1933.

———. *Origins of Early Semitic Ritual.* London, Oxford University Press, 1935.

———. *Babylonian and Assyrian Religion.* London, Hutchinson, 1953.

———, (ed.). *Myth, Ritual and Kingship.* London, Oxford University Press, 1958.

———. *Middle Eastern Mythology.* Harmondsworth, Penguin, 1963.

Hopper, R. J. *The Acropolis.* New York, Macmillan, 1971.

Hoyle, P. *Delphi.* London, Cassell, 1967.

Hutchinson, R. W. *Prehistoric Crete.* Harmondsworth, Penguin, 1962.

Huxley, G. L. *Early Sparta.* London, Faber and Faber, 1962.

Jacobsen, T. In *The Intellectual Adventures of Ancient Man,* ed. by H. Frankfort. Chicago, University of Chicago Press, 1946.

———. "Primitive Democracy in Ancient Mesopotamia." *Journal of Near Eastern Studies,* vol. II, 1943, 159–172.

———. *Toward the Image of Tammuz.* Cambridge, Mass., Harvard University Press, 1970.

James, E. O. *The Old Testament in Light of Anthropology.* London, Macmillan, 1935.

252   When God Was a Woman

————. *The Origins of Religion.* John Heritage, 1937.

————. *Prehistoric Religion.* London, Thames and Hudson, 1957.

————. *Myth and Ritual in the Ancient Near East.* London, Thames and Hudson, 1958.

————. *The Cult of the Mother Goddess.* London, Thames and Hudson, 1959.

————. *The Ancient Gods.* London, Weidenfeld & Nicolson, 1960.

————. *Seasons, Feasts and Festivals.* London, Thames and Hudson, 1961.

————. *The Worship of the Sky God.* London, University of London Press, 1963.

Jastrow, M. *Religion of Babylon and Assyria.* New York, Atheneum Press, 1898.

Kapelrud, A. S. *Baal in the Ras Shamra Texts.* Copenhagen, 1952.

Karageorghis, V. *Mycenaean Art from Cyprus.* Nicosia, 1968.

————. *The Ancient Civilization of Cyprus.* London, Barrie & Jenkins, 1970.

Keller, Werner. *The Bible as History.* London, Hodder and Stoughton, 1956.

Kenyon, Kathleen. *Archaeology in the Holy Land.* Tonbridge, Ernest Benn, 1960.

Kitto, H. D. F. *The Greeks.* Harmondsworth, Penguin, 1951.

Klein, Violet. *The Feminine Character.* London, Routledge & Kegan Paul, 1946.

Komisar, Lucy. *The New Feminism.* New York, Franklin Watts, 1971.

Kramer, S. N. *Sumerian Mythology.* Philadelphia, University of Pennsylvania Press, 1944.

————. *Sumerian Myths, Epics and Tales.* Princeton, Princeton University Press, 1957.

————. *History Begins at Sumer.* New York, Doubleday, 1958.

————, (ed.). *Mythologies of the Ancient World.* New York, Doubleday, 1961.

————. *The Sumerians, Their History, Culture, and Character.* Chicago, University of Chicago Press, 1963.

————. *The Sacred Marriage Rite.* Bloomington, Indiana University Press, 1969.

Kursh, H. *Cobras in the Garden.* Wisconsin, Harvey Press, 1965.

Landes, G. "The Material Civilization of the Ammonites." *Biblical Archaeologist.* September, 1961.

Langdon, S. *The Sumerian Epic of Paradise.* Philadelphia, University of Pennsylvania Press, 1915.

————. *Tammuz and Ishtar.* London, Oxford University Press, 1914.

————. *Semitic Mythology.* Francestown, N.H., Marshall Jones, 1918.

Larousse. *New Larousse Encyclopedia of Mythology,* ed. by F. Guirand. London, Paul Hamlyn, 1960.

Lawson, John. *Modern Greek Folklore and Ancient Greek Religion.* London, Cambridge University Press, 1910.

Layard, A. H. *Nineveh and Babylon.* London, British Museum, 1853.

Leach, Maria. *Standard Dictionary of Folklore.* New York, Funk and Wagnalls, 1949.

Levy, Rachel. *The Gate of Horn.* London, Faber and Faber, 1963.

Lewis, H. D. and Slater, R. L. *The Study of Religions.* Harmondsworth, Penguin, 1969.

Lissner, Ivar. *The Living Past.* New York, Putnam, 1957.

Lloyd, Seton. *Mesopotamia, Excavations on Sumerian Sites.* London, 1936.

———. *Ruined Cities of Iraq.* Iraq, Dept. of Antiquities, 1942.

———. *Foundations in the Dust.* London, Oxford University Press, 1947.

———. *Early Anatolia.* Harmondsworth, Penguin, 1956.

———. *The Art of the Ancient Near East.* London, Thames and Hudson, 1961.

———. *Mounds of the Near East.* Edinburgh, Edinburgh University Press, 1963.

———. *Early Highland Peoples of Anatolia.* London, Thames and Hudson, 1967.

Lommel, A. *Prehistoric and Primitive Man.* New York, McGraw Hill, 1966.

Luckenbill, D. D. *Ancient Records of Assyria and Babylonia.* Westport, Conn., Greenwood, 1927.

Macalister, R. A. S. *Bible Sidelights from the Mound of Gezer.* London, Hodder and Stoughton, 1906.

———. *Gezer Excavations.* London, Palestine Exploration Fund, 1912.

Mallowan, M. E. L. *Twenty Five Years of Mesopotamian Discovery.* Iraq, British School of Archaeology, 1956.

———. *Early Mesopotamia and Iran.* London, Thames and Hudson, 1965.

———. *Nimrud and its Remains.* Glasgow, Collins, 1966.

Marinatos, S. *Crete and Mycenae.* London, Thames and Hudson, 1960.

Maringer, Johannes. *The Gods of Prehistoric Man.* New York, A. A. Knopf, 1960.

Marshak, A. *The Roots of Civilization.* New York, McGraw Hill, 1972.

Marshall, John. *Mohenjo Daro and the Indus Civilization.* London, Probsthain, 1931.

Matz, F. *Crete and Early Greece.* London, Methuen, 1962.

Mellaart, James. *Anatolia.* Cambridge, 1962.

———. *Earliest Civilizations of the Near East.* London, Thames and Hudson, 1965.

———. *Catal Huyuk.* London, Thames and Hudson, 1967.

Menan, Aubrey. *Cities in the Sand.* London, Thames and Hudson, 1972.

Mendenhall, G. "Biblical History in Transition." In *The Bible and the*

Ancient Near East, ed. by G. E. Wright. New York, Doubleday, 1961.

Mercer, S. *The Religion of Ancient Egypt.* London, Luzac, 1949.

Montagu, Ashley. *The Natural Superiority of Women.* London, Macmillan, 1970.

Moortgat, A. *The Art of Ancient Mesopotamia.* London, Phaidon, 1967.

Morenz, S. *Egyptian Religion.* London, Methuen, 1973.

Moscati, S. *Ancient Semitic Civilizations.* London, Paul Elek, 1957.

_____. *The Semites in Ancient History.* Cardiff, University of Wales Press, 1959.

_____. *The World of the Phoenicians.* London, Weidenfeld & Nicolson, 1968.

Murray, Margaret. *The Witch Cult in Western Europe.* Oxford, Clarendon Press, 1921.

_____. *The Splendour that Was Egypt.* London, Sidgwick & Jackson, 1949.

_____. *The Genesis of Religion.* London, Routledge & Kegan Paul, 1963.

Mylonas, George. *Eleusis and the Eleusinian Mysteries.* Princeton, Princeton University Press, 1961.

Nethercot, Arthur. *The First Five Lives of Annie Besant.* St. Albans, Rupert Hart-Davis, 1961.

Neumann, Erich. *The Great Mother.* New York, Pantheon, 1955.

Nilsson, Martin. *The Minoan-Mycenaean Religion and its Survival in Greek Religion.* London, Lund, 1927.

_____. *Greek Popular Religion.* New York, Columbia University Press, 1940.

Norbeck, Edward. *Religion in Primitive Society.* London, Harper, 1961.

O'Faolain, Julia and Martines, Lauro. *Not in God's Image.* London, Maurice Temple Smith, 1973.

Ohnesfalsch-Richter, G. *Ancient Places of Worship on Cyprus.* Berlin, 1891.

_____. *The Bible and Homer.* London, Asher & Co., 1893.

Olmstead, A. T. *A History of Palestine and Syria.* Chicago, University of Chicago Press, 1931.

Oppenheim. A. L. *Ancient Mesopotamia.* Chicago, University of Chicago Press, 1964.

Palmer, L. *Mycenaeans and Minoans.* London, Faber and Faber, 1961.

Parke, H. W. *Greek Oracles.* London, Hutchinson, 1967.

Parrot, Andre. *Sumer.* London, Thames and Hudson, 1960.

_____. *The Arts of Mankind.* London, Thames and Hudson, 1960.

_____. *Nineveh and Babylon.* London, 1961.

Pendlebury, J. *The Archaeology of Crete.* London, Methuen, 1939.

Persson, A. W. *The Religion of Greece in Prehistoric Times.* Berkeley, University of California Press, 1942.

Petracos, B. *Delphi.* Athens, Hesperus Editions, Delphi Museum, 1971.

Petrie, Wm. Flinders. *The Status of the Jews in Egypt.* London, Allen & Unwin, 1922.

_____. *Life in Ancient Egypt*. London, Constable, 1923.

_____. *Religious Life in Ancient Egypt*. London, Constable, 1924.

_____. *Egypt and Israel*. London, Christian Knowledge Society, 1925.

Piggott, S. *The Dawn of Civilization*. London, Thames and Hudson, 1961.

Porada, E. *The Art of Ancient Iran*. New York, Crown, 1962.

Poulsen, F. *Delphi*. London, Glyndendal, 1921.

Powell, T. G. E. *Prehistoric Art*. New York, Praeger, 1966.

Pritchard, J. B. *Palestinian Figures in Relation to Certain Goddesses Known Through Literature*. New York, Kraus-Thompson, 1943.

_____. *Ancient Near Eastern Texts Relating to the Old Testament*. Princeton, Princeton University Press, 1950.

_____. *The Ancient Near East*. Princeton, Princeton University Press, 1958.

_____. *Archaeology and the Old Testament*. Princeton, Princeton University Press, 1958.

_____. *The Ancient Near East in Pictures*. Princeton, Princeton University Press, 1969.

Ramsay, W. M. *Cities and Bishropics of Phrygia*. Oxford, Clarendon Press, 1895.

Ransome, H. *The Sacred Bee*. London, Allen & Unwin, 1937.

Rassam, H. *Ashur and the Land of Nimrud*. New York, Eaton & Mains, 1897.

Reverdin, L. and Hoegler, R. *Crete and its Treasures*. New York, Viking Press, 1961.

Robinson, T. H. In *Myth, Ritual and Kingship*, ed. by S. H. Hooke, London, Oxford University Press, 1958.

Rose, H. J. *The Handbook of Greek Mythology*. London, Metheun, 1928.

Rowe, Alan. *The Topography and History of Beth Shan*. Philadelphia, University of Pennsylvania Press, 1930.

Russell, D. S. *Between the Testaments*. London, SCM Press, 1960.

Saggs, H. W. F. *The Greatness that was Babylon*. New York, Mentor, 1968.

Sakir, Cevat. *Asia Minor*. Ismir, Turkey, Ismir Publications, 1971.

Sanders, N. K. *Poems of Heaven and Hell from Ancient Mesopotamia*. Harmondsworth, Penguin, 1971.

Sayce, A. H. *The Hittites, Story of a Forgotten Empire*. London, Religious Tract Society, 1892.

_____. *The Religion of Ancient Egypt and Babylon*. Edinburgh, T. & T. Clark, 1902.

Schaeffer, C. *The Cuneiform Texts of Ras Shamra-Ugarit*. From Schweich Lectures of 1936, Oxford, 1939.

Scholem, G. *On the Kabbalah and its Symbolism*. London, Routledge & Kegan Paul, 1965.

Seltman, C. *The Twelve Olympians*. London, Pan Books, 1952.

_____. *Women in Antiquity*. London, Pan Books, 1956.

Smith, Homer. *Man and His Gods*. London, Jonathan Cape, 1953.

Smith, Sidney. In *Myth, Ritual and Kingship,* ed. by S. H. Hooke. London, Oxford University Press, 1958.

Smith, Wm. Robertson. *The Religion of the Semites.* London, A. & C. Black, 1894.

———. *Kinship and Marriage.* London, A. & C. Black, 1903.

Sormani, Guiseppi. *India.* New York, Greystone Corp., 1965.

Speiser, E. A. *Akkadian Myths and Epics.* Princeton, Princeton University Press, 1957.

Spiteras, Tony. *The Art of Cyprus.* New York, Reynal, 1970.

Strong, D. *The Classical World.* New York, McGraw Hill, 1965.

Strong, D. and Garstang, J. *The Syrian Goddess.* London, Constable, 1913.

Tanner, Leslie (ed.). *Voices from Women's Liberation.* New York, Signet, 1970.

Taylour, W. *The Mycenaeans.* London, Thames and Hudson, 1964.

Ussishkin, D. "The Necropolis at Silwan." *Biblical Archaeologist.* May, 1970.

Vaerting, M. and Vaerting, M. *The Dominant Sex.* London, Allen & Unwin, 1923.

Van Buren, Elizabeth, D. *Clay Figures of Babylonia and Assyria.* Hartford, Conn., Yale University Press, 1930.

———. "The Sacred Marriage in Early Times in Mesopotamia." *Orientalia,* vol. 13, 1944, 1–72.

Van Loon, M. N. *Urartian Art,* Istanbul, 1966.

Vieyra, M. "Istar de Nineve." *Revue d'Assyriologie,* vol. 51, 1957, 83–102.

Von Cles-Reden, Sybelle. *The Realm of the Great Goddess.* London, Thames and Hudson, 1961.

Von Matt, L. *Ancient Crete.* London, Thames and Hudson, 1967.

Von Oppenheim, M. *Tell Halaf.* New York, Putnam, 1931.

Waldstein, W. *The Argive Heraeum.* New York, Riverside Press, 1902.

White, Anne T. *Les Grandes Decouvertes de l'Archaeologie.* Quebec, Marabout University Press, 1942.

Whiting, Pat. In *The Body Politic,* ed. by M. Wandor. London, Stage I, 1972.

Widengren, George. In *Myth, Ritual and Kingship,* ed. by S. H. Hooke. London, Oxford University Press, 1958.

Willetts, R. F. *Cretan Cults and Festivals.* New York, Barnes & Noble, 1962.

———. *Everyday Life in Ancient Crete.* London, Batsford, 1969.

Wilson, Horace H. *The Great Mother.* London, Oriental Translation Fund, 1840.

Winton-Thomas, D. *Documents From Old Testament Times.* London, Nelson, 1958.

Witt, R. E. *Isis in the Graeco-Roman World.* London, Thames and Hudson, 1971.

Wollstonecraft, Mary. *A Vindication on the Rights of Woman.* London, Everyman, 1792.

———. *A Vindication of the Rights of Woman with Strictures on Political and Moral Subjects.* 1833.

Woolley, L. *History Unearthed.* Tonbridge, Ernest Benn, 1958.

———. *Excavations at Ur.* New York, Thomas Crowell, 1965.

Wright, G. E. (ed.). *The Bible and the Ancient Near East.* New York, Doubleday, 1961.

Yadin, Yigael. *The Scroll of the War of the Sons of Light.* London, Oxford University Press, 1962.

———. *Hazor.* London, Weidenfeld & Nicolson, 1975.

Zimmern, H. *Babylonian and Hebrew Genesis.* London, 1901.

Additional References

Revised Standard Bible. London, Nelson, 1952.
The Jerusalem Bible. New York, Doubleday, 1966.
New English Bible. London, Oxford University Press and Cambridge University Press, 1970.

Aeschylus	Homer
Apollodorus	Lucian
Diodorus Siculus	Pausanius
Euripedes	Plutarch
Herodotus	Philostratus
Hesiod	Sophocles
	Strabo

Index